THE BUILDING OF ELIZABETHAN AND JACOBEAN ENGLAND

THE BUILDING OF ELIZABETHAN AND JACOBEAN ENGLAND

MAURICE HOWARD

Published for
The Paul Mellon Centre for Studies in British Art
by
Yale University Press • New Haven and London

In memory of my grandparents
CHARLES and MARY JANE MINTER
SAM and FLORENCE HILDA HOWARD

Designed by Elizabeth McWilliams

Printed in China

Library of Congress Cataloging-in-Publication Data

Howard, Maurice.
  The building of Elizabethan and Jacobean England / Maurice Howard.
     p. cm.
  Includes bibliographical references and index.
  ISBN 978-0-300-13543-5 (cl : alk. paper)
  1. Architecture, Elizabethan – England. 2. Architecture, Jacobean – England.
3. Architecture and society – England – History – 16th century. 4. Architecture and society – England – History – 17th century.
5. Buildings – Remodeling for other use – England. I. Title.
  NA965.H69 2007
  720.942'09031 – dc22

                          2007025317

A catalogue record for this book is available from The British Library

Frontispiece: Leycester's Hospital, Warwick. The lower floor gallery on the eastern side of the courtyard.

Contents

Acknowledgements

A book such as this is indebted to the many scholars and colleagues with whom I have worked, shared in the organising of conferences and discussed issues over a long period of time. Their published work is duly acknowledged in the footnotes and from amongst them I would like to mention three in particular. Malcolm Airs first charted the existence of the richness of material other than country houses in this period, and his efforts to bring scholars of early modern architecture together at conferences over many years puts us all in his debt. Christy Anderson has given me the courage to look at issues concerning architecture in its widest intellectual context. Robert Tittler has more citations in the bibliography than anyone else; without his reaching out to public buildings and their contents from his original base as an historian I would not have understood the urban story of this period and much else besides. The colloques and study trips shared with European colleagues over many years opened up the riches of Renaissance architecture in Europe; I would like to thank especially Jean Guillaume, Monique Chatenet, Claude Mignot and Koen Ottenheym. Steve Hindle's conferences on the built environment of early modern England at the University of Warwick happened at a crucial time. Also deserving thanks for a multitude of things are Steve Burman, Richard Burrows, Rosalys Coope, Nicholas Cooper, Tarnya Cooper, Nicholas Doggett, David Gaimster, Claire Gapper, Mark Girouard, Andrew Hadfield, Raphael Hallett, Tara Hamling, Karen Hearn, Paula Henderson, Deborah Howard, Nick Humphrey, Eve Lacey, Ann Matchette, John Newman, Janet Pennington, Sylvia Pinches, the late Annabel Ricketts, Alexandra Shepard, Christine Stevenson, Margit Thøfner, Mary Whiteley, Edward Wilson and Lucy Worsley.

Great Libraries and Record Offices provide both our books and documents and the expertise to locate and contextualise them. I want to thank the staff of those places I have thought of as home in recent years: the

National Art Library at the Victoria and Albert Museum, the Society of Antiquaries, the Institute of Historical Research, the University of Sussex Library, and amongst many Record Offices where earlier work went on that helped formulate the general conclusions of this book, especially those of Hampshire, East Sussex and West Sussex.

One's 'home' university is the most vital source of support. All my colleagues in the Art History Department at the University of Sussex, past and present, deserve my deepest thanks, but I would especially like to acknowledge Liz James, Simon Lane, Nigel Llewellyn, Sarah Maddox and Michelle O'Malley for their particular and sustained support and encouragement, both academic and personal. The AHRC-funded Material Renaissance project of 2000–03, headed by Michelle O'Malley and Evelyn Welch, provided stimulus, new comparative reading and set standards of attention to completing the task in hand. It was a privilege to learn from and act as internal examiner to some of the project's Ph.D. students. Twenty-five generations of students on the course 'Elizabethan and Jacobean Culture and Society' in the former School of Cultural and Community Studies brought me into contact with questioning minds from a range of arts and social science disciplines.

For research leave to work on this project I must thank the University of Sussex and the Arts and Humanities Research Council. The University has also been generous with support for illustrations.

On the production of the book Sophie Hartley proved an expert picture researcher, and at Yale University Press Gillian Malpass, Emily Angus, Ruth Thackeray and Elizabeth McWilliams have steered the course with great skill and experience.

Finally, the personal debts. Amongst close friends, Mary Eminson, Todd Gordon, David Johnson and Margaret Williamson have listened, sympathised and counselled. My parents have as always been a rock of support, and at a challenging time in their lives.

'Transformation': An Introduction

In a painting by the Flemish artist Cornelis van Dalem in the Alte Pinakothek, Munich (fig. 1), people are shown at work against a backdrop of ruins; their abode and housing for animals have been thrown up in the precinct of a ruined building which might well be an abandoned monastery. It is not clear, given the origin of the painting in the Low Countries, whether if this was the case, the monastery has been quietly dissolved and left to become ruinous or whether it was sacked in a bout of religious upheaval. There is no image of this kind at this period in England but living among or alongside ruins must have been the everyday experience of large numbers of people during the decades after the Reformation of the 1530s. It was to be at least a century before anyone in England sought to represent this traumatic episode of the past in this way, as a form of landscape painting drawing on contemporary material; from a later seventeenth-century viewpoint, old monasteries were historically romanticised and clearly something from a distant past, not at all like the style of modern buildings.[1]

This book covers a timespan stretching between two periods of political experiment. During the first, the 1530s and 1540s, England's religious establishment was overturned by Henry VIII and the country's relationship with Europe for ever changed thereby; extraordinary legislative means were used to carry out the king's wishes. The government held its nerve, met with comparatively little resistance, and won. During the second, the 1630s and 1640s, the Personal Rule of Charles I used all-but-forgotten forms of legal expediency to keep the country's finances afloat; stress was laid on reviving a sense of continuity with medieval forms of worship (believed by the majority of the population to have been long thrown off) and a promotion of elite forms of culture took place at the royal court as part of a re-engagement with European powers. The government lost its nerve, prompted conflict and ultimately surrendered its right to exist. Both periods were marked by destruction of the built environment that left very visible

1 Cornelis van Dalem, *Landscape with Farmsteads and Ruins*, oil on wood, 1564. Munich.

2 Clarendon House, East Grinstead, West Sussex. A four-bay hall-house originally built in the mid-15th century with an open hall in the central two bays. In the 1560s a continuous upper floor was made and gables added.

signs, namely ruins in the landscape, which contributed more than any other factor to a deeply different – and disturbing – sense for contemporaries of their place in historical time.

The century between these two periods, however, is usually confidently and broadly brushed as one of positive improvement in the country's building stock. During the decades since the publication in 1953 of W.G. Hoskins's article on the issue of the 'Great Rebuilding', many historians have challenged the basis of his argument.[2] They have severally stressed the need to factor in regional variations, moved his dates around, posited a second phase of rebuilding later in the seventeenth century, and suggested more sophisticated ways of measuring advances in the technology of building and the means of measuring the comfort of individuals that new houses offered. This book argues that the premise that a great change took place remains secure through one particular word underpinning Hoskins's argument. It is the 'transformative' quality of the effort expended on the buildings he discusses that is certainly undeniable. There were new houses, built from scratch. But, far more importantly, there was a lot of making new from old materials: the flooring of halls open to the roof to create at least one, more private upstairs space; the deployment of visible signs of luxury and comfort such as the fireplace (its stack often prominent for display purposes on the main façade of the house) and glazed windows; all these things customised old structures into modern dwellings (fig. 2).

The 'Great Rebuilding' as historically constructed, however, has been a selective one, since it effectively considers only the most widespread form of building, the house, and predominantly in the rural environment. The building or refurbishment of houses is certainly the most telling way of measuring changes in general prosperity and the desire to emulate perceived peer groups. However, the broader picture of building enterprise is also significant, through individual and collective investment in urban societies. Whether by actual sums of cash or local support and pressure on local authorities, dilapidated churches were restored, new town halls were built, schools and almshouses founded, town walls, gates and bridges kept in repair. Other types of building were maintained or begun by central government, including royal palaces, government offices and houses of justice, and coastal defences. In the period after the Reformation, cathedrals (to a limited extent) and the two universities (to a great extent) were also major players in commissioning new or refurbished buildings. Some of these types of public building have been well documented and explored but are rarely considered alongside each other. This book does not attempt to chart that broad and complex narrative in its entirety but seeks to explain how new forms of building came into being through a series of themes. These are the processes of rethinking the past and making new from old materials, the language that was invented both to describe and celebrate buildings and their meaning for different groups in society, how buildings created a sense of community in the urban environment and the way that disputes and upheavals concerned with the ownership of buildings prompted visual records of entirely new kinds.

It has been argued, often by inference or rather default, that the 'high ground' of building history in England between the Reformation of the 1530s and perhaps as late as the early nineteenth century is that of the country house, a phenomenon that truly betokens 'architecture', a word hitherto avoided in these introductory remarks. In fact the dominance of the country house is taken for granted in the most influential book since the 1950s on the history of building (in Britain as a whole) between that crucial date of 1530 and 1830.[3] It is assumed that the history of the country house is a progressive and linear development. The rules of classicism were first scrutinised through intellectual debate between patrons and architects and then ever more ingeniously adapted and applied. This is especially true of a 'high period' of production between about 1660 and 1800, from which many examples survive. There were, it is always acknowledged, excursions into the making of other great public buildings but they are somewhat isolated, determined by exceptional circumstances, or unfulfilled: these included the rebuilding of St Paul's and the City of London churches after the fire of 1666 and the intensive work on designs for a royal palace in the 1630s, 1660s and 1690s, all only partly realised. This has resulted in a narrative which has become plotted through issues of style: throughout this long period one style, namely the classical, as it was applied to country houses, became so dominant that some of the writing of its history in England sets out to show how every builder was focused on getting the rules of classicism right, of making its message ever more sophisticated and rarefied. Other historians have discerned a more complex pattern of fits and starts in the comprehension of rule and practice in continental Europe, sometimes the rejection of its precepts and always a willingness to experiment and mix its various forms (fig. 3).

In the century after the Reformation, a number of styles – if that is the right or most helpful word to use in this context – jostled with each other for prominence and appropriateness not just for great houses but for a huge range of public and other private buildings. Some of these were introduced through the treatises and pattern books of continental Europe but the residue of the past suggested other styles, other solutions. The key issue here, then, is one of transformation. What are the transformations happening at this time which presage what is to come and in fact themselves continue throughout the period? First, there is an issue about the extent to

3 Charlecote House, Warwickshire. Passage through the gatehouse, 1560s, with classical shell niches below and a more traditional rib vault with pendants above.

4 St James's Palace, London, originally built for Henry VIII in the 1530s. The gatehouse and chapel range to the right are from that time, 18th-century additions on the left.

which people regarded buildings as structures intended to last. The Royal Works provide the most abundant source of documentation for the early sixteenth century and these present an astonishing amount of information about running repairs, even to relatively new buildings (fig. 4).[4] It seems that whenever the king was absent from one of his many houses even for some months, let alone years, an advance guard went ahead to repair roofs, windows, shutters and entrances; the practice of the constant removal of the royal locks from one building to another to ensure security in the royal apartments is therefore with hindsight also a somewhat symbolic action, as if the building were incomplete at all times when the king was absent. Some of this activity was certainly due to Henry VIII's constant demand for changes to the palaces and to different queens consort needing new arrangements, but equally one must look to the building practices of the period that did not necessarily see the process as creating something more than semi-permanent. The undeniably temporary palace built for the Field of Cloth of Gold in a matter of weeks in 1520 on the one hand and then even the greatest of Henry's palaces on the other may not be as far apart on the sliding scale that encompasses buildings for occasion and buildings to last as one might at first imagine. Royal accounts also provide information on one other factor concerning the temporary nature of these structures and it concerns the matter of the disguise, often justified by the need for preservation, of the surfaces of structures. Buildings were conventionally rendered and constantly painted, sometimes to obscure completely, at other times to heighten or modify the colour of the building material, such as the pink often applied to red brick, examples of which sometimes survive today in trapped roof spaces where gable ends have been added to. Such practices continued throughout the century. Accounts for the time of Elizabeth I show a great deal spent on Whitehall Palace for re-painting the walls with black and white work in the 'antique' style. Elizabeth is well known for not adding to the stock of her father's palaces, rather she slowly dispersed her holdings of many of them, but there was continuous replenishment of what remained by these means of re-painting and thereby the re-presentation of an already established building.[5] Both the maintenance of the fabric and the covering, decorative order of these buildings were constantly under refurbishment.

The urban environment too was in a state of constant flux and remodelling, partly because of the generally poor state of repair in England's towns and cities, but also because, in the period after the Reformation, the very purposes of traditional buildings were in question and their relative significance one to each other was changing. What is remarkable, however, is the way in which new meanings for buildings were carved out of the legacy of the past. Churches were adapted and re-organised to meet the needs of reformed religion, civic buildings were sometimes rebuilt but more often encased with new façades to promote at least the image of substantial wealth and settled conditions. Just as the coming of the royal court transformed a great palace for a short period, so the calendar year that was followed in towns and cities was re-shaped to meet new civic expectations in the wake of the dismissal of old, Catholic, festivities; the appearance of the urban environment on special occasions could temporarily change.[6] There are written records of the streets of London decorated on the occasion of state visits by foreign sovereigns, of coronations and triumphal processions, when windows were thrown open and expensive chattels displayed; equally something is known about the reverse side of that coin, the occasions of public funerals and public punishments, when windows and gates were barred. The lost wall painting once at Cowdray House of the coronation procession of Edward VI, recorded in an eighteenth-century copy, is a rare sixteenth-century visual record of such a celebratory occasion (fig. 5). In varying degrees, the streets of the capital were 'decorated' to suit each of these purposes and the townscape was transformed anew for each occasion. In this, England shared common practices with other European countries, though it is clear that after the Reformation the medieval Catholic practices that survived in parts of Europe afforded a richness of traditional display not seen in England.

This book opens with an account of the impact of the dissolution of the monasteries and the processes of adaptation that these buildings inspired not only in the resolution of their own transformation but in the evolution and modification of other buildings as well. It then addresses issues of how buildings were altered to suit new rituals of behaviour, of language and of

patronage and moves towards a conclusion about the changing representation of buildings. A consideration of one type of structure can encapsulate here much of what follows: it is one whose practical role remained both critical for the internal security of the country from the end of the Middle Ages to the time of the Civil Wars of the 1640s, but also whose symbolic value underwent a sea-change. Historians often talk of the castle at the end of the medieval period as being 'in decline' and certainly many were left dilapidated in parts of the country now more settled than in earlier times and less subject to the threats of over-mighty subjects some centuries before. Under the Tudors, the Crown's northern castles in particular were left to decay, no longer serving the needs of medieval peripatetic kings.[7] Yet it has also been noted that some later medieval castles exaggerated their display of defence simply to project the image of strength and power; within their stout walls castles were constantly adapting to new standards of comfort and luxury.[8] Written around 1535–43, John Leland's notes towards what was eventually published as his *Itinerary* repeatedly remark on this new aspect of remaining castles. Sometimes old features of the castle were turned to pleasurable uses: at Belvoir, in Leicestershire, 'the dungeon [his word for the keep] is a fair round tower now tournid to pleasure, as a place to walk yn, and to se al the country aboute, and raylid about the round [waull], [and] a garden [plot] in the middle'.[9] At other places, new ranges of buildings added comfort and convenience, so at Durham he describes how Bishop Tunstal 'hath also done cost on the dungeon and other places of the

5 *The Coronation Procession of Edward VI* (detail), pen and watercolour, 18th-century. Copy of a lost wall painting at Cowdray House, West Sussex, showing Cheapside festooned with carpets and fabric for the occasion. Copyright The Society of Antiquaries of London.

6 Framlingham Castle, Suffolk. Early 16th-century brick chimneys built over the range of apartments that once stood against the east side of the curtain wall.

7 Raglan Castle, Gwent. The great gatehouse range of the 1460s was preserved in the transformation of the inner part of the castle by the Somerset family, Earls of Worcester, in Elizabethan times.

castel, and hath builded a goodly new gallery and a stately stair to it, and made an exceding strong gate of yren to the castelle'.[10] The explicit addition of new features for comfort is seen in the now-ruinous state of the castle of Framlingham, in Suffolk, where the Howard Dukes of Norfolk inserted fireplaces into old ranges around the curtain walls, probably in the 1520s (fig. 6).[11] More spectacular adaptations of old castles were a feature of the later sixteenth century, notably at Kenilworth, as discussed in the context of Robert Dudley's building patronage in chapter 4, and at Raglan, over the border in Wales where the Somerset family, Earls of Worcester, transformed the medieval stronghold into a country house within its walls; these were castles adapted for entertaining and receptions on the grandest scale (fig. 7).[12] By the beginning of the seventeenth century, some new castles appear, not now defensible strongholds, but places constructed deliberately to evoke the past, sometimes playfully doing this on a reduced scale.[13] For this evocation of the past yet in a new guise, no building quite rivals the 'Little Keep' at Bolsover, in Derbyshire, begun about 1612 for Sir Charles Cavendish; it really is like a little 'villa' at the end of a long new curtain wall and it shares with the Italianate sense of 'villa' the aspect of surprise, for within are a series of rooms evoking the loves of the classical gods, denying and counteracting the medievalising aspect of the exterior (fig. 8). When one asks how contemporaries viewed such buildings and how they were prepared for the visual exploration of assumption and expectation, one needs to turn to the language to which buildings were subject by this time. The literate of Elizabethan England would have been familiar with

8   Bolsover Castle, Derbyshire. The 'Little Keep', built 1612–21.

9   A moated castle on a valence with hunting scenes. English, from the Sheldon looms, silk and wool with some silver thread, early 17th century, about 25 cm high. Victoria and Albert Museum, London.

poetry of the time, in which the word 'castle' could as much have a symbolic meaning, perhaps the 'tower' in the mind where love for another was 'imprisoned', as the described reality of an existing medieval building. The fantasy of 'castle' appears many times in the decorative and applied arts of the day, an image ethereal and indeed symmetrical as few working medieval castles actually were (fig. 9). The people of Elizabethan and Jacobean England embraced buildings of the past and transformed them, making sense of the political and religious upheavals of the time that threatened the fabric of the past with redundancy. We could learn much from both their practicality and their sense of imagination.

I

'Bare Ruin'd Choirs' Re-visited

When the Augustinian nunnery of Lacock, Wiltshire, surrendered to the royal commissioners William Petre and John Tregonwell in January 1539, it must have seemed a baffling blow to the community of nuns, now dispersed and pensioned off: just two years earlier, after the first Act of Parliament suppressing the smaller monasteries, it had been licensed to continue. The new owner, Sir William Sharington, was left in possession by the commissioners, though he did not actually purchase the property until the following year, for £783. Sharington's work on the site was forthright and disregarding of the past since he pulled down the church and built up a new service court to the north of the cloister. He is reputed to have sold the bells of the church to rebuild nearby Ray Bridge in order to divert people and traffic from a path close to his house. In other ways, however, the people of Lacock would have enjoyed some continuity because Sharington needed local services and experience to run his house and farmland. The bailiff remained in post, as did the auditor and steward of the manor courts. The monastic receiver-general was still in post at Sharington's death in 1553 (fig. 11).[1] The dissolution of the monasteries was a profound break with the past but it was complicated and the history of both public and domestic building enriched as much by this cataclysmic event as the fabric of the medieval church was obliterated by it. This chapter is about the progress of that complex transformation.

The de-commissioning of the monasteries in sixteenth-century England offers a unique slice through both the built and the ideological 'archaeology' of the building practices of the age. In the massive and multi-directional conversion that took place one gets a particular insight into the expectations of this period as to how buildings should look and function. The dissolution involved a huge re-shaping of the built environment of early modern England and its story has conventionally been told in terms of a sudden and unexpected move by government, giving opportunity for the

10   W. Capon, cross-section of the nuns' dormitory at St Helen's, Bishopsgate (before 1799, published 1817). The hall of the Leathersellers' Company and its plaster ceiling of 1610 are above the 13th-century undercroft of the medieval nunnery. Copyright The Museum of London.

11 Lacock Abbey, Wiltshire. The south side of the cloister range, with William Sharington's mid-16th-century tower at the right and later windows and insertions. The Augustinian nunnery church stood in front of this range.

display of rapacity and greed by all who sought to gain from it. Great regret for the loss of a built heritage and its furnishings (both domestic and liturgical but especially for books and manuscripts) was almost immediately expressed. 'Bare ruin'd choirs' still populate the English countryside and also in towns and cities such as Coventry, Gloucester and Whitby (fig. 12). Ruinous buildings are a highly evocative symbol of destruction. The political decisions that swept away centuries of monasticism in a few short years have been portrayed as a swift and violent change the like of which is unparalleled in English history and a form of imposed governmental tyranny.[2] Although violence also attended reform movements across northern continental Europe, the particular progress of dissolution in England is not really like that of any other reformed country, including that of the nearest kingdom, Scotland.[3] Strangely, while the dissolution was undeniably part of the process of the English Reformation, it seems with hindsight to have been somewhat detached from religious, doctrinal debate; the monasteries were part of an old order of church establishment that was soon gone and both Catholics and Protestants benefited from the resources made available. But the true narrative is not a linear one. Historians have

come to discuss the English experience not as a single event but in terms of a series of 'Reformations' with the legal, ideological basis for a reformed church arising over a period of a century.[4] Similarly, the despoliation of the built heritage of the Church did not happen all at once. Certainly the suppression was swift and brutal; two Acts of Parliament in 1536 and 1539 effected the closure of the eight hundred or so monastic houses, though between these dates a great many of them surrendered voluntarily.[5] Yet this action was not entirely without precedent: in earlier times languishing individual monasteries, or small groups of them, had been suppressed for a range of particular purposes, notably the endowment of colleges.[6] More-over, the dissolution was part of a wider, opportunistic expropriation of the wealth of the established Church; it was accompanied by the Crown's taking the opportunity to mix policies of bullying and offers of genuine exchange to move the bishops out of some of their prime properties wher-ever this was to the king's advantage.[7] Later, in 1547, the chantries, with all their attendant properties and lands, were suppressed (fig. 13).[8] The need to stress England's 'difference' and signal the firm break with Rome was reiterated in the years after 1570, following the papal bull that excommunicated Elizabeth I; this constituted a second act of separation after the series of changes of the 1530s and, initiated as it was by England's enemies, may have been the spur to a second wave of destroying or adapting as yet un-reconstructed monastic fabric after the initial moves of the 1530s and 1540s.[9]

The moment one looks a little more deeply behind the undeniable story of destruction and vindictiveness towards the monasteries at various times during the sixteenth century, the story gets more complicated, less gratuitously violent and more sensitive to contemporary needs of buildings in different ways. This is evident whenever ex-monastic sites have been examined by archaeologists. While there are discernible similarities of usage, every former monastic site has presented the investigator with a distinctive solution to the individual fabric; there was no common template for alterations to buildings that had belonged to the same monastic order, or been situated within a given region, or constructed in a common building material, even though attempts have been made to look at groups of buildings in these ways.[10] What can be drawn are some broad patterns and differences on account of political and social circumstances. To cite one regional example, hardly any great families completed a large-scale monastic conversion in the westernmost counties of England, where most monastic buildings and estates passed into gentry hands; in the counties surrounding London, however, the prestige of impressing fellow courtiers with new country houses resulted in far more ambitious programmes of building by those of high rank at court.

The rapid and cost-effective changes of the first years after the suppression are revelatory of how people expected certain kinds of building types to function because the very speed of conversion encouraged conformity with prevailing norms. This is especially true with regard to domestic structures. Thus a large monastic space might be suitable for a hall, a working kitchen would hardly be abandoned, and most crucially a cloister garth with its surrounding buildings signalled 'courtyard'.[11] The first and most significant aspect of such exploration is that the earliest solutions were but the beginning of a process; within a generation, or even less time than that, initial solutions were reversed, altered or rethought. These changes were not always inspired by external influences; the former monasteries were not prey simply to the changes of fashion initiated by other, new buildings. Rather, the structures themselves often encouraged their own refashioning as they suggested new solutions to practical problems of orientation, of plan and room sequences, of access, and of movement between floors. Thus they were not the passive respondents of radical change in other new buildings but themselves motivated new owners into doing that refashioning. As discussed below, the monastic past was sometimes, and for good reason, allowed to resurface first in literary form and then in the very fabric of the buildings themselves, initiating a new sense of pride in the past. But over a

long period of time there is a progressive and continuous development of learning from the key buildings of England's past, one by which the legacy of monasticism was neither entirely forgotten nor consistently abused.

New owners and the specialist craftsmen who executed their wishes have left the historian with one, and the most important, kind of evidence in the form of standing structures, or lost structures that have left some record. But there are other ways by which the process of transformation became the engine for novelty and change. The first thing concerns the documentation of that process. There is no complete set of building accounts for any one monastic conversion, perhaps because, unlike the building of some brand new country houses for example, the transformation was never thought to be completely 'finished' and also because the work was carried out rapidly and with an emphasis on the new owner's immediate convenience.¹¹ The first priority after dissolution was to reserve for the Crown the most valuable materials, the movable church furniture in precious materials, the lead off the roofs and the bells. After that, complex deals were made to sell the site, whether in parts or as a whole. However fragmentary the accounts, the tentative instructions and wishes of owners, the letters passing between like-minded entrepreneurs in this opportunistic game, a new language for building can be discerned, pinpointing the struggle to adapt and to allow new forms to emerge from this palimpsest. New, recognisable formulae had to be developed and new terminology adopted to become the future verbal currency. This process was part of a broad reshaping of how buildings were described, documented and accounted for in financial terms in early modern England, and from the outset there was something of a struggle to get it done efficiently and precisely. The language of making and re-making buildings here merges seamlessly into that of the description of buildings, a topic addressed in chapter 3.

The second thing that the great transformation of monasteries caused was an opportunity for speculation and risk in the building market.¹² The wealth of buildings that became available were a key, and for some people decisive, card in the game played for social recognition and status. In the decades between the 1530s and the 1580s the process of acquiring and adapting a monastery was not concerned, as is often imagined in analysing the acknowledged ingenuity of some great new country houses of the Elizabethan period, with outward aspect, with self-advertisement through style or fashion. The monastic conversions were not outwardly architecturally innovative and many bore the outward aspect of their origins for many years to come: radical transformations of country houses that were once monastic, such as the eighteenth-century transformation of Woburn in Bedfordshire, were already challenged by an increasingly antiquarian appreciation of these buildings and there were already arguments for preservation. In the sixteenth century it was rather that these buildings and their roles as bargaining tools were associated with reputation and the standing of the individual's credit. Holding a series of properties would yield income through the lands attached and through the privileges and nominations to minor offices they included. There was a sense of holding a 'portfolio' of investments which were expected to yield and produce income, only one or two of which might make the site of a permanent residence or other form of enterprise (such as industrial manufacture, the storage of goods, or subcontracting for the purposes of quarrying). But they were also a bargaining factor in all manner of deals and bids for positions of authority and power. How the individual handled these processes would make or break his or her reputation for moral probity. False moves or clear acts of damaging the public good led to a series of famous court cases in sixteenth- and seventeenth-century England. When, for example, Sir William Sharington severely impaired his reputation as a servant of the state by abusing his privileges as the vice-treasurer of the Bristol Mint in 1549, the money he had spent on his houses, and most especially Lacock Abbey, became drawn into the judgement of his felonies.[13]

The Acts of Dissolution

Historians have offered different interpretations of the causes of the two Acts of Dissolution. One school of thought sees that of 1536 as simply a softening-up exercise in preparation for the second (1539), something of a trial run to see how the country reacted. Reform of the monasteries (though not their wholesale suppression) had often been discussed in early Tudor England as part of a wider humanist reform programme. Another view argues that a crisis in 1534 and a threat of invasion did at that point cause the government to look at the monasteries as a source of capital, but it is easy to read the pattern of events with hindsight back from the wars with France of the 1540s and 1550s (which absorbed so much of the monastic revenues accrued by the Crown), as if these events were the planned outcome of such a windfall.[14] The process became a self-fulfilling one; if the government propagated the notion that monastic communities were potentially hotbeds of resistance to the most important aim of reform thus far, the placing of the king at the head of the English Church in place of the pope, then the refusal of a relatively small number of high-profile abbots to accept the surrender, followed by their public humiliation and execution, justified the government's case. As discussed below, certain systematic campaigns of destruction followed each Act of Suppression, but it is important to note here that it was widely expected for the physical monastic fabric to continue in some form once the buildings had been sufficiently decommissioned, thus making the re-gathering of their religious communities an impossibility. Indeed, the Crown was challenged through a series of individual appeals to allow the saving of some monasteries for community use because it was argued that these particular sites played a wider role in their localities or were very remote. Sir Thomas Audley suggested the foundation of colleges at the monastery of St John's at Colchester and at the Augustinian priory of St Osyth's, also in Essex: 'bothe these howses be in the ende of the shire [. . .], where litel hospitality shalbe kept, yf these be dissolved. For as Seynt Jones lakkyth water, and Seynt Osyes stondeth in the mersches, not very holsom, so that fewe of reputation, as I thynke, wil kepe continual howses in eny of them oonlez it be a congregation, as ther be nowe.'[15] Royal commissioners on their visitation of monasteries in the spring of 1536 praised Ulverscroft in Leicestershire and the Augustinian house of Northampton both for hospitality and relief of the poor. Ulverscroft 'standith in a wildernesse in the fforeste off Charnwood & refressith many pore people & waye faryng people'.[16]

The government was well aware of the dangers of so potentially traumatic a break in the pattern of ownership and habitation of buildings, and the farming of their estates, such that particular steps were taken to ensure continuity. The 1536 Act is particularly revealing in this respect since it decrees that 'all and singular persons, bodies politic and corporate to whom the King's majesty, his heirs and successors, hereafter shall give, grant, let or demise any site or precinct with the houses thereon builded [. . .] shall be bounden by the authority of this Act. [. . .] to keep or cause to be kept an honest, continual house and household in the same site or precinct, and to occupy yearly as much of the said demesnes in ploughing and tillage of husbandry.'[17] It may be that the placing of this clause towards the end of the provisions was concerned principally with the huge number of granges, farmhouses and other buildings on the monastic estates rather than the monastic buildings at its centre, but it signals an expectation of continuity nevertheless. Indeed, it is arguable that it was only specifically the monastic church that was singled out as the key building to de-commission. In the long negotiation and special pleading that took place in 1536–7 as Lord Lisle, the king's deputy at Calais, sought to get his hands on the priory of Frithelstock, in Devon, his agent John Husee warned: 'The very house of ffrystock, as it is now left, by every man's report is scant worth a mean farm, for the house of the priory is pulled down and nothing standing but the house for the farmer.'[18] The pre-dissolution presence of lay patrons on monastic sites and the wish of new owners in many cases to preserve and re-direct the goodwill of the local populace from the monastery towards themselves meant that there was often active preservation of buildings in working use. Deliberate destruction on any large scale was determined at particular sites by political circumstances, by the isolation of the property from proximate settlement or by the conflict of urban interest groups with the monastery in their midst (in larger towns, perhaps several monasteries).

Costs of purchase, costs of conversion

It is important to look at the balance sheet of investment both financial and in terms of aspiration to political power by all the parties interested in the opportunity that the dissolution provided. For the Crown, the immediate benefits were financial since, contrary to many assumptions about the king 'giving' away this seized patrimony, even the most favoured courtiers bought their new properties, albeit at favourable rates, and in some cases very swiftly after the monastic community had been evicted. Sometimes, especially in the case of some of the royal commissioners on the ground – for example Sir William Sharington at Lacock, Wiltshire, or Sir Thomas Wriothesley at Titchfield, Hampshire – new owners were in possession of the site within days of the religious community's ejection (fig. 14).[19] In other

cases, the Crown, in the person of Thomas Cromwell or one of the chief officers of the Court of Augmentations in charge of the processes of taking properties and selling them on, were evasive or allowed other parties seemingly to compete, not necessarily to up the price but to keep courtiers guessing at the seeming whim of the royal will. Many gained equivalent properties to those they asked for, but not the specific sites they requested. The battle undertaken on behalf of Lord Lisle by his agent for Frithelstock, mentioned above, was largely due to the machinations of Richard Rich, Chancellor of the Court of Augmentations, which effectively blocked the decision for many months; clearly Rich had his own reasons for exercising his power over someone who ostensibly outranked him.[20]

In addition, monastic sites and estates became a means by which the king was able to place his intimates and most trusted servants in parts of the country where their ear to the ground on his behalf was most necessary. In a key position near the Sussex coast, the great Benedictine abbey of Battle in Sussex was sold to Sir Anthony Browne, the King's Master of the Horse, in order to plant a magnate and trusted servant in this area for the purposes of defence and of settling the local area. Browne duly obliged, notwith-

14 Titchfield Abbey, Hampshire. Sir Thomas Wriothesley's Caen stone gatehouse of 1538, driven through the nave of the former monastic church.

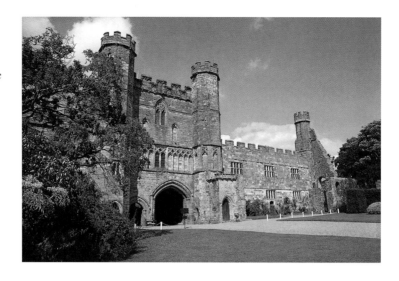

15 Battle Abbey, East Sussex. The 13th-century gatehouse to the abbey, with Sir Anthony Browne's new court house for the town to the right, built about 1550.

standing that he inherited from his half-brother Sir William Fitzwilliam the great (and recently built) West Sussex house of Cowdray just a few years later. At Battle, Browne extended the range to the east of the thirteenth-century abbey gatehouse to provide a court house for the town, a very visible sign of the meeting of the private and domestic, for this stood at the edge of the outer court of the monastery, now the main court of Browne's new house (fig. 15). He was buried in the local parish church, just outside the old perimeter wall of the abbey, beneath a splendid tomb chest proclaiming his courtier status by its taking the cue of style from the monument to Henry VII in Westminster Abbey.[21] Following the disturbances of the Pilgrimage of Grace in 1536–7, Charles Brandon, widower of the king's sister Mary and now married to a Lincolnshire heiress, Katherine Willoughby, was prevailed upon to sell his estates in East Anglia, including his very new house at Westhorpe in Suffolk, and move to a new power base in Lincolnshire.[22] He rebuilt the great house of Grimsthorpe but the symbolic significance of his new position was embodied in the grant of historic sites such as Tattershall Castle and the site of the abbey of Barlings, just outside Lincoln. At the latter, research published in 2003 has shown that Brandon lived in a newly built house alongside gardens incorporating monastic ruins. He thus became the king's vice-regent placed in an historical cathedral city with a very pointed reminder to all of the royal power to impose order and change the landscape.[23] Monastic property also served the Crown's purpose for other administrative arrangements in the transformation of the Cistercian house at York into King's Manor, the seat of the King's Council in the North, sealed in significance by Henry's staying there with Queen Catherine Howard on his progress in the north of England in 1541.[24]

Two key issues emerge concerning the buyers of monastic sites: who were they and what prices did they pay relative to their income? The most thorough analyses of the first question have concluded that one should beware of believing in the creation of an entirely new class of estate owners. Established aristocratic families did rather well and a relatively small number of courtiers, many of lowly origin, established great family seats thereby. The speculators standing between these two groups form no single body but the actions of the most successful of them show a deliberate policy of holding properties across a variety of geographical locations and of holding on to these properties only as long as they yielded a viable income.[25]

The costs of monastic conversion are significant because they reveal attitudes to long-term investment and the willingness, or not, to spend on these new, and politically risky, properties. It is apparent that few expected to be put to great expense but warnings were issued nevertheless about the dangers of spending too much in an unfamiliar market. The conversion of monasteries tells a great deal about the low expectation of new owners who were not willing to spend large sums on adaptation. Agents and other officers of new owners, men who actually visited the site and sometimes supervised building works, were constantly advising their patrons that this or that building was already suitable as a means of keeping costs down. Nevertheless, coming in to such properties could be expensive if the debts that the new owner took on were of some magnitude. Commissioners advised Thomas Wriothesley that at Titchfield the house had general debts of £200, specific debts to the king of 200 marks (or £133) and that 'the expense of alterations will be 300 marks (£200) at the least and thus your entry will be expensive'.[26] The Royal Works afford the best documentation of the actual costs of construction and these buildings also offer a more accurate sense of whether the use of the site was expected to be temporary or more permanent, if sporadic, since the State Papers give a rich record of later use not traceable for other classes of society. At St Augustine's, Canterbury, one particular royal visit promised use but possibly no further such occasions were foreseen: here the abbot's quarters, of stone, were comfortable and modern enough to serve as the king's lodging, but a new range had to be built rapidly in timber to receive Anne of Cleves on her way to London in the closing days of 1539, at a cost of £650.[27] At Rochester, much more of the site was re-used; accounts speak of 'the King's lodging called the late dorter' and 'the great hall which was the frater before' and two series of payments totalling £418 and £819 respectively chart the completion of this work.[28] At Dartford, however, a former nunnery at first simply plundered for its materials but by 1542 reconfigured as a hunting seat, a radical rebuilding cost £6600 later in the decade.[29]

Even the highest of the king's servants did not need quite the extensive provision of a royal court, except that Edward Seymour, Duke of Somerset, Protector to the young Edward VI, did have something of those pretensions.

His cofferer's roll shows that in two years Somerset spent over £5000 on building works on the site of the former Bridgettine abbey of Syon.[30] Here it seems that a radical transformation took place when Somerset's new courtyard house, to this day still the basic shape of the present house as transformed by Robert Adam between 1760 and 1773, was built over the nave of the abbey church, entailing much destruction. Somerset had similarly destroyed and ruthlessly used the materials not only from former monasteries but also from bishops' houses (commonly called Inns) in the city of London for the construction of his town house.[31] A rare record of expenditure (though the statements may not be totally trustworthy) survives from a difficult political moment in 1549, when the owner of Lacock came before an enquiry. As mentioned above, Sir William Sharington was arrested for fraud in connection with his post as vice-treasurer of the Bristol Mint and his expenses were identified: 2000 marks (£1333) on building works at Lacock in the previous three years.[32] Clearly some owners and their employees took pleasure in a certain value for money. New owners were conscious of achieving a new house that was not as draining as building totally from scratch. Agents at Titchfield flattered Wriothesley by saying: 'Many do preyse yor worke, som so highly that they say no man in England without exception for the quantitie of it shall have a strong or more boatful nete and pleasaunt house altho they or he shuld spend three thousand pounde more than yo shall. [. . .] Never no work hath done in so short space with so few workmen.'[33]

The state of the buildings and deliberate destruction

The readiness of the grantees of monastic sites to convert the buildings as found suggests a sense that the general state of the monasteries was sound and adaptable. Much of the decay reported by the pre-dissolution visits of royal commissioners in 1535–6 is part and parcel of the general picture of moral dilapidation that they sought to paint.[34] Pleas of poverty were frequent, and monastic communities sometimes argued that the state of their buildings was bound up with necessary income from elsewhere to sustain and modernise them. The Dominican friars of Guildford, burdened with the cost of a recent 'House of Honour' established there by the king in 1528 and struggling to complete gardens associated with this building, put it thus:

> havyng no londys Rents nother tenmentys for the mayntenace of theyr sayd hows and co'vent but lyvyth by charyte and almes of all true crysten people the wiche charyte and almys we Receave not so plantefull as we have yn tyme passyd wherthrough the sayd place hathe sustained great scarcyte and penury as well often tymes wanyng towards their bodily sustenacyon as yn mayntena'ce of theyr Ruyno' house and buyldyng.[35]

The deliberate and thoroughgoing destruction that came to be associated with the dissolution happened only at selective sites. Removal of the whole site, or even the aim to do so, was rare, though it seems that some systematic removal took place in Lincolnshire after the rebellion known as the Pilgrimage of Grace of 1536–7.[36] At Lewes, East Sussex, it would seem that Thomas Cromwell's employment of the Italian Giovanni Portinari to pull down the greater part of the Cluniac priory was motivated by the re-sale value of the Caen stone, though it may also reflect particular concern about this priory's historic role as the mother house of an order perceived as especially foreign (fig. 16).[37] At other sites, a programme of systematic destruction did not aim at the total obliteration of all the buildings. Similar stories of the deliberate pulling down of walls to that of Lewes are evident at Reading in Berkshire and at St Augustine's, Canterbury, but at both places by no means all the site was destroyed. Moreover the difficulties in pulling down walls and the inventiveness of the overseers in achieving this at Lewes, Stanley in Wiltshire and Reading suggest that such activity was uncommon and that techniques of destruction were improvised, sometimes with tragic results. At Stanley excavations in the south transept have revealed that

16   Southover Grange, Lewes, East Sussex. Built in 1572 with Caen stone taken from the dissolved Cluniac priory nearby. The connecting porch between the wings is much later in date.

pillars of its east wall were sunk into pits, suggesting that the wall was destroyed only by props and mining; a skeleton found beneath the masonry was evidence of the fate of one of the workmen.[38] The mining of sites continued; gunpowder was used during the reign of Edward VI to remove Bishop Stillington's chapel at the cathedral of Wells, though the permission granted to Sir John Gates for this procedure anticipated not a quick result but more than four years of demolition.[39] Destruction was in most cases a long and arduous process and the removal of stone left indelible marks. At St Albans, Hertfordshire, indentations made by the wheels of carts as stone was transported out of the chapter house into the cloister have been found in archaeological investigation.[40]

All this material had potentially a new purpose; re-cycling building materials was a familiar exercise in early Tudor England and in this sense the destruction of the monasteries simply formed part of a much wider interchange and re-use. A careful study of centuries of transporting stone has demonstrated the range of uses to which material was put in Lincolnshire, sometimes casual as hardcore, sometimes functional in the transportation of an entire feature to serve the same purpose elsewhere, sometimes retaining iconic value when worked stone was perceived to have symbolic significance.[41] In many cases new owners would destroy only in part in order to re-use building stone on site, as did Sir Anthony Browne at Battle in Sussex and Sir Thomas Holcroft at Vale Royal, Cheshire.[42] Other sites became quarries for local towns, sometimes continuously, sometimes only on sporadic and time-defined licence from the Crown; the abbey of Reading suffered systematic destruction at the time of the Somerset Protectorate when, between 1550 and 1553, stone was removed for the building of St Mary's church and then later, in Elizabeth's reign, licences were issued to the town for the removal of stone for the repair of bridges (fig. 17).[43] A sense that the 'stock' of building stone was somewhat finite emerges whenever stone is needed for structures that can be built in no other way. Fortifications are the most significant case in point here: Caen stone from the abbey of Bradsole in Kent was used for the building of Sandgate Castle in the 1540s and at the same time the abbey of Meaux afforded material for fortifications at Hull.[44] It was rumoured that near Dover in 1541 'the king's men are demolishing churches and religious houses near the sea, to convey the materials to Guines (in the Pas-de-Calais) for the fortifications.'[45] In many cases, individual features of monastic buildings such as windows and complete free-standing gatehouses were transported elsewhere, rarely it seems because they were believed of symbolic value but because their building material or their sound construction made them still practicable. A whole series of forty clerestory windows from Rewley Abbey near Oxford were used in the new bowling alley constructed at Hampton Court after their removal in 1537.[46] A window now at Samelsbury Hall, Lancashire, is likely to have come from Whalley Abbey.[47] The bay window added to the

Great Hall at Gainsborough Old Hall, Lincolnshire, has the appearance of being monastic in origin.[48] Perhaps one of the most emphatic of all the examples to survive is the fourteenth-century gatehouse moved by Sir Richard Williams from one monastic property, Ramsey Abbey, Huntingdonshire, to another, the former priory of Hinchingbrooke, where it eventually served a similar purpose to its original function, as the entry to the outer court of the newly converted house just as it had once given access to the abbey (fig. 18).[49]

Just as monasteries had been suppressed before the two Acts of Dissolution, giving at least some sense of continuity to the dramatic happenings after 1536, so the transformation of monastic fabric also had a context within wider building enterprise in the later sixteenth century. Even wilful despoliation was not confined to the first phase. John Stow describes how William Paulet, later Marquess of Winchester, preserved the church of the Augustine Friars in London, dividing it in half. In 1550 the west end was granted to the community of Dutch nationals living in London whilst the east end with choir, steeple and side aisles was used for storage until his son, inheriting in 1572, sold the monuments and paving stones from the east end for the small sum of £100 and changed the storage space into a stable.[50] Conversion was not therefore always as simply practical and summary as some of the first campaigns of the 1530s might suggest. Making

17 (*above left*) St Mary's, Reading, Berkshire. The church tower, built in 1550–53 with chequered flint and stone removed from the site of the town's former Benedictine abbey.

18 (*above right*) The late medieval gateway from Ramsey Abbey, Huntingdonshire, moved after the dissolution to serve as the entrance to another former monastic site, Hinchingbrooke, in the same county.

living and working spaces from these structures proved a lasting challenge for the rest of the century and beyond.

Monasteries in the hands of the Crown

As argued above, the royal use of former monasteries is a useful case of both reaction and inspiration because they are so well documented relative to many other buildings. Because the Crown retained a significant handful of sites, there built up an expertise in the problems of conversion, most notably at the hands of James Nedeham, the king's Surveyor of Works, responsible for both Dartford and Rochester.[51] It is clear from the beginning of the dissolution process that commissioners had an eye to those sites that might be suitable for the king's use. At the time of the dissolution, Henry VIII hardly lacked residences; between 1536 and 1539 he was building extensively at no fewer than twenty-three other properties, plus work at several former bishops' town and country houses. Major work was happening at Whitehall, Hampton Court, Oatlands and Nonsuch (the last begun in 1538, using for its foundations stone from the priory of Merton). It is clear that some former monastic properties, along with several former bishops' palaces, were seen as potential staging posts for the king on certain journeys, particularly those that stood on the road to Dover.[52] In some cases, for example the Benedictine abbey at Reading and the Dominican priory of Guildford, it seemed natural that the king would keep such properties at which he had lodged before the dissolution. The former College of Bonshommes at Ashridge was used as a home for the royal children, being situated on elevated ground and therefore believed to be salubrious and protective of the dynasty's future.[53] In two cases, the Crown's retaining or resuming ownership of former monasteries gave Mary I the chance for some restitution in her five-year reign (1553–8). The Bridgettine nuns returned to Syon, which had passed back to the Crown at the attainder of the Duke of Somerset in 1552, though investigation of the site has made it clear that the vast church had been substantially removed.[54] From 1557, after the death of Anne of Cleves (grantee of the site ten years earlier), Dartford was for two years the home of Dominican friars.[55] Moreover, there was some transfer of property back to the church via its prominent figures, if only for the short period of Queen Mary's reign: St Augustine's, Canterbury, was granted in 1556 to the papal legate, Cardinal Pole, having already served as a seat of Archbishop Cranmer in the previous reign.[56] Other properties were useful as sites to lease to courtiers and it was eventually by these means that almost the entire monastic patrimony of the Crown was alienated through lease, usually followed by sale within a generation.

None of the former monastic properties was kept in constant repair during Elizabeth's reign and thus there was a slow process of dispersal.

Rochester had been sold as early as the reign of Edward VI to Lord Cobham, who sold it on to the dean and chapter of the new cathedral of Rochester, having made as much as he could from the dispersal of some of its building materials.[57] Ashridge, having long ceased its duty as a royal nursery, was sold to Thomas, Lord Ellesmere, in 1575.[58] St Augustine's, Canterbury, was leased to Lord Cobham in 1564 for thirty years and then James I granted some materials from the site to Robert Cecil towards the building of Hatfield; the whole of the site was then sold to Edward, Lord Wooton, in 1612.[59] The future of Dartford was discussed as part of the exchange between James I and Cecil in 1606 and it, too, was sold in 1612, to Robert Darcy.[60] At St Albans the Crown kept for its own use the buildings of the outer court, even after relinquishing most of the former monastery in 1553, because its position on the road north from London provided a staging post. It was last repaired by the Crown in 1607 and dispensed with shortly thereafter.[61] Only the Cistercian abbey of York, converted into a seat for the King's Council of the North, survived in Crown hands throughout the seventeenth century.[62] The Crown was always in the forefront of weighing up the cost benefits of holding on to such property. In 1598 squared stone from Dartford was taken for building works at Whitehall. But it was clear that a piecemeal dismemberment of an already dilapidated building was not going to be a good return. In 1601, when the sale of Dartford was first contemplated, it was pointed out to the Crown that the site might be sold for almost £1500 but the value of the materials was a mere £154, stressing the fact that these buildings were past their sell-by date as simply either quarries for building stone or repositories for storage, save for very local, short-term needs.[63]

Monasteries in towns

The fate of monastic sites in the urban environment provides one of the most emphatic pieces of evidence of continuity between their state in medieval times and their post-dissolution conversion, while also stressing the ways in which former monastic buildings could inspire solutions to urban development that were quite distinctive. The relationship between townspeople and civic authorities on the one hand and the monastery, or series of monasteries, in their midst, varied from place to place. At Reading, the Benedictine abbey was always an integral part of urban life; the meeting of the town's market at its gates was so fundamental a fixture that the arrangement continued beyond the dissolution.[64] At Bury St Edmunds, on the other hand, town and abbey had grown rather apart in the century preceding the 1530s; the town had somewhat turned its back on the abbey and had taken over many of its extramural urban initiatives by the early sixteenth century.[65] Research into significant sites within what is now under-

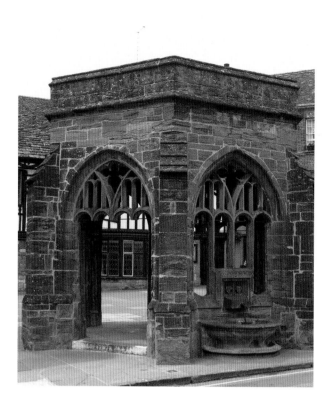

stood as Greater London has revealed a highly active interface between town and monastery in the late Middle Ages. The remains of tenements built in monastic times on the east side of both St Mary Clerkenwell and St Mary Spital, Bishopsgate, suggest that these foundations expanded at their outer edges either for the use of abbey servants or for revenue from lets. Certainly at the Clerkenwell site, seventeen tenements yielded some 12 per cent of the institution's total income by the 1520s. At St Mary Spital the tenements flanked a roadway from the hospital building almost in the form of a terraced street. These buildings did not disappear at the Reformation but continued in use possibly as late as the eighteenth century.[66] High-ranking tenants lived in such places, including aristocrats and court functionaries, reminding one that before the building of great town houses along the Strand in the second half of the sixteenth century it was necessary for such people to live as comfortably as they could in such buildings, perhaps only for part of the year, in order to be in attendance at the royal court or during the Law terms.

The leading role of the monasteries in providing for urban water supplies meant that town governments were anxious to preserve and take over this key facility at the Reformation; indeed they had often collaborated in organising this resource with the religious foundations. The built fabric of this

provision thus became integral to the town at this time. At the end of Half Moon Street, Sherborne, Dorset, the north side of which is made up of sixteenth-century tenements, the edge of the former abbey precinct is marked by the early sixteenth-century conduit, originally built by Abbot Mere for the lavatorium in the abbey cloister but moved here to serve the town after the Reformation (fig. 19).[67] At Lincoln the city authorities collaborated with the Greyfriars as late as 1535 for the building of their new conduit and conduit head in such a position as to serve both the friary and the city. At the dissolution the one demand of the city of the monastic precinct was the continuance of the conduit head, which almost certainly stood at the southern end of the precinct.[68]

The 'open door' policy of many urban monasteries in late medieval England had often extended to the monastic church itself. At a significant number of sites the monastic church became the parish church in the 1530s, not always as a new departure but underpinning and legalising a long-established tradition. Malmesbury, Wiltshire, and Dorchester on Thames, Oxfordshire (at Dorchester, unusually, the whole of the monastic church officially became the parish church after the dissolution), are among the most significant cases of customary use becoming formalised (fig. 20).[69] At the Franciscan friary of Chester merchants and sailors had helped pay for

20 Malmesbury, Wiltshire. The parish church, formerly the nave of the abbey church, 12th century, with 14th- to 15th-century windows.

rebuilding the church in the early sixteenth century in return for permission to store sails and equipment in the aisles, suggesting that in the decades before the dissolution the monastic choir alone was proving to be sufficient space for the friars in which to worship.[70] It is significant too how often even small parts of the monastic complex had roles to play in the new shape of the town after the dissolution. The former abbot of St Albans Abbey, now a schoolmaster, purchased his monastery's Lady Chapel to use as a school in 1551, while the former gatehouse of the abbey served as a town gaol.[71] Turning parts of the monastic complex to urban use was often initiated by the town even as the suppression was taking place. The commissioner John Freeman wrote to Cromwell in October 1538 that 'the whole town' of Grimsby begged to have use of the church of the Austin Friars as a storehouse for anchors and cables.[72]

At Reading the re-tooling of the monastic legacy proved especially practically oriented towards changing civic needs: over several decades it became clear how much of the monastic fabric would survive and to what different purposes it could be put along with a sense of where the town's future centre of gravity would be in the new, post-Reformation setting. In September 1538 the royal commissioner John London appealed to Cromwell on behalf of Reading that the church of the Greyfriars be allocated as a new town hall, while the rest of the site could serve the king's usual purpose at commodious sites he did not wish for himself, namely as a prime site for a leading courtier: 'And if it please the King's grace to bestow that house upon any of hys servants, he may spare the body of the churche, wich standith next the strete very well; and yet have roume sufficient for a great man.' The town's wish was finally granted in 1542. In 1560, however, when Elizabeth I presented a new charter to Reading, a new urban prosperity was beginning to emerge. It was centred not around the former Greyfriars but rather in the parish of St Laurence, just outside the gates of the great Benedictine abbey at the eastern end of the town. In this district the new urban oligarchy lived and here the chief market continued, as in monastic times. Since the *hospitium* of the old abbey had survived and had served as a school, it was here that the town hall eventually moved in 1578, moving the school to the lower floor. It was as if Reading had relocated to its former centre of activity.[73] Towns became adept at putting monastic and chantry foundations to a variety of uses, both communal and mercantile. At Beverley, Yorkshire, a suppressed chantry chapel became a gaol.[74] Enterprising citizens sometimes put buildings to commercial use. The transformation of monastic buildings at Malmesbury by the clothier William Stumpe has become especially famous because of John Leland's graphic description not only of the transformation of the monastic cloister but of Stumpe's enterprise in housing his workforce: 'At this present tyme every corner of the vaste houses of office that belongid to thabbay be fulle of lumbes to weve clooth yn, and this Stumpe entendith to make a stret or 2.

21 Newcastle-upon-Tyne, Tyne and Wear. A range of the cloister buildings of the former Blackfriars, adapted to secular use. Medieval, with post-dissolution adaptation, 16th to 19th century.

For clothier in the bak vacant ground of the abbay that is withyn the towne walks.'[75]

The piecemeal adaptation of single ex-monastic buildings was therefore frequent and widespread in urban settings. The impact of monastic foundations on cities and towns, however, was both deep and broad. This came about when monastic spheres of influence lived on, sometimes resulting in the creation of a 'quarter' of like-minded citizens, crafts workers and small manufacturers within the town. Stow recounts how the former nuns' hall and adjacent houses at St Helen's, Bishopsgate, were bought by the Leathersellers' Company for their common hall. They also maintained seven alms dwellings for the poor in the former great court.[76] The former Blackfriars at Newcastle-upon-Tyne was bought from the Crown by the mayor and burgesses in 1544. The church was most likely pulled down at this point and the cloister area leased to nine crafts companies for their meetings in 1552. All nine stayed here until the nineteenth century and some of the original internal transformations of the sixteenth century still remain (fig. 21). Most interesting is the way that the unit let to the tanners had the original stair up to the refectory; this was retained and became the template for other units since they all sublet ground-floor spaces for a variety of purposes and needed secure access to the upper floor for their own gatherings, though even then only periodically so that upper floors too were put to several uses. Two ranges of the cloisters of Newcastle Blackfriars remain to this day, serving as shops and workshops in the spirit of the original post-Reformation use.[77]

In some instances, former monastic sites provided a spaciousness and plenitude of ground area around new dwellings that would otherwise have been impossible. The familiar pattern is one of making the most, financially and spatially, of the profitable return on urban development. A post-monastic grand house close to a block of tenement buildings, for example, can be seen in the 1590s plans of Holy Trinity, Aldgate, London, where Sir Thomas Audley's house in the outer court of the former Augustinian friary stood cheek by jowl with the tenements carved out of the floored crossing space and east end of the monastic church.[78] In other towns and cities, empty space was more generously allowed to remain. The church and steeple of the Carmelite house at Chester was demolished in 1597, when Thomas Egerton built a town house over the east end of the site, while at the western end a set-back house was erected and survives in a later form. There was thus open ground here around both large town houses.[79] But former monasteries also encouraged the perpetuation of the notion of 'precinct' when the establishment had in medieval times built up a 'territory' that was then sustained after the Reformation. At the Austin Friars in London, stone from the church provided the basic material for grand courtier houses nearby, some of which survived until the nineteenth century, the most famous of them being that of the Marquis of Winchester, chief grantee of the monastic site. Houses of lesser status in brick and timber surrounded these quasi-country house establishments. At St Bartholomew's, Smithfield, the equivalent of three parallel streets were laid down. Such precinct areas were possible only through the land being released all at once at the Reformation.[80] Previous conclusions that the upheaval of the period created an immediately rapacious and cut-throat land market need to be corrected in the longer view of the century as some aspects of the monastic past reasserted themselves and cut across radical redevelopment.

Urban survivals of the physical remains of the broad outlines of the monastic complex allow something of a meta-view, of the whole or partial retention of sequences of spaces, of interconnecting ranges, of inner spaces and the ground left around them: former monasteries clearly provided a new resource for the towns and cities of England that helped shape these communities for the rest of the century. Medieval towns were lacking in large indoor spaces for communal use. The convenience of large covered spaces released at the dissolution was a great advantage, enhancing a sense of the town as a place where people gathered and introducing what historians have described as the beginnings of leisure activities that attracted local gentry and their money. Such spaces could also serve as emergency headquarters in other ways. The remains of the former abbey of St Albans was one of many places where authorities from outside the city would assemble when plague made their regular gathering sites dangerous. In 1589 the assizes moved here from Hertford and in 1594, with plague in London, the law courts moved here from Westminster Hall for the Michaelmas term.[81] Former urban monasteries thus set something of the programme for new urban identities and purposes by providing large places where people could gather and through the potential released by their sheer ground area. To turn to particular architectural features that survived and their influence on the future, however, it is notable that monasteries provided very focused solutions to problems as each post-monastic building project was undertaken. Since this evidence is to a great extent dependent on recent excavation of standing buildings, this topic is best explored by examining country houses formed out of monasteries in rural areas or at the edge of small towns, where the survival rate of pre-dissolution structures is greater than those in densely populated urban areas.

The cloister and the courtyard house

To consider the plan of these establishments first: it has been argued that while in one sense the monastic cloister was the inner spiritual sanctum of the establishment, only its inner focus signified that contemplative life. Its western range usually accommodated the most public face of the religious house, its abbot's or abbess's dwelling; this was often the most comfortable part of the complex, often renewed and made more luxurious in the early years of the sixteenth century with a range of attached guest lodgings.[82] So on one side the cloister partook of the inner life of the monastery while on the other its western range formed one side of the public, outer court. In this it replicated the basic system of the conventional courtyard house. Many new, post-dissolution owners with any pretension to grand living used the cloister in that way. It could not, however, be used quite as it stood. First, whether to preserve or demolish the cloister walks had to be decided. In some, seemingly hasty, programmes of conversion, such as Wriothesley's house at Titchfield, they were immediately removed. This is despite the fact that early Tudor houses had long experimented with covered walkways, open on one side, towards or around gardens.[83] There are also instances in early Tudor houses, most notably at Hengrave Hall in Suffolk, of corridors running around the inner walls of a newly built conventional courtyard, giving privacy and convenience to what would otherwise be single ranges of rooms, one leading into the other.[84] Sir William Sharington apparently got the point at Lacock, perhaps initially because he found here a three-sided cloister rebuilt within living memory and in good order (fig. 22). More than this, he took the cue from the ground-floor cloister to build parallel corridors to give access to new suites of rooms carved out of spaces on the first floor.[85] There is the notable example of Sopwell, Hertfordshire, converted for Sir Richard Lee, where the cloister walks were initially destroyed and then seemingly replaced (as corridors) in a second round of modifications some years later.[86] Sometimes just one or two of the cloister walks proved convenient to retain when the house was completely re-orientated or made outward in aspect. At Forde, in Dorset, the gradual

22 Lacock Abbey,
Wiltshire. A view towards
the north-east of the
15th-century cloister, with
the walks retained and
new galleries built above
c. 1550.

transformation took the one newly built arm of the early sixteenth-century
cloister to lead from the Great Hall (formerly the hall of the abbot's lodging)
to the chapel, carved out of the chapter house.[87] Moreover at Forde, as at
Lacock, one of the early post-monastic owners also took advantage of the
cloister arm as a convenient passageway by duplicating its use through
creating a corridor above it. While the chapter house had been the place of
business, discussion and congregation in the old abbey, it now became the
new house's place of worship. This was certainly also the case at some
houses, though such use might not have been continuous since the Reformation; for example at Newstead, in Nottinghamshire, bought from the
Crown by Sir John Byron in 1540, the present nineteenth-century chapel
stands in the space of the monastic chapter house.[88] Making the cloister
walk a feature of the outside of a house, as at Forde, also became a solution to those properties, particularly developed for the first time, or rede-
veloped, in the seventeenth century, where only one or two ranges of a
cloister garth survived. A similar arrangement survives at Vale Royal,
Cheshire. Here the first post-monastic owner, Sir Thomas Holcroft, did
some radical removal of building ranges, leaving the Cholmondley family
in the early seventeenth century with just two major ranges left from the
monastic buildings.[89]

However, a converted space which created the sense of a cloister walk had one further significant and long-term influence through its link to the idea of a loggia in front of the hall range. As time went by, only the grandest – usually aristocratic – houses still needed multi-courtyard houses. New houses tended more and more to use smaller courtyards as light wells for what was essentially a compact house plan. In fact, where transformation was necessary it often came about with the rationalisation and restructuring of the house. As patrons wanted more evenly spaced windows on the inner façades of their courtyard houses, the old medieval and early Tudor convention of the great bay window to the hall became less fashionable. Some houses of a new kind, for example Kirby in Northamptonshire of the 1570s (still a courtyard house), and houses of a lesser pretension, such as Danny and Parham in Sussex (with extended frontage, now on an H- or E-plan), went to great lengths to express visual continuity. The window openings of the hall were repeated across the façade, beyond the (usually now central) hall door, even if these big windows gave largely on to kitchens or service spaces.[90]

In the courtyard space the problem of how to designate the most significant range was solved, particularly around 1590–1620, by the building of a loggia or open arcade before the hall, which at once signifies authority and effects both a kind of unity to the façade and a dignified entrance to the hall range. This is found where older buildings were being adapted and modernised, as far apart as Knole in Kent, a multi-courtyard house, in the great reordering for Thomas Sackville, Earl of Dorset, about 1605, and at Chillingham Castle in Northumberland, an example of the four-square northern fortified house. This idea passed sometimes into those houses where the entrance range was removed, revealing a three-sided house, a type of plan that reached its grandest form in the post-1600, Jacobean period. Perhaps the greatest example of all is at Hatfield, where the great loggia of Robert Cecil's house of 1605–1612 is now on the garden side of the present house, but this was originally the entrance front, backing on to the Great Hall behind it. In effect, here at a newly built house, this is the development of a solution used at earlier buildings where the cloister had been opened up and only part of it retained as a front to the house. The idea of the colonnade, giving both dramatic splendour to the hall range and a practical way of moving people about, both between the two ends of the Great Hall itself and from one projecting wing to the other is a significant monastic legacy.[91]

Access and floor levels

In the layout of the larger houses, monastic features also gave a lead to country houses in terms of floor levels. One important aspect of the visual appearance of the cloisters was that they often disguised the existence of changing floor levels between abutting ranges with different functions. Nevertheless the greatest domestic spaces of the monastery, that is to say the frater, dorter, abbot's or abbess's lodging, were upstairs, prefiguring the way in which Elizabethan great houses were themselves to develop their sequences of upper-floor spaces, just as houses of far more modest dimensions were increasingly using upper levels for bedrooms and private space. Crucially, however, it was the means of access that enabled change to take place, and here the plan of monasteries afforded new ideas about getting from one floor to another. In the conventional great houses of the end of the Middle Ages turret stairs had been used, tucked into the corners of courtyards, to convey people from ground to first floor. Entry to the most important space, the Great Hall, was at ground-floor level. When converting a monastery the transformation of an upstairs frater into the hall, or needing to get the visitor into the upper floor of the lodgings in the west range, had to be facilitated by an external staircase. These constructions were not usually grand or pretentious but they involved a decision about the prominence of this new architectural feature because it necessitated a compact single-flight structure to stand before the building range. Such stairs were constructed at Newstead for the Byrons, at Norton, Cheshire, for Sir Richard Brooke, and at Vale Royal.[92]

The traditional form of spiral stairs in turrets set into the corners of old courtyard houses certainly eased the problems of communication from ground to upper floors, helped the internal security of the house and, just occasionally, sometimes facilitated the passing from one place of leisure (an upper-floor gallery for example) to another (a garden or a private court). But they were essentially features of a kind of building where ranges around the court were separate from each other and served different functions for the house. From the mid-sixteenth century, newly built houses sought a more continuous flow of activity around the upper floor, around the courtyard if that still existed, or into the projecting wings of an open house. In very grand country houses, the staircase became part of a sequence of significant rooms, leading from the hall up to rooms of state for entertaining and housing important guests. The monasteries and their absorption into secular domestic life may have energised this change and suggested new solutions. In monasteries, stairs had been built integrally into ranges for the highly practical purposes of daily life and ritual. Wherever they were retained, new secular owners evidently learned from the past and in this way influenced new arrangements for staircases in domestic space. Two seventeenth-century plans of monastic sites clearly reveal this development. At Chetwode, Buckinghamshire, the remains of the small Augustinian priory are now the parish church and the adjoining Priory House. The church is simply the chancel of the former priory and the house stands on what was the eastern range of the cloister buildings, incorporating some

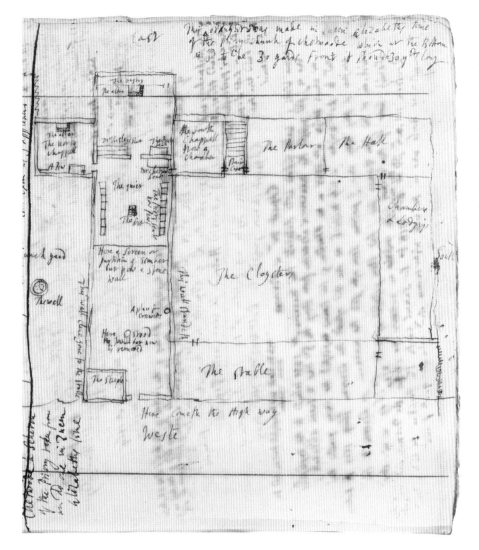

23 Plan of Chetwode Priory, Buckinghamshire, copied in the 19th century from a document made during Queen Elizabeth's reign. A staircase has been inserted in the narrow space of the monastic slype between the former south chapel and chapter house (indicated here as the post-monastic parlour). The Bodleian Library, University of Oxford, MS Willis, fol. 82r.

remains of them. However, in Queen Elizabeth's time, the buildings were differently used. Among the Willis manuscripts at the Bodleian Library there is a plan recording the sixteenth-century arrangements, showing three sides of cloister buildings in domestic use, with a staircase inserted where the narrow monastic slype would have been (fig. 23). An even simpler record of the priory of Chicksands, Bedfordshire, a house that now demonstrates the basic footprint of a cloister-into-courtyard house, shows how by the seventeenth century the passage entrance to the cloister in the western range, and thus from the outside world, had become 'the passage to the garden'. What is likely to have been the stair down from the frater to the south cloister is also still in use.[93]

Some of the seventeenth-century conversions betoken a new attitude to the past, involving as they sometimes did accepting the challenge of an old monastic site when a great family already had a fully developed country house elsewhere. One of the most interesting is the renewal of the fabric of the abbey of Woburn by Francis Russell, 4th Earl of Bedford, begun in the late 1620s, three quarters of a century after his great-grandfather, John Russell, courtier at the time of Henry VIII, first gained the reversion of the property. It is unclear how much Woburn was used by the Russell family in the sixteenth century, since for much of the time it was tenanted. The 4th Earl's major building operations were largely confined to a new, modestly sized north range, on the site of the south-western area of the monastic church. This range, with its grotto flanked by parlours, still survives. How the seventeenth-century earls used the rest of the house is recorded in an inventory of 1700 and in two plans and a view of the west front drawn by John Sanderson in the late 1740s, just before Henry Flitcroft's great transformation of the house. This shows a remarkable adaptation of the monastic layout, especially in the south claustral range, where the monks' arrangements of kitchen, warming house and frater were clearly turned into an assemblage of servants' quarters for working and eating that made optimum use of the medieval legacy.[94]

The longer view: the late sixteenth century and beyond

Changes over time also prompted a more general re-shaping of the surviving monastic buildings. It is fascinating to note the ways in which this places the transformations within the broader context of country-house history. In the seventeenth and eighteenth centuries many rambling late medieval and early Tudor multi-courtyard houses were scaled down drastically, both for economy of maintenance and for the management of much smaller households, to preserve only the core of the old house. However, this often required the formation of new kinds of service buildings in separate courtyards (or informal collections of buildings) away from the main house. Certain practical needs, such as stables and storage buildings, were still paramount, so that at The Vyne, Hampshire, the scaling down of a huge, early Tudor multi-courtyard house in the seventeenth century led, shortly thereafter, into the building of new, free-standing service buildings to make up the loss.[95] Where owners of former monastic property downsized from the provisions of a community house they faced similar problems, even at this early stage. At Battle, after the suppression of 1538, Sir Anthony Browne and his successors chose to use the outer court of the Benedictine abbey as the core of the new mansion, developing the former abbot's lodging in the western range of the cloister and giving the outer court's southern side a dramatic new focus with the construction of a new guest range. While the abbey church was largely pulled down, this refocusing of the site meant that the owners had to think about service provision, which is why other buildings, the dormitory for example, originally in the eastern arm of the cloister, were retained, but partly subdivided.[96]

The transformations discussed above were therefore not immediate responses to the dissolution but the objects of a second campaign of building which occurred when the dust had settled politically and when the buildings themselves had suggested their own solutions; these were not immediately apparent to those anxious to settle on the site in the years immediately after the dissolution. But in some cases the time-frame is even broader than this. Some sites were left completely undeveloped, or used for subletting or storage, only to become great houses many decades after they ceased to be monasteries. Issues of class and political factors caused these delays. While courtiers felt sufficiently confident to take risks and commence large-scale conversions in the 1530s and 1540s, evidence suggests that the gentry classes waited well into the later decades of the century until the religious settlement looked more permanent.[97] Perhaps too by 1600 tastes had changed and the political elite wanted new fashionable houses

24 Buckland Abbey, Devon. The crossing tower, with nave to the left, of the monastery converted into a house by the Grenville family in the 1570s. The transformation would have disguised much of the earlier monastery and was perhaps even rendered; the crossing arch and monastic stonework were unpicked by 19th-century restorers.

25 Forde Abbey, Dorset. From left to right, Abbot Chard's Great Hall, the new 'solar' tower built by Sir Edmund Prideaux in the mid-17th-century, the late medieval north cloister walk.

undetermined in their scale or appearance by pre-existing fabric, whereas less affluent people, perhaps less subject to the whims of fashion, were still attracted by the good value of what remained of the monastic legacy. On another level, effecting a transformation after a delay of perhaps half a century must have been determined chiefly by practical considerations, for after many years of dilapidation and licensed robbing of materials by local people, owners could only now make a house from the strongest part of the building to survive. Buckland Abbey, Devon, shows one of the most startling examples of the nave-and-crossing area of a monastic church, developed by the Grenvilles in the 1570s, more than thirty years after the initial grant to the family (fig. 24). It was of course not the first monastery where the church itself offered the main living space: in the years after 1536 the nave of the Augustinian house of Mottisfont Priory, Hampshire, was floored to provide the grand rooms for the new house of William, Lord Sandys; and at Sir William Paulet's Netley Abbey, also in Hampshire, the nave was transformed into the Great Hall during the same period. But both of these remained courtyard houses using much of the former claustral ranges, whereas at Buckland forty years later the main great house was

formed entirely from the monastic church. In a sense this can be said to foreshadow the more compact, high houses of the late Elizabethan age, most especially those associated with the name of Robert Smythson at a building such as Worksop Manor Lodge.[98]

Other later developers found not one but several surviving ranges, sometimes attached to, sometimes isolated from, each other. At Forde Abbey, one of the most eloquent of all former monasteries in the way it reveals externally a continual process of transformation for more than a century after the dissolution, some decisions had been taken soon after the Reformation, as discussed above. Then in the mid-seventeenth century Sir Edmund Prideaux completed a transformation that had taken more than a century, thus creating one of the earliest proto-Romantic silhouettes of a house of monastic origin. The porch to Abbot Chard's late fifteenth-century hall is balanced with a late version of a medieval solar block; here Prideaux housed his new saloon on the upper floor, and he kept the already established use of the one late medieval cloister arm to lead from hall to chapel (figs 25 and 26). The informal grouping of old and new structures at Forde must have been a significant prototype for eighteenth- and especially

26 Forde Abbey, Dorset. Detail of the late medieval cloister walk leading to the chapter house at the right, converted into the chapel of the post-monastic house.

nineteenth-century owners of former monastic houses who wished to celebrate the origins of their buildings by unpicking the post-dissolution changes and revealing monastic features.[99]

As early as the seventeenth century, regret for the passing of the monasteries was evident in many literary genres. In fact the loss of these religious houses and the remains of many within the landscape helped to shape attitudes towards the past, towards a growing English, anti-foreign nationalism and towards the shaping of new kinds of writing and an antiquarian construction of history. An evidently ruined past was an eloquent way of giving that distance from a 'history' that had to be reconstructed and mythologised, as in Shakespeare's history plays. Moreover, this was not a tale of destruction that could be set at the door of an outsider, as Spanish rule and destruction of history infiltrated itself into the psychology of Dutch nationalism. This English awareness of history was reflected in the slow but significant development of the representation of the monasteries. Occasionally there is a glimpse of something terrible and brutalised, as in the sketch of Shaftesbury Abbey in the 1565 survey of the lands of the Earl of Pembroke.[100] Estate maps owe their existence and rapid development in the later sixteenth century to the massive re-ordering of dissolved landholdings and the build-up of large new estates, which necessitated owners having a visual record of what they owned.[101] It is notable that many new houses of the period are quite conventionally depicted in these maps, usually by an abbreviated sketch of something turreted and rather fantastical, while older properties are often depicted in sufficient detail to supply some conjectural evidence about the appearance of the post-monastic house and what its original extent was. These images also help to show how monastic houses were conventionally adapted and assimilated; several examples from the seventeenth century show the use of series of gables along the inner façades of the house, demonstrating how this feature could disguise old non-aligned roof levels.[102] But most surviving early visual representation, certainly in England, functioned simply as a practical way of recording. Only towards the end of the seventeenth century do painted and printed representations of converted monasteries begin to appear, usually at houses where a modern, classical front or range has been added. In these images they are often surrounded by formal gardens and parks, which falsify the original sense of a working house, at one with the working order of the monastery that came before it.

But for the third and fourth generations, a century or so after the dissolution, there was about to be a further assault on buildings that would make many great domestic houses, indeed all buildings in urban settings, vulnerable in a way that the monasteries were a century before. The Civil Wars of the 1640s brought a great deal of destruction, both when houses found themselves in the theatre of conflict and in the form of systematic despoliation of houses whose owners had backed the wrong side. Some owners, for example Sir John Winter at Whitecross in Gloucestershire, deliberately razed their own houses to prevent their enemies taking possession. Monastic conversions, now fully assimilated into the building landscape, suffered alongside their newer counterparts. At Lilleshall, Shropshire, a house formed out of part of the former abbey buildings became a royalist garrison. This was bombarded and then assaulted by the Parliamentarians in 1645. A century after the dissolution, England was once again dotted with new ruins, some of which were never repaired.[103]

2

'All This "New" Building':
The Urban Landscape

It has become commonplace to discuss the issue first raised by W. G. Hoskins under the heading 'The Great Rebuilding', whereas his article of 1953 was in fact entitled 'The Rebuilding of Rural England'.[1] To some extent Hoskins was thereby making it clear that many of the issues about the larger towns, but most importantly the city of London, would not be caught up in the profound message that he wished to put across. His 'rebuilding' was essentially focused on the greater spread of the country's domestic building stock in the farmhouses and dwellings of classes of people that covered a range from the reasonably solvent farmer to the minor gentry. Hoskins's point about the transformation of buildings by the insertion of floors, the adding of wings of privacy and convenience, the infilling of fireplaces and the building of chimneys sits well with the stress on transformation argued here. Hoskins's concentration was, however, on the domestic infrastructure of the countryside. Commentators on his argument since the 1970s turned the debate towards urban evidence to make specific points or sought to see whether the basis for this change is supported by contemporary documentation.[2] When one turns to the urban environment, one finds – alongside new arrangements in domestic dwellings – that other new forms of building emerge there; such forms also pose questions about their role in a great rebuilding. New urban structures were determined in shape and function by a society coming to terms with a new, post-reform mentality. There was thus a demand for new places of assembly for political debate and commercial transaction and new forms of social interaction. Provision was needed too for the sick and elderly and the punishment of offenders. The attempts of government to secure the allegiance of the country to the religious settlement meant that devices of control were put in place which sought to empower local officials loyal to the Crown, to determine certain patterns of behaviour among the populace and to enforce conformity.[3] The government also sought actively – and creditably allow-

27 Steyning, West Sussex. In Church Street, the brick porch of the grammar school, founded in 1614, with wings converted from 15th-century buildings of the fraternity of the Holy Trinity, to which gables were added *c.* 1600.

ing for the distance of time from a modern viewpoint – to relieve the poor by giving communities the tools to pay for housing, food and work.[4] This chapter is concerned with the success or otherwise of this policy and investigates both new initiatives and continuity with the past through urban housing, churches and public secular buildings.

Concerning housing, successive governments were aware of the dangers of visible decay in the urban infrastructure in the form of uninhabited dwellings, vacant plots, dilapidated town walls and gates and poor means of access caused by roads and bridges being in need of repair. Ultimately, however, the government could be no more than admonitory since the citizens of the towns themselves were the only people in a position to re-shape the environment. From this re-shaping, particular building types bear the distinctiveness of the period. Public buildings (churches, town halls, almshouses, schools and the many other structures needing constant repair, ranging from town gates and defences to bridges, lock-ups and conduits) marked the power and the patronage of local dignitaries with money to spare and charity to dispense. Private developments show the affluence with which certain classes chose to live and their encouragement of the formation of new streets marked a new turn towards a different kind of town. In these developments, new building technologies and the local importation of materials from elsewhere often changed the skeletal form of built structures. Only once that had been done can the imposition of aspects that might be described as stylistic, inspired by rivalry with buildings elsewhere and sometimes directed by the appearance of prototypes in the increasing literature on building, could be said also to have transformed the outward aspect of the town. Practical needs always preceded stylistic innovation.

England and Europe: the ideal town and the role of decorum in building

Historians who have examined the phenomenon of urbanism from a pan-European angle have stressed certain aspects of exceptionality about England at this time. Unlike most other states in continental Europe, England never built a single, planned new town of the sort initiated by the active patronage and self-aggrandisement of other great European powers. There had never developed in England a sense of fierce urban independence, most manifest in continental Europe in the notion of the city-state, and the Reformation, with its resulting drive for religious conformity, did not encourage this any further. For England as a nation, inland defence was less necessary than elsewhere in Europe and though the coastal forts built by Henry VIII in the 1540s formed a ring of seaward defences, none of them spawned a particularly large, significant town on its doorstep. Berwick-upon-Tweed was perhaps the only significant garrison town along the protected border against the Scots.[5] Planned towns seem to have come about only in later centuries and for different reasons to do with their situation and economy; even Whitehaven, often described as the country's first town with a gridiron plan has been shown to have evolved into that shape only slowly and under the careful management and enterprise of Sir John Lowther after he reached his majority in 1663.[6] This meant that the most invigorating and challenging inspirations to innovation, the world of the ideal city found in the pages of a series of Italian and French treatises on architecture, were not going to be realised in England. London alone offered some response to that degree of urban planning in the early seventeenth-century formation of streets and squares, most emphatically realised in the development of Covent Garden, but these happened through energetic private initiatives and were not the responsibility of government.[7] Essentially, for all the upheavals of the post-Reformation, English towns in the century after 1540 were settled places, even though some small towns effectively disappeared in the shakedown after the disappearance of the monasteries, or became very impoverished. Cerne Abbas, in Dorset, had a wealthy abbey; its annual revenues in 1535 amounted to just over £576. The town then lost revenue from travellers and pilgrims to the abbey after the dissolution of 1539 and by the time of John Norden's *Survey* of 1617 he notes poverty, squatters on common lands and the guildhall falling to ruin.[8] Nevertheless, the broader history of the urban fabric at this period is of fundamental importance in the emergence of many towns from an extended period of decline, both of population and local trade and enterprise (fig. 28). Buildings had to reflect not necessarily a burgeoning new prosperity

28 Elm Hill, Norwich, 16th-century rebuilding was slow until the influx of Dutch and Walloon weavers accelerated the pace in the 1560s and 1570s.

but a turn towards a new identity; in many cases the dissolution forced this upon them.[9] The absence of the ideal, planned city does not mean that in some less visible and less architecturally startling ways there was not the formation of groups of buildings that were visually and spatially related to each other. The links, however, are not to do with the visible signs of architectural hierarchy and order, with each building given its appropriate ornament, the sort of advice on building that the fifteenth-century Italian architect and humanist-scholar Leon Battista Alberti had advocated. Alberti, and the architectural theorists who followed him, had quite clear ideas about the classical orders of architecture and their appropriateness for different kinds of public and private buildings. If the high principle of 'decorum' was absent, however, people in England were exercised by the issue of what was 'decorous' and a significant battle raged about the most sensitive building of all in the post-Reformation world, the place of worship, in terms of its physical shape.

For the theologian and philosopher Richard Hooker there was a clear distinction between the appearance of a church, to take the primary, historic communal building, and any other structure. In *Of the Laws of Ecclesiastical Polity*, the first four books of which were published in 1593, he asked: 'Can we judge it a thing seemly for any man to go about the building of an house to the God of heaven with no other appearance, than if his end were to rear up a kitchen or parlour for his own use?' This is contradicted by the Puritan position that the appearance of a church need not follow different building principles since 'there is no more holiness in the church than in their kitchen, nor in the Lord's table than in a dresserboard'.[10] How Elizabethan and Jacobean communities organised their churches to follow reformist services and remain the fulcrum of the community is one of the essential enquiries of this chapter.

Status, class and benefaction in the post-Reformation town

Promotion of the town's interests was determined by the self-perception of status. Many towns at this period agitated for the status of incorporation, which meant securing a charter from the Crown which gave privileges, the rights of holding markets, and dignity for town officials in both their public and private capacities. However, the achievement of borough status was not simply to do with visible achievement and measurable success. The process was often part of a long transition from one kind of town to another, during which the pre-Reformation religious ritual and calendar year was unravelled and replaced by secular activities, along with the provision of new identities through stress on new trades, commerce and social gatherings. Towns were not necessarily places of established new wealth when their status was upgraded into a corporate borough, and buildings were erected not always at times of affluence but at a perceived 'take-off' juncture which their newness and physical presence in the town could accelerate and celebrate. Incorporation did not always accompany grants of new wealth to support it, nor did it necessarily come at a time of settled conditions; in the case of Barnstaple, Devon, for example, though a charter of incorporation was granted by Queen Mary in 1557, the manor was then sold to a stranger to the town.[11]

As discussed in chapter 1, the developments concerning the changes wrought by the dissolution were the chief means whereby towns at this time saw the coming of interlopers, new minor gentry who saw themselves as stakeholders by virtue of their property interests, as well as new professional classes and, in towns within reach of London, courtiers. There has been much debate as to how far these newcomers led to a new zoning or demarcation of the town between social classes.[12] There is in fact as much evidence for mixed areas as there is for the exclusivity of parts of the town around a particular occupation or trade. It is generally believed that the government's concern for overcrowding in the really quite fixed urban framework as the population increased was as much due to the multi-occupation of large properties by wealthy families as the sufferings of the very poor.[13] There were certainly many and telling disputes about boundaries as incomers invaded, as territory was increasingly subdivided; such disputes were exacerbated by the often vague intimations of dividing lines between sites as left by the rapid sale and exchange of ex-monastic properties (fig. 29).[14] It is noteworthy that the first of the English colonies arriving in the New World made sure that they defined the boundaries of their properties before any cultivation took place, a measure of the behaviour and mores of the country they left behind.[15]

The issue of boundaries and areas claimed by one class rather than another is an important one for building not just because of the debate about the 'quarters' of the town, about the clash between 'east' and 'west' ends, but because it elides into a wider debate about the degree to which new urban classes were keen to adopt a degree of social responsibility. Historians have divided here; one view of the medieval past is to propose it as quite different from the aggressive, post-Reformation present of Elizabethan and Jacobean England, an earlier age of medieval community against one where the dictates of consumerism were paramount.[16] What price, what value in this environment then was given to the foundation of schools and almshouses, to the upkeep of the church or the management of the streets? There has been much debate about this through the examination of common civility in this period and through the notion of hospitality. So another issue for this chapter is that of the role of local government in initiating and managing public endowments. In many instances, town governments themselves took on almshouses, schools and other public works.

29 A map of houses in Tothill Street, Westminster, belonging to Christ's Hospital along with adjacent properties. Annotations of exact measurements amd of ownership and leasehold here demonstrate the complexity of property-renting in 16th-century London. It is attached to a lease of 1586 and was drawn by Ralph Treswell, the painter-stainer who was at the time estate surveyor to the courtier Sir Christopher Hatton. Revised annotations were probably made when the original leaseran out. By kind permission of Christ's Hospital (photo: Guildhall Library, City of London), GL MS 13507.

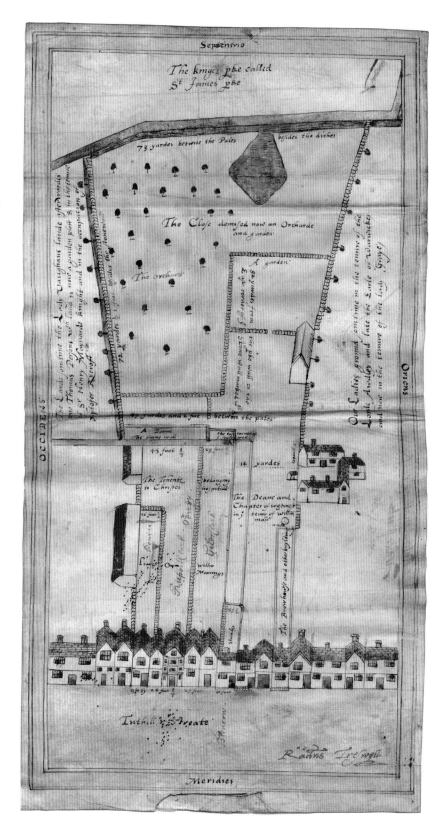

Were their investments any more sound than the risky private endowments that, as described in chapter 4, were sometimes prone to the carelessness or disinterest of the heirs of benefactors? And did town governments have a policy of improvement that spanned across different building projects?

The central government of Tudor and early Stuart England was always anxious about the perceived state of decay of buildings in towns and cities. But the most acute sense of crisis came in the great decade of reform from 1534 onwards, when a series of rebuilding statutes sought to remedy the situation in groups of identified towns.[17] Three major motives have been put forward as the prompt to government decrees to control and ameliorate the situation. First, decayed properties and empty sites complicated the legal jurisdiction over lands transferred in the course of the monastic dissolution. Second, for towns to flourish, corporate owners needed to get the greatest profits out of sound buildings; where decay was present, it had to be put right. The third reason is the most complex and least tangible. Governments were concerned about disaffection in centres of population and the need to create a sense of urban well-being that would encourage trade and commerce. This touches on the more general context of direct intervention: acts encouraging rebuilding (in the first instance by penalising decay itself) were part of a wider government concern about the state of society and it sought continually to control matters that were perceived to threaten public order on the streets as well as support systems of deference and ensure the paying of dues. Sumptuary laws were similarly recurrent throughout the century. These regulations were intended to impose a hierarchy of materials of dress that were deemed appropriate to class and position; the fact that they had so often to be reactivated suggests that they were continually flouted.[18] Yet the government's perception of the urban problem remained one that now appears to be essentially static; the town was a fixed and contained location, both physically and ideologically, and government did not have a mind-set that grasped the concept of inbuilt change and development.

What did happen, however, was that some town governments and more especially particular individuals realised at least a schematic skeleton of the interdependence of urban resources and facilities that led to money being spent on the maintenance of buildings and the recasting or even total rebuilding of others. A sense of a composite infrastructure emerges for example as early as 1535 in the legacy of Richard Phelips of Hereford. Six times mayor of the city between 1509 and 1532, he understood that the customs and tolls levied at the gates of the city meant heavy charges on local trading so that merchants were going elsewhere. Houses were left untenanted and the town walls unrepaired. In granting to the present mayor and citizens income from his lands and tenements for twenty years to offset these tolls, he hoped to revive the city's trading fortunes. Such 'joined-up' thinking seldom occurred at this level of urban society; it is a rare instance of someone taking account of the interconnectedness of trade, the buildings that served the city and the need to fix what was going wrong.[19]

Spaces for worship: Protestants and the dangers of old church buildings

In terms of public building, a town living under a reformed church would surely need to take care of its places of religious assembly. It may seem extraordinary that in post-Reformation England so little time, energy or resources were put to the building, or even the complete refurbishment or visual transformation of the country's churches. This seeming inactivity took place against a fierce debate as to what constituted an appropriate space for Christian worship. There were different opinions within the newly established post-Reformation church, between different sectarian groups and even among Catholics (now bereft of officially recognised spaces for worship). Some argued whether a dedicated space for worship had to exist at all. According to those who wished to break with the established Church and follow radically simplified services, all old church buildings were by their nature idolatrous because they were built with notions now abhorrent to their religious position. The churches of old Catholic Christendom embodied the notion that some parts of the church were holier than others and this was made evident to the congregation through subtle distinctions of architectural ornament.[20] Old churches had undergone ritual initiation ceremonies that had designated a hierarchy of meanings within the building and its immediate surroundings of churchyard and adjacent streets. Buildings near to the church had met all kinds of needs of servitors and priests of the church, indulging themselves with earmarked accommodation and spaces reserved for elaborate preparations of ritual. For post-Reformation separatists, modern churches must not fall into the errors of Judaism and its luxurious synagogues; the extravagance of the Temple of Jerusalem was cited as an example. The new church was in danger of using the old church in the same way. The comparison of the Anglican use of old churches with Jewish buildings was the charge of Henry Barrow, in his *Brief Discoverie of the False Church*, written in the Fleet prison in 1587–90 and smuggled out page by page to be published in the Netherlands. All the faults of the synagogue are replicated in his view by the Elizabethan established Church still inhabiting the carcass of the medieval building. He pays particular attention to condemning the continuing separation of functions, the sense of mystery to the faithful and privilege to the church officials that division of space within the building allowed:

> They have their aisles, and their body of the church: they have also their
> cells to the side of the walls, their vestry to keep the priests' ministerial
> garments, where they are to attire and dress themselves before they go

to their service: they have their treasury. [. . .] They have also their holiest of all, or chancel, which peculiarly belonged to the priest and choir, which help the priest to say and sing his service. They have their rood loft as a partition between their holy and holiest of all. The priest also hath a peculiar door into his chancel, through which none might pass but himself.[21]

Ultimately the outright rejection of buildings of any form as the true repository of holiness was rooted in the notion of the inner 'building' residing within the individual. As the seventeenth-century founder of the Quakers, George Fox, was to record in his *Journal*:

> These steeple-houses and pulpits were offensive to my mind, because both priests and people called them the house of God, and idolized them; reckoning that God dwelt there in the outward house. Whereas they should have looked for God and Christ to dwell in their hearts, and their bodies to be made temples of God; for the apostle said, 'God dwelleth not in temples made with hands.'[22]

Scruples originating in firmly held beliefs aside, there sometimes was a ruthless and proprietorial exploitation of churches by local magnates using them as if part of their own patrimony, or deciding what was best and quite ignoring the church's wishes. Adrian Stokes, the second husband of the widowed Frances Brandon, Duchess of Suffolk, pulled down the spire and removed the lead from the roof of the church of Astley in Warwickshire and Sir Francis Walsingham ordered the demolition of the chancel of the church at Carisbrooke, on the Isle of Wight, telling the townspeople that the chancel was room enough for worship. Far many more others, however, were not to strip but to replenish churches in one way or another, as explored below. The Catholics too had a fundamentalist position on spaces for worship, but compromised in the age of persecution with makeshift arrangements.

Spaces for worship: The Catholic compromise

It is a curious fact that even Catholics were sometimes forced to think of the non-corporeal sense of the place of worship since they were now living in a country that did not allow open celebration of their faith. Catholicism survived in pockets of England that were relatively remote and underpopulated; it has been argued that in upland areas of the north of England, isolated by moorland, Catholics practised their faith more or less openly in their houses, but they were fewer in number in the Dales, where nascent industry flourished so that newcomers could break the bonds of local loyalties and tolerance.[23] In Northumberland the Ratcliff family practised their faith openly at Dilston and Francis Ratcliff built a chapel beside their house in 1616. A few very powerful families, especially a group living in a swathe from West Sussex through Hampshire into Wiltshire and Dorset, celebrated

30 Baddesley Clinton, Warwickshire, a 15th-century moated house with Elizabethan changes. It was rented in the late 16th century by the recusant Anne Vaux; hiding places for Catholic priests were made using passages into the moat and sewers.

Mass only a little less overtly. Sometimes chambers for holding the Eucharist were created high in the house. The higher the social status of the Catholic family, the more likely they were to worship more or less openly within the house. At Battle Abbey, Sussex, the Montagues had a chapel with a stone altar and a pulpit, while at their house of Great Harrowden, Northamptonshire, the Vaux family had a richly appointed chapel with candlesticks, crucifix and vestments; only in 1611 were these seized from the house. But other Catholics at this period improvised settings for celebrating Mass wherever they could not risk maintaining either overt or secret spaces.[24] On the borders of Wales there was a strong centre of recusancy around Monmouth, and further north a group of country houses of the west midlands was vividly exposed in 1605 in the depositions following the Gunpowder Plot (fig. 30). The Jesuit Robert Southwell recommended the dedication of one room of the house for services or, failing that, even a garden or orchard nearby.[25] Catholics imprisoned together in numbers made their jails into places of worship, paying as they did for their keep and thus sometimes exacting privileges from their jailers.[26] But their crucial difference from the Puritans and all radical Protestant separatist groups was that Catholics made associative links with their prayers; they maintained the presence of ritual even in the most unlikely circumstances and certainly through means that Puritans would have described as idolatrous. Even when Catholic individuals suffered the fate of martyrdom, the procession to execution might be turned into a semblance of Christ's last journey to the Cross. If attendance at Protestant services became absolutely necessary to avoid huge fines or imprisonment, the rosary would be kept hidden in a pocket and Catholic prayers inwardly recited. Catholics always emphasised quite the opposite idea to the Puritan sense of the omnipresent opportunity to worship, stressing that the space of ritual had somehow to be separate, even where a physically separate, enclosed space proved impossible.

The government and buildings for worship

For Queen Elizabeth's government the true temple of the church was indeed the community of the faithful, but the designation of space in which to worship did involve separating off a certain area. It had to be distinctive from other kinds of building and the government's position was laid down in the *Second Book of Homilies*, which also underlined the sense that God was found in particular in his Temple. This is expressed in a way that does use the decorum of building types to make its point:

> if we lack Jesus Christ, that is to say, the Saviour of our souls and bodies, we shall not find him in the market place, or in the guild hall, much less in the house or tavern amongst good fellows (as they call them), so soon as we shall find him in the temple, the Lord's house, amongst the teachers and preachers of his word, where indeed he is to be found.[27]

So the government did what it always resorted to in its search for a passive population, a *laissez-faire* attitude to the prevailing built legacy, superimposed with a prescribed means of behaviour through regulation. A pervasive nervousness, not about what things looked like but how people used and perceived them, directed all areas of attempted government control.

Thus government regulation attempted to remove from the physical body of the church and its surroundings a great many of the associated events that had sheltered there in medieval times, for example the performance of mystery plays. This was by and large achieved, though it would be wrong to assume that the Puritans were the first to castigate such activity in church. However, churches were to remain centres of multifarious activities after the Reformation, even as the government sought by injunction to remove regular gatherings, whether of the communally enjoyable type (plays, fairs) or the judicial (secular courts and inquests). The latter were banned because in the revolution of the 1530s the Church had been divested of secular power; to pass judgement and possibly pronounce punishment within church walls would imply the continued existence of such authority.[28] The constant repetition of injunctions suggests, as mentioned above, that the wishes of government were only fitfully obeyed. The church remained, however, communal in the sense that it occasionally provided space for services that found no home elsewhere or were awaiting more permanent housing nearby, for example libraries and schools; it also served in times of crisis for the distribution of poor relief, or temporary storage, or even as a venue for sudden conscription when there was no standing army. A particular focus of the government's attack was on the church ale, held on particular anniversaries or as part of the wake and burial of an individual; these feasts had proved the mainstay of sums of money for maintenance of the church in medieval times. As explored below, churchwardens had the option of requesting the community for a church rate for such a purpose, but this proved difficult until increasingly enforced by law in the early seventeenth century.

Paying for the fabric of churches

In many ways, the cathedrals, both old and those newly established after the Reformation out of former abbeys, were an important test of the government's intentions.[29] New hierarchies were set up to govern these communities but often the fabric was left in a state of poor repair. By and large, in the century after the Reformation, the building fabric of the cathedrals was neglected, with very few programmes of major rebuilding or restoration. The history of the maintenance of the fabric of St Paul's following the collapse of the spire in 1562 is one of general prevarication and neglect.[30] At the parish church level, it is perhaps a sign of the government's success in maintaining control that the physical body of the church remained largely whole; that there was – albeit for some time uncertainly delineated by rules about furnishings, candles and vestments – a crude and physically damaging programme of sorts; the country's old churches were whitewashed, the royal arms were placed prominently in view and there was a prescribed core corpus of books housed in all of them.[31] The government did not encourage the building of new Protestant temples or preaching halls; the sole exceptions were the new churches for alien communities and the anomaly of Leicester's church at Denbigh, discussed below and again in chapter 4. In England the bare maintenance of the medieval legacy of the fabric of churches signified that the established Church was to be seen as one, continuous with the past, and remaining unified. Just as it can be argued that the infrastructure of provision for public building suffered somewhat, town for town, parish for parish, in the century or so before the Reformation, when local resources were being spent so lavishly on churches, between 1540 and 1640 churches in their turn took second place to investment in public secular buildings.[32] It is also plain that the standing of the church in terms of its temporal 'establishment' and thus the buildings that expressed that power, was damaged by the Reformation; clergy incomes were reduced, some parishes removed or merged, and a whole section of ecclesiastic presence disappeared with the abolition of the chantries and their priests.

Sources of income for the maintenance of the church fabric in the late sixteenth century were paltry. Some churches retained lands but most under

Elizabeth were dependent on the church ale and to a lesser extent on the occasional church rate, a specific levy for the fabric of the building.[33] The fact that the church rate was exceptional is shown time and again by the arrears recorded in churchwardens' accounts for non-payment. Parishioners rich and poor left comparatively little in their wills for the upkeep of churches compared with sums bequeathed for poor relief.[34] A survey of wills in Wiltshire provides a microcosm of the range of bequests. Small sums were left for repairing glass, but only rarely any amounts, and these often small, directly for the essential fabric. In 1553 William Nottyngham, yeoman of Amesbury, for example, left 20 shillings for the repair of the south aisle of his local church. Bequests were more often directed to remedy the particular inconveniences of the individuals concerned or the families they would leave behind, as in 1575 when the widow Christian Rabbetts alias Willoughby left Baverstock church no money for its fabric but 5 shillings to mend the way from the church to her house. Legacies towards the upkeep and replacement of bells are plentiful, suggesting that post-Reformation citizens saw their maintenance as important: regular bell-ringing would serve to commemorate these individuals, somehow substituting for the pre-Reformation opportunity to leave money for obits and masses. Legacies for the bells varied from large to small according to means, and did not always take the form of a direct monetary bequest: at Bishopstone in 1559 the widow Jane Kyng left 'to the repayring of the bell ther late decayed 1 bushel of wheat and 1 bushel of barley'.[35]

It was the role of churchwardens to supervise expenditure. Their accounts are a rich source of information, though largely revealing a legacy of patchy attention to the fabric. Medieval arrangements for the division of responsibility still operated. The traditional role of the parish was in looking after the nave and church tower, while upkeep of chancels fell to the church authorities (fig. 31). At the church of Charing, in Kent, fire swept through

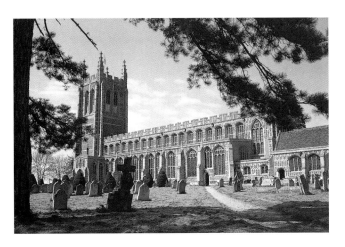

31   Holy Trinity, Long Melford, Suffolk, rebuilt in the late 15th century by the town's prosperous clothiers.

the building in 1590 and while the parishioners saw to the completion of the nave by 1592, only in 1620 did the dean and chapter of St Paul's complete their responsibility for the rebuilding of the chancel.[36] After the Reformation there was a sense that certain aspects of the church, its upkeep and internal arrangements, were privatised to an unprecedented degree: individuals paid for their own self-satisfaction and aggrandisement by buying space to sit in the same place on a regular basis; they commissioned their own private pews where they could get away with it; and they commissioned their funeral monuments. These last did not necessarily have to be any more prominent in size or novelty of style than their medieval predecessors; many wealthy parishioners still asked for modest brasses or simple inscriptions on a flagstone. However, many late sixteenth-century patrons did build huge superstructures on a scale unknown in medieval times. The de-commissioning of the centrality of the altar in Protestant worship, the removal of the screen and the rood loft meant that funeral monuments, eschewing religious imagery and celebrating secular achievement, now often claimed prominence as the most striking object of church furnishing (fig. 32).[37] People of modest means often simply wanted to be buried in a par-

32   St John Lateran, Hengrave, Suffolk. In the chancel and the north chapel are the late 16th-century tombs of the Kytson family. Wealthy merchants in Henry VIII's time, by Elizabeth's reign they were ennobled and marrying into the highest aristocracy.

ticular place within the church because to the present community it had become associated with them and it thus became another means of preserving memory within the space: in 1562 the will of Robert Nelson, innkeeper in the parish of St Thomas at Salisbury, asked to be buried near to his pew; and in 1558 William Stileman asked at Steeple Ashton that he be buried 'in the quire where I do kneel'.[38] For those comparatively few places which did have a national significance, sometimes the raising of money as revealed by the churchwardens' accounts did yield a wide geographical and social response. One such place was predictably Cambridge, which benefited from the dispersal of its graduates, especially among the parish clergy. In 1593–4 the sum of £179 12s. 7d. was raised towards the steeple of Great St Mary's from 193 donors; accounts included local aldermen and tradesmen but also knights and squires from various counties and even a total of £11 11s. 10d. from 'straungers whose names I cold not take'.[39]

Adapted churches

During Elizabeth's reign the building of a completely new church on reformist lines was rare because it would be expensive and because government did not encourage or give a particular lead towards the rebuilding of spaces for worship. However, rearranging medieval interiors, the pushing out of external walls or adding a note of classical stylistic distinction all testify to new ideas about places for worship, albeit usually prompted by a state of near-dereliction of the fabric. There was some experimentation in Edward VI's reign with radical re-organisation with a call for the table to be moved to a part of the church where all communicants could see and hear, though this was often found to be the choir or chancel; the word most frequently used to inform the decisions of the congregation in any particular church was 'convenient', thus allowing for conditions of space and light.[40] Under Elizabeth the 1559 Book of Common Prayer called for morning and evening prayer to be 'in the accustomed place of the church, chapel or chancel, except it shall be otherwise determined by the ordinary of the place'.[41] Many ministers did indeed have their seat in the nave and read the offices from there. The bottom line was that worshipping with the Elizabethan prayer book was a corporate activity, replacing the medieval church as 'a mysterious succession of self-contained rooms'. In some instances, rethinking the space of the church, de-emphasising the axiality and processional aspect of the Catholic ritual, meant turning the oblong space of earlier churches into a shape as close to approximating the square as possible. One of the most striking means of adaptation occurred at those churches where Elizabethan communities changed the nature of the interior through the construction of a new row, or new rows, of columns in such a way as to challenge the medieval, ritual use of the space. Often this

33 St Mary's, Winkfield, Berkshire. The interior, showing the row of octagonal columns of 1592 that run through the centre of the church and support the new double-span roof.

involved rebuilding the roof whose heightening or widening also changed the distribution of light within the building. A striking example of this is at Winkfield, in Berkshire, where in 1592 a row of wooden octagonal columns divided up the space of the fourteenth-century church into two equal areas, with a new roof of two high-pitched spans. Just as it is hard now to envisage the arrangements of nave and (possibly) side aisles before the late sixteenth century, it is equally difficult to understand how the new, Elizabethan double-aisled nave related to the altar area, since the whole of the east end of this church was rebuilt in the late nineteenth century. It is nevertheless striking how the row of columns brazenly blocks the former, central, pre-Reformation way to the high altar (fig. 33). Elizabethan expenditure stopped there. No attempt was made at this point to alter the window openings and it was a generation later, in 1629, that a new brick, south-west tower was constructed in place of the earlier wooden one. This example may well be typical of the Elizabethan period as it doubtless followed severe disrepair of the medieval roof; necessary repair and the use of comparatively cheaper timber combined to serve up something that was

34 St Etheldreda's, Hatfield, Hertfordshire. The Tuscan arcade of two bays (a third was added much later) built to separate the choir from the newly built north chapel for the Cecil family in about 1618.

radically new in its emphasis of the 'squareness' of the church and a de-emphasis on earlier axiality.[42]

Many examples of new arcades at this time betray a willingness to engage with a style approaching the classical. The columns of Winkfield are hardly fully 'classical' in design though they are baseless to the floor and the capitals are simple with consoles above these between the springers of the arches. The use of a simple classical order ('Tuscan' being a mere approximation in many cases) was the preferred style for a number of instances where a new run of columns, sometimes in wood, sometimes in stone, was used to separate the chancel of a church from a new chapel to south or north, often the burial place of a leading local family. The nave arcade of about 1610 in Hatfield church leading into the space of Robert Cecil's tomb is one example of this, as is the single Tuscan column to the Morison chapel at Watford of 1597 (fig. 34). The most striking example of a complete new church employing the classical order is the church at Standish in Lancashire, put to contract with the mason Lawrence Shipway in 1582. Malcolm Airs has suggested that a careful compromise was intended here. The strength of the Tuscan order reflects something of the simplicity of the forms of reformed worship while replacing the plain forms of late Gothic piers, thus also forming a link with the past.[43]

Sometimes radical adaptation could give the semblance of a new church. At Brooke church, Rutland, a substantial rebuilding took place, leaving the Romanesque central arcade as a spine but building up the outer walls of the church anew (fig. 35). Though the church furnishings have clearly been moved around, the survival of pulpit and tester board, pews and rails from the Elizabethan period testify to a new communal character to the church and the attempt to refurnish according to new worshipping practices. The Jacobean period was to take this yet further: it is from the early seventeenth century that a remarkable legacy of wooden furnishings survives. The creation of four almost equal spaces within the church at Brooke determined the use of the church in ways ancillary to worship, as they became the setting for meetings and harvest

35   St Peter's, Brooke, Rutland. The south side, showing the chancel wall and porch extending the medieval church, *c.* 1579.

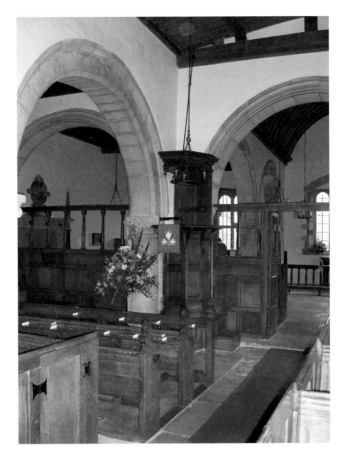

36 St Peter's, Brooke, Rutland. The central pillar of a medieval church interior extended to form four more or less equal spaces of nave, chancel, north aisle and north chapel.

suppers. Thus they re-established something of the varied and communal, non-worshipping use of the church interior that had been commonplace up until the Reformation (fig. 36).[44]

New churches and their patrons

In relatively few instances during Elizabeth's reign, churches were completely rebuilt. The church of Holcot, Bedfordshire, was reconstructed about 1590 (two of the bells are dated 1593) and serves as a significant test case of the potential for a new style. Indeed the windows are largely mullioned and transomed in a way reminiscent of contemporary domestic buildings; the outer door to the south porch (the rest of the porch later rebuilt around it) and a round-headed door on the south side of the chancel both have scrolled ironwork and the former has the initials R. C. for Richard Chernock, both father and son of that name being buried in the church. The ceiling is tunnel-vaulted and to explore what an earlier writer

37 St Nicholas's, Holcot, Bedfordshire. The tower of the new church, about 1590, with straight heads to the windows.

might have meant by the reference to a 'Renaissance' feeling, the square plan of the tower, its three unadorned stages divided by clear string courses and affording a grounded 'dialogue' between horizontal and vertical, does lend a sense of an opposition to the soaring, upward thrust of many late Gothic towers (fig. 37). This was however already adumbrated in many pre-Reformation churches of the early part of the century, where more squat towers were sometimes also used, as at Barton-under-Needwood in Staffordshire, built in 1517 at the behest of Dr John Taylor, chaplain to Henry VIII. A closer look at Holcot also suggests that the medieval footprint of the earlier church was adhered to, so that the rebuilding never radically altered the basic plan.[45]

Some distinguished patrons left their mark on a parish church in such a way as to have invited the question as to whether a distinctively reformist programme was at work here by figures prominent at court. The new church at Denbigh, built by Robert Dudley, Earl of Leicester, has been described as a 'prodigy' church but no one has ever argued for a wholeness of Protestant direction here; the exterior was Gothic in style, the interior classical.[46] It is a rare instance of a building whose influence may not have been international but whose context certainly was: with the arrival of Dutch immigrant communities into London, their places of worship were purpose-built or single spaces adapted to meet the reformed demand for a unified, non-processional space. This was most evident at the Austin Friars, where the Dutch community was granted in 1550 just the nave of the former monastic church.[47] At Easton Royal, Wiltshire, another patron with strong reformist family credentials, Edward Seymour, Earl of Hertford, the son of Protector Somerset, built a new parish church in 1591. He had a vested family interest here because the Seymour family tombs, moved by this time to Great Bedwyn in the same county, had been housed either in the former Trinitarian friary on this site, or very close to it. The surviving nave of the late Elizabethan structure has simple arched lights to the windows, surmounted by hood moulds.[48]

A new classical style was used not in terms of an overall restraint or guiding hand to the building as a whole, but more often in particular ways, at special points of reference. As with the point of entry at many newly built country houses of the period, sometimes a new porch to the church was constructed using a form of classical language that is far more emphatic than anything on the rest of the structure. In the case of domestic architecture, the porch often uses an elaborate arrangement of columns or applied pilasters to frame heraldry, or indeed essentially to replace it. It has been suggested that the symbolism of number is expressed at Kirby Hall in Northamptonshire through the use of seven attached classical columns on

38 St Leonard's, Sunningwell, Berkshire. The porch to the church, traditionally said to have been built about 1550.

39 The removal of images from the church and the formation of the new church congregation, from John Foxe's *Actes and Monuments*, 2nd edn, 1570. The Bodleian Library, University of Oxford.

the front of the porch, an allusion to the Book of Proverbs, 9, 1: 'Wisdom hath builded a house: she hath hewn out her seven pillars', making Kirby the House of Wisdom.[49] It is important therefore to ask how style is used at the entry to churches in this way, and to what purpose. Perhaps the most startling example of this is the porch at the church of Sunningwell, Berkshire (fig. 38). This has often been attributed to a decision that may have been taken by the parish priest in the years around 1550, the presumed date for the porch, since it was the reformist John Jewel. As Bishop of Salisbury between 1560 and 1571 he made it his duty to repair the cathedral's fabric, including pavements, window glass and the replacing of Purbeck marble pillars in the cloisters.[50] Something of the intention here is echoed in the simple, basilical forms of places of worship for the new reformed church as envisioned in contemporary representations of the church as 'establishment', such as the columned hall church seen in the 1570 edition of Foxe's *Actes and Monuments*, where a Protestant congregation gathers around the preacher and a woman symbolically leads a child into the church. Such new initiatives of church building that are practical and only occasionally reach into stylistic concerns through the choice of new forms are part of ongoing refurbishment (fig. 39).[51]

Churches and 'Gothic'

Towers and porches were the most prominent additions to older churches, as were chapels at the east end of the church paid for by private individuals or families; these new structures offered opportunity for dedicated heraldry or an inscription that reveals a date of construction.[52] During the Elizabethan period there are many examples too of the building of new chancels, the addition of aisles to the nave and other such means of increasing the internal volume of the church or renewing dilapidated structures. Many of these are dated and in some cases documented through churchwardens' accounts, but they give themselves away also by either a careful echoing of the style of the older architecture or through parallels with other kinds of building, most especially domestic architecture. The key to this is often seen in window openings; some additions to churches have surprisingly domestic-style windows with simple arched lights or a hood-mould. Since additions to churches continued into the seventeenth century, window design of this period has become a key factor in judging date and style (fig. 40). It is often the springboard for argument about the power and intention of a style labelled the 'survival' – or more accurately the 'revival' – of Gothic.[53]

40 Holy Trinity, Berwick-upon-Tweed, Northumberland, from the south, 1650–52, built by the London mason, John Young. The church originally had a Gothic west window and the battlements seen on the aisle topped the entire structure. The 'stepped' windows, all originally with flat tops to the lights, show the merger of classical elements yet soaring Gothic proportions also seen in London churches.

The debate over the meaning of Gothic style as it manifested itself in the early seventeenth century is of course coloured by hindsight of the imminent Civil War and the fact that a major Puritan charge against the government of the early Stuart kings was that religious practice moved back towards rituals now described as High Church. Critics of the period came close to charging these practices with proto-Catholicism and icon worship. The revival of Gothic might at first therefore suggest the return to medieval practices of style and design. Against this interpretation, it can be argued that the chief protagonist of this movement, William Laud, Archbishop of Canterbury from 1633, looked if anything not to medieval style but to current continental Baroque, or rather to a northern European version of it as shown in the porch of St Mary's, Oxford, built in 1637. Laud was less concerned about the restitution of the physical appearance of the medieval church than restoring its lands and goods. He stressed England's separation from European Roman Catholicism by agreeing with the concept that somehow it was the Roman church that had changed direction through the edicts of the Council of Trent after 1563, so that it was the English church that now expressed a true continuity with the Christian past.[54] This was but the latest chapter in the attempt to look beyond and before the supremacy of Rome in European Christendom to an early church that expressed true Christian belief. Thus any simple equation of new High Church practices with 'Gothic' would be misplaced. In fact, a case has been made for Gothic being the true style of Republicanism, its origins based in a style that preceded the Norman conquest of England and the subsequent royal assertion that the land was held by conquest and that parliamentary institutions were a concession by the king rather than a right of the people. The new Gothic of this time can therefore be seen as something creative, replenishing an old tradition.[55]

Occasionally the programme of building in the revived Gothic style was on a grand scale and built as a gesture to a particular political moment. The church of Arthuret, Cumbria, arose from 1609 after more than half a century in ruins, symbol of peace in the border regions following the union of the English and Scottish crowns under James VI and I. Indeed the church was paid for by subscription from all over the country at the king's order. Its singularity of design and close following of the Perpendicular style nevertheless creates an evenness of line and shape unknown in the churches of the period that inspired it from a century and a half before. At Charles Church, Plymouth, begun in 1640 and providing services as early as the following year (thus still within the time limit of Charles I's rule), the grandeur of scale is greater than any other Gothic revival church of the first half of the seventeenth century. But more common is work in the Gothic style at small churches for rural parishes and in privately endowed chapels. Here the distinctiveness of the Gothic is particularly apparent in the design, and especially the tracery, of the windows where the geometric qualities of

Decorated tracery are given new complexity and ingenuity. In Dorset there is a group of churches, including those at Leweston, Folke with its three-bay aisles and Minterne Magna with its north chapel, which shares a very localised design of window, with the central opening of the five lights higher than the rest (fig. 41). Some Gothic-style churches are on a scale to seem almost like private chapels and indeed in some cases their origins have the patronage connections of such an intention, as at Groombridge, Kent, where John Packer erected a private chapel beside the road near his house in 1625. The intention of suggesting that Gothic was a native style to be proud of seems evident here since its porch inscription celebrates the fact that Prince Charles's visit to Madrid in 1623 had not resulted in marriage into the Catholic Spanish royal family. The style features too in a number of private chapels attached to churches built as family burial chapels, as at Beoley in Worcestershire. It has, however, equally been stressed that the incidence of Gothic in certain areas of local church building in early seventeenth century England may be explained by the surviving traditions of local craftsmen, suggesting something of a continuity with a pre-Reformation past.

Urban secular initiatives: the town hall

While the church formed the religious heart of every community, other buildings expressed its daily and earthly needs. The centre of administration, power and regulation was the town hall, though that term encom-

Market
Harborough, Leicester-
shire. The grammar
school, founded in 1607
and built in 1614, with
19th-century pargeted
plasterwork and bell
tower.

passes a great variety of buildings given other names in contemporary
records. This is very much to do with the multi-functional nature of such
structures, sometimes incorporating not just the seat of town government
but also a place of trade on the ground level and, in varying numbers and
combinations, perhaps a jail, or lock-up, storage space for grain, an
armoury, even sometimes a schoolroom. Occasionally just one of these
functions took place above an open ground-floor area with an external
aspect that might be mistaken for the usual form of town hall, as at Market
Harborough, Leicestershire, where the grammar school founded in 1607
and built in 1614 looks like conventional town halls elsewhere (fig. 42).
There has been considerable attention paid to the medieval origins of
various forms of structure and debate about how far examples both surviving or once recorded can be classified under broad types. Basically there
are two: first, it could be a free-standing structure with a room or rooms
raised over an open space, commonly built in timber but a candidate for
transformation into the classical form of a room raised over a double back-

to-back loggia, on columns or piers with applied orders. Access to the upper floor was via a secure staircase block to which only officials would gain entry. Second, it could be a building that was structurally part of a street, with a closed-in ground floor, marginally or emphatically distinguished from other buildings to each side of it.[56] Robert Tittler, a leading historian of the Tudor and Jacobean town hall, has pared down a complexity of late medieval precedents to these two forms; he estimates that at least 202 town halls were rebuilt in 178 different towns, in the broad period from 1500 to 1640, with a further number of thoroughgoing re-fits of most or substantial parts of the building. It could be argued therefore that approximately half the towns in England had such a 'new' town hall during this period.[57] There were highs and lows of activity, not every decade showing as much rebuilding as another, just as other historians have shown similar ebbs and flows for country-house building across the early modern period. However, since no one has looked as thoroughly as Tittler has at the equivalent previous century and a half or a similar subsequent time-span, it is difficult to argue whether these numbers were significantly greater than before or after. The body of information and interpretation on these buildings might make it seem possible for them to take their place alongside great domestic structures as the 'architecture' of their age. Yet they remain elusive when that very term is applied to them. Architecturally they betray little serious stylistic development; their appearance remains in the vernacular tradition because no serious amounts of money were spent on them and because those who initiated their building were reluctant to employ expertise from any great distance. Only a few town halls, whether lost or surviving, have any great individual distinction. They are on the whole small and compact, rarely grand and imposing, frequently of no more than three bays. The lost town hall of Hereford, with its eight bays by four, was a rarity.[58] It is rather in the exploration of the multi-functional purposes, their situation within the town, the circumstances of any new commission, and their symbolic encapsulation of individual aspirations and exercise of power that these buildings have the richest information to offer.

The role of individuals in promoting and initiating the rebuilding of such a public structure is often key to their physical situation, their purpose and most especially the way that they are ornamented; provision of funds through the generosity of an individual might determine also the possibility of their subsequent maintenance, if indeed they ever came to completion. Robert Smyth, a member of the Merchant Taylors' Company of London, for example, gave very specific instructions about the biblical texts that were to be placed on the bressumers (lintels) supporting the upper floor of the grammar school in his home town of Market Harborough.[59] The famous market house built at the behest of Sir Thomas Tresham at Rothwell in Northamptonshire is certainly an example of a building where failure to complete came about because the town did not follow the donor's

initial lead. It shares a likeness of form and style less with other market halls of the period than with other buildings, notably Tresham's house at Rushton, his lodge of Lyveden New Bield and the extraordinary warrener's lodge, or Triangular Lodge, also built for him. All these share a concern for expressing the ornament of the building in symbolic terms. Notably, however, the building at Rothwell was unfinished at Tresham's death and the local community did not immediately find the cash to continue work on it so that it was not finally roofed until 1895 (fig. 43).[60] The vulnerability of privately funded public buildings recurs across a variety of endowments. Sometimes it is unclear whether self-promotion within the local community or a genuine sense of public service prompted these actions. Thanks to Robert Tittler's research, the figure of John Pitt has emerged as the key figure in the building of the new town hall at Blandford Forum, Dorset, in 1593.[61] A modest property-owner and trader, Pitt played a vital role in raising about £255 for a new building within and from a relatively small town of maybe 600 to 800 inhabitants. It certainly helped the town gain its own special identity, though not immediately; the first charter of incorporation came some twelve years later, in 1605. With only modest pretensions, Blandford Town Hall very much matched the series of buildings raised by Tresham in that any reconstruction of its appearance suggests a two-storey building very like other contemporary structures, including local

gentry country houses. It may have been a rare example of a free-standing closed type of town hall, without an open ground floor.

The multi-functions of town halls reaches down to the smallest examples. It is worth noting the way in which the accretion of a series of purposes to this type of building reflects a growing concentration on the power and authority residing there. In small communities it is difficult now to grasp the full sense of the enormous localised power that servants of the Crown exercised and the fact that their very presence symbolised powerful forces of order. At Titchfield, in Hampshire, a small sixteenth-century market hall, now reconstructed at the Weald and Downland Museum at Singleton in West Sussex, included not only the usual upstairs meeting place but an open walkway on the upper floor where officials could amble and survey the town and on the ground floor there was a lock-up for prisoners (fig. 44). The situation of each town hall was therefore crucial for their significance as the seat of power. They often stood at one end of the town, perhaps tucked in to the triangle formed by the confluence of narrow streets. They could be near to the parish church, but were equally often at the other end of town from it. The market house at Ledbury, Herefordshire, although now hemmed in by later buildings yet on the same street line as the original structures around it, still evokes the close proximity of buildings always found here from the time of its construction, begun after 1617 (fig. 45). Identity of place was signalled by plas-

45 Ledbury, Hereford-
shire. The market house,
begun in 1617. The street
lines around the structure
have changed somewhat
but this was always
hemmed in by adjacent
buildings.

46 Leominster,
Herefordshire. The town
hall, built in 1633. Moved
from its original location
in the High Street. The
inscription running along
the lintel of the ground
floor equates the use of
columns with gentry
support for the country.

terwork decoration, heraldry or the placing of a public clock, perhaps the first in the community and by its very situation therefore suggesting a control of time and people by the civic rulers. But few town halls as clearly signalled the dominance of a local powerful elite as the inscription on the hall of Leominster, Herefordshire, dating from 1633 (fig. 46): 'like columnes do upprop the fabrik of a building so noble gentri dos support the honour of a kingdom'. This example reflects the particular political situation of a disaffected local gentry in the decade during the personal rule of Charles I.[62]

The town hall and classicism

The mention of columns in the inscription at Leominster raises particular issues for the adoption of classicism. In a sense, the governing class there were acknowledging one of the fundamental aspects of the usefulness of the classical orders for all kinds of ornament, whether on a building as a whole, or just perhaps its porch, on the title page of a book, or surrounding the coat of arms in wood or plaster over a fireplace. The classical orders frame things well, give order and proportion to messages needing to be directed at the audience whether in the street, passing through the country house or in the schoolroom. The use of classicism for conveying the message of these public edifices is sporadic and inconsistent. However, since the message is best delivered with at least a facing of stonework, there are, or rather were, some notable examples in the west of England where good stone was readily available from the Somerset–Dorset limestone belt.

The use of classicism as the framing device to messages of power and authority is nowhere more explicit than at the celebrated guildhall of Exeter (fig. 47). It is curious that this, by the accident of survival the most significant example of classical ornament on a civic building of the Elizabethan period, is no more than a frontispiece to the building behind it, resembling more than anything the porch to a country house, albeit here on an aggrandised scale. Since Exeter is of the 'second type' of town hall running between two streets, it is also the show frontage to a long-established building; it is a new look to an essentially old-fashioned structure. With its multi-layers of mouldings, it resembles some of the great tomb canopies over funeral monuments of the period, which signals that the primary intention of this chosen style was to frame heraldic messages both by figurative and colouristic means. Technical examination of the structure has revealed traces of paint and the fact that the choice of different stones was partly governed by rendering a different hue to parts of the building and then emphasised by the application of colours from the city's arms.[63]

Yet there were free-standing structures that began to engage with classical forms. As early as 1542, when John Leland was travelling the country and putting together the notes that survive today as his *Itinerary*, he stated

that the market place of Salisbury 'is very fair and large and well watered with a running streamlet; in a corner of it is *domus civica*, no very curious piece of work, but strongly built of stone'.[64] Around 1580 this already stone-built structure was replaced by the one shown on John Speed's map of the city of *c.* 1610, where it appears as a vignette (fig. 48). Later pen and wash drawings, including those produced by Francis Grose shortly before the destruction of the building in 1780, appear to show that at some point the open ground floor was filled in and new arcades were built to project out into the market square.[65] In the 1620s Bath had a new guildhall on the site of a Tudor market house in the middle of the High Street. Here too the classical orders were employed, with superimposed rows of what appear to be Doric half-columns expressing the bays. Interestingly, the style is a compromise and it is less clear than on some of the church refurbishments of the 1620s and 1630s (described above) why the classical orders are here combined with perpendicular arches and windows; the side elevation as revealed in a drawing of about 1750 indicates that the former function of market house suggested an appropriate reference to the past by repeating its origial arched openings. Crucially here the rather singular building that first was put up proved inadequate for the differing purposes of civic responsibility since an extension was later added on its south side.[66] Something of the character of this survives at the mid-seventeenth-century market house at Tetbury, Gloucestershire, where a similar extension was found necessary, though here the style is simpler and bolder, with straight-headed openings to the ground floor and round-headed arches on the north elevation. This simplicity is echoed in the simple ground-floor columns (fig. 49).

What caused the move towards buildings of a more thoroughgoing classicism? The story is most likely to begin not with a conscious turning to a new style for its own sake but through allowing other forms of building to suggest different solutions, part of the ongoing process of transformation that crosses building types. A key element of this was undoubtedly competition, which sometimes suggested rivalry with, and therefore copying, civic

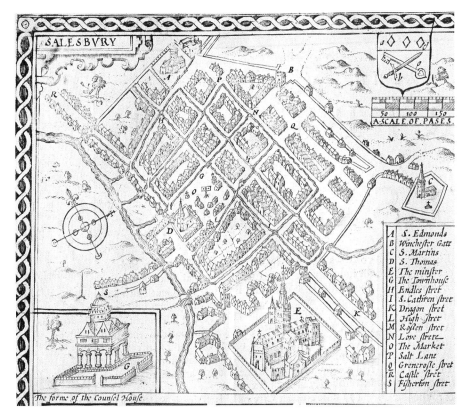

48 John Speed, map of Salisbury, *c.* 1610, with the 'Counsel House' in the bottom left-hand corner. From John Speed, *The Theatre of the Empire of Great Britaine* (1611–12), 1676 edn, vol. 1, p. 14. Copyright The Society of Antiquaries of London.

49 Tetbury,
Gloucestershire. The
Tuscan order of the
ground floor of the
market house, 1655.

buildings either in close proximity or in neighbouring towns, but sometimes doing this by offering a deliberate difference. At Norwich, a new shire house, or meeting-place for county officials rather than town government, went up between 1577 and 1586 on a site close to the castle keep. It is difficult to reconstruct the appearance of this building but it seems to have been a simple, block structure with an attached open arcade. It was built of timber with some use of brick and tile. Resources were concentrated on internal fittings, providing comforts expected by the Norfolk justices who used it, many of them travelling to the city and needing a semblance of home during their daily duties in the shire house, so that its closest equivalent was the domestic architecture of the period. It certainly looked very different from the Norwich Guildhall, with its elaborate heraldry and display of timber-framed features, and there is evidence that rivalry between different power interests within the city emerged through these distinctive kinds of building.[67] If the case of Norwich exemplifies rivalry within one city, later in the seventeenth century, and thus beyond the scope of this book, the building of the County Hall at Abingdon bears witness to a further dimension of rivalry (fig. 50). This was built as a direct challenge to Reading, in the south of the same county of Berkshire, a town with which Abingdon was battling for the honour of housing the county assizes. By the second half of the seventeenth century it was ever more apparent that the erection of distinguished public buildings both for civic government but equally for reception and entertainment, for example theatres, baths where natural springs were available and assembly rooms, were important means by which money came into the town. Abingdon County Hall was one of the most pre-eminent of a whole series of buildings in which many towns had invested. In that scenario, the distinctions of demarcation through stylistic means, through using the classical orders to express subtleties of hierarchy that Alberti had called for, could at last come about.[68]

'A faire schoole house': education in the towns

Elizabethan England, however, was more concerned with continuity than innovation and no species of community building raised this issue more fundamentally than the local school. The motivation for particular forms of instruction came certainly from the top, from the government, but during this period there was remarkable negotiation over site, building costs and future endowment between the various forces that sought to resolve the issue of the need for schools.[69] Private endowments usually led to quite personalised instructions through the schools' statutes; these often appear to have an affinity with earlier chantry endowments, or certainly some of the sense of needing to perpetuate the memory of the donor, here in a new guise. The government led on policy, the church nominated key officers, but it was local governments and individuals who ultimately made the provision happen. Education was now introduced as a necessary part of public policy because the Tudor regime needed to ensure that all were true to religion in ways that were coterminous with loyalty to the State. Only since the debates of the convocation of the Canterbury province of the church when it met at St Paul's in 1529–30 was it generally accepted that, beyond the tasks of divine service and prayer, secular clergy were obliged to teach and lead the young; this was driven not so much through the desire for religious conformity but as a means of ensuring the supremacy of English, the language in which grammar was to be taught.[70] Elizabeth found it convenient to continue the policy adopted in the previous reign of her Catholic sister Mary in putting the appointment of all schoolmasters under the control of diocescan bishops, themselves of course appointed by the Crown.[71]

Before the Reformation, different types of school were in operation sponsored variously by monasteries, chantry foundations and private benefactions; central and local government had to come to grips with how and whether these were to continue. In towns dominated by a significant abbey, such as Reading, Evesham or Bury, the abbey owned the schoolhouse and monks appointed the master. Local members of the monastic orders often also served as the trustees of privately endowed schools as at Cirencester, Faversham or Lewes; at the last of these the prior himself was responsible for the appointment of the master.[72] The idea that it was important for these schools to survive did not automatically endure the upheavals of 1536 and 1539; some were indeed confirmed in their continuity by the Crown, others were re-founded under Edward VI, yet others continued thanks to private finance. The dissolution of the chantries by the act of 1547, two years after the government of Henry VIII had first formally proposed a bill to bring this into effect, proved more distinctly disruptive. The traditional role of chantry foundations in education was more direct, attached to the aims of the foundation and more transparent than the less continuous associations of the monasteries. And whereas the push for reform in the case of the monasteries paid only lip-service to the notion that resources would be released for the public good, including the education of the young, the dissolution of the chantries was more deliberately excused and indeed justified by the claim that more money would thus come to education. Most chantry schools did in fact survive in a new guise, from 1550 generally known as the 'free grammar schools of Edward VI'. There were, however, fewer new foundations than originally envisaged and they now concentrated more specifically on secondary education, to the loss of teaching the very young.[73] Clearly schooling was now directed specifically at two things: the training of the sons of gentry class to fulfil roles in government and society that suited their station; and of those from mercantile and urban classes to staff the bureaucracy of local government. The provision of a trained professional class, rather than of priests, was just as true of the schools provided for under cathedrals of the new foundation. Although they were often housed in former monastic buildings within the cathedral precincts, their relation with their cities was stronger than that of their predecessors before the Reformation.[74]

51 Ashbourne, Derbyshire. The grammar school, founded in 1585, with building continuing until at least 1603.

In the years immediately after the accession of Elizabeth, many towns petitioned for the foundation of grammar schools, in many cases re-foundations of schools recently suppressed. Mansfield, in Nottinghamshire, applied in March 1561, the same month in which Kingston-on-Thames, Surrey, received its letters patent. For many such arrangements, existing buildings were brought together under one governance, making the best of available property. For Kingston, the royal grant, to be held as of the honour of Hampton Court, is an especially detailed description, providing places for worship, rooms for study, rooms for accommodation, space for preparing food, and the physical means by which all these elements could be brought together:

> all that our free chapel called Marye Magdalene chappell, in Norbiton in Kingston with its garden on the east, and a little chapel called St Anne Chappell; a small study [unum parvum le Studie] and an inner chamber with the Hawkes Mew over it and S. Loye's chapel on the south side with a little place underneath it; and an old kitchen and a chamber adjoining it; and a parlour [solarium] called a loft above the same kitchen and chamber and another under the kitchen, on the west side of the chapel,

situate across the footway leading from Kingston to London; and a house next to the kitchen; also the yarde on the North, and another yard on the west, and a passage called a gallery [deambulatorium vocatum 'a galorye'] above the yarde leading from S. Anne's chapel to the small place, and 2 chambers called the Masters lodging; also a cellar and 4 small chambers under the Masters lodging.

It was no simple task for the bailiffs and freemen of the town because this repeated a grant of fourteen years earlier to one Richard Taverner, with whom they had to discuss terms to remit the last seven years of his lease, but this they effected through exchanges of property and further endowments.[75] These rather makeshift arrangements of buildings for the foundation of schools were slowly overtaken by the purpose-built structures first envisaged by scholars of early Tudor England, in whose eyes schools had a very definite and customised shape in order to meet their ideals.

While the many foundations known as 'Queen Elizabeth's grammar schools' gained the royal stamp of approval, they were largely paid for and initiated by local people who pressed each case, though sometimes the later presence of a powerful benefactor assured the schools' future.[76] This is what happened at Godmanchester, Huntingdonshire (fig. 52). The much-altered remains of the school retains a plaque with the queen's name over the door but the chief mover of the foundation was a local man, Richard Robins. The school was founded by letters patent in 1561, though legal challenges to his will went on for more than twenty years until in 1586 the estate which Robins had bequeathed was passed to Sir Walter Mildmay, later Chancellor of the Exchequer, who then re-granted the governors two rent charges from the estate amounting to £20.[77] The Grammar School of Leicester also began life as a collective enterprise, but later came under the benefice of the Earl of Huntingdon, who was probably responsible for the content of new statutes drawn up in 1573 when the school moved out of the redundant church of St Peter into newly built premises.[78] What followed here, as it did at Shrewsbury, originally also a local initiative, was that the school took on a wider significance under this noble patronage. At this period schools in England became what they have been ever since, namely either a direct service to the local community or something rather more nationally significant than that, since in some cases their individual fame and reputation meant that pupils came from a wide geographical area to study there.

The significance of what is now known as a 'catchment area' is exemplified by the case of Salisbury. In 1548 the chantry commissioners declared the town to be without a school but that chantries there were awarding stipends to priests teaching at Trowbridge and Bradford-on-Avon (about 25 and 28 miles distant respectively). After the suppression of the chantries these arrangements continued. In 1569, however, it was decided that Trow-

53 Oakham, Rutland. The south front of the grammar school, inscribed *Schola Latina – Graeca – Hebraica Ao 1584*.

bridge and Bradford did not need scholars since they were 'but upland towns and not a resort of gentlemen and merchants'. The stipends were then combined and a school at Salisbury at last financed, suggesting that educational institutions were felt appropriate where the local population met the right social, aspirational character.[79] So some schools in relatively large towns, such as Ashbourne in Derbyshire and Shrewsbury, can be said to have initially served local gentry and the sons of merchants; others, often in such small places as Felsted in Essex or Oakham (fig. 53) and Uppingham in Rutland, became schools of national renown, widening their limited local catchment.[80] In most cases, however, this was begun by the deliberate arrangements put in place by founders; hence Richard Rich ordained for Felsted that boys from his Essex-wide, indeed south-east-wide estates, should have preference. Rich's wider patronage at Felsted is discussed further in chapter 4.

While many Elizabethan and Jacobean schools therefore were re-foundations and some of their buildings were a legacy from the past, there was a rationalisation of their plan and arrangements that matched the avowed educational ambitions of the age. It has been suggested that many of them appear to have been situated in side streets rather than the main streets of the town, though sometimes a newly built school or one with a new frontage presented a bold architectural statement. A key aspect of instruction and emphasising the school as community is clear from the way in which adequate lodging for the schoolmaster and often the usher became incorporated into new school building, with an attached residential range at right angles to the main schoolroom block or a separate house nearby. Schoolrooms were conventionally on the upper floor of a long block and sometimes lower-storey rooms were let out for commercial purposes. The formation of a school around a courtyard, as at Guildford, for example, is usually found in larger rather than smaller urban environments; such a plan matches something of the domestic integrity of a gentry or merchant house of the period, and was perhaps intended as much for security as anything else. It is notable, however, that this may have been the preference of a mix of local interest groups rather than those foundations where a local magnate determined both the statutes and the physical form of the school. In surviving written testimony on schools and their organisation, order and necessary division of age and precedence is first outlined in Erasmus's description of John Colet's foundation of St Paul's School, London, as early as 1509. It had four apartments: one for young children to be taught the principles of religion; two spaces for lower boys and upper forms, divided only by a curtain, 'to be drawn at pleasure'; and a chapel. 'The School has no corners, or hiding places; nothing like a cell or closet.'[81] This encouragement of a shared religious value and experience rather than the cloistered cell emerges in the number symbolism employed representing the communal aspects of Christ's ministry; at St Paul's nine classes or forms of

seventeen pupils apiece added up to 153 pupils, the number of fish believed to have been caught by the first, mutually supportive Christian community, Christ's apostles.[82] The earliest surviving school that seems to echo the spirit and form of St Paul's is usually said to be that at Berkhamsted, Hertfordshire, originally built about 1544 through the bequest to his home town of John Incent, former Dean of St Paul's. This has the emerging convention of plan typical of many later schools, with a long block flanked by accommodation at each end for master and usher (fig. 54).[83]

Among many Elizabethan texts on education, Richard Mulcaster's *Positions* of 1581 has taken on a pre-eminence in the history of schools because he looks at the school experience as a holistic training. For Mulcaster, the integrity of what was to be learned and the conditions under which that could best take place were all of a piece, so that he pays more attention to the provisions for building and good situation than other writers. His description of the ideal school runs thus:

> I could wish that grammer schooles were planted in the skirtes and suburbes of townes, neare to the fields. . . . There might not be much want of room. . . . To haue a faire schoole house aboue with freedome of aire for the tongues, and an other beneath for other pointes of learning, and perfiting or continuing the Elementarie entrances, which will hardly be kept, if they be posted ouer to private practicing at home: to have the maister and his familie though of some good number conueniently well lodged: to have a pretie close adioyning to the schoole walled round about, and one quarter if no more couered aboue cloisture like, for the childrens exercise in the raine weather, as it will require a good minde and no mean purse.[84]

Mulcaster's description encompasses the ideals of good education but also the geographical location and multi-building arrangements under which that can happen. Schools were perceived as integral to the communities they served, and an equal part of the fabric of its social housing.

The almshouse and the hospital

For Mulcaster, the siting of a grammar school on the outskirts of a town meant good air and space for work, housing and recreation. Traditionally another major social provision of towns, the hospital or almshouse, was also situated on the outskirts, though for a different practical reason, the keeping of sickness at bay.[85] Many late medieval foundations were set up in the wake of the Black Death of 1348–50. They were often placed at the city or town gates, for example St Thomas, Southwark, at the approach to London Bridge, or those at the five gates to Bury St Edmunds. Almshouses and hospitals were also part of a rethink of the past, like schools, in the wake of the Reformation. Their provision certainly met a perceived need but they were even more closely tied to an awareness of both altruistic care for the under-privileged and as a means to perpetuate the names and good works of the individuals who paid for, or simply contributed towards, them. They have become something of a touchstone in the work of many historians as to whether wishing benefit on the poor was genuine or whether patrons of new foundations were simply attempting to replicate the sums formerly spent on now proscribed obits and masses for their souls after death, by appearing to support the most immediate good cause. Post-Reformation funeral monuments are inscribed in abundance with reference to the good works undertaken for the poor and infirm during the deceased's lifetime. W. K. Jordan, one of the most respected historians of this area of research, concluded that the surviving evidence shows a rather patchy response across the substantial number of counties that he examined. Philanthropy was not as embedded or as regularly dispensed as the lavish inscriptions seem to imply and funds given by private individuals often ran out, leaving the local community to continue providing for the foundation or letting it decay.[86]

The issue of the poor was yet another concern that the central government took in hand in order to regularise and set rules for conduct. Through a series of Acts of Parliament, the poor were defined as a series of groups, not all of which merited help and support.[87] The poor were indeed, in the biblical sense, the rich man's burden; the inscription 'Hee that giveth to the poor lendeth to the Lord' and the date 1638 is found on the north wall of the entrance passage to the Jesus Hospital at Bray, Berkshire, founded in 1627.[88] Yet they were also stereotyped into 'deserving' and 'undeserving' classes: the former were the infirm, wounded soldiers, widows of prominent men who had served the community, those who had served but fallen on hard times (the former minister of All Saints, Dorchester, for example, was described as 'very poor' at his almshouse);[89] the latter included the able-bodied but idle, the vagrant or anyone who had moved parish and was therefore suspect. The making of such distinctions was, of course, like the charge of witchcraft, prone to highly local prejudice and the settling of old scores, so that who got service at the almshouse or hospital very much reflected the collective goodwill and sense of well-being in local communities.[90]

Like other kinds of building considered in this chapter, almost every aspect of the development of almshouses and hospitals was prefigured or even fully formed by medieval precedent, whether concerning the nature of endowment, the plan of the buildings or the way in which patrons guarded their singular identification with these buildings as their personal project. It has been noted that in the fifteenth century the giving of indiscriminate doles was giving way to particular endowments for specific buildings.[91] What changed was the way these foundations began to operate in post-Reformation society and the channels by which their endowment was celebrated. Patrons became increasingly fastidious about the conditions of their bequest. Numbers of endowments were significant and the English evidence for such activity appears to have been greater than in some European countries, such as France, though probably less than in the mercantile communities of the Dutch Republic.[92] Local rivalries may well have spurred some to give; the county of Buckinghamshire enjoyed no fewer than twenty-two almshouse foundations in the course of the sixteenth and seventeenth centuries.[93] There was certainly a spurt after the Act of 1598, which allowed benefactors to found almshouses (along with houses of correction) without the process of obtaining charters or letters patent.[94]

These buildings fall into different physical types, all of which had largely been established before the Reformation. Indeed some 'new' hospitals and almshouses adapted pre-existing monastic or guild buildings, stressing a continuity with the past. The Great Hospital of Norwich was duly dissolved at the Reformation but re-founded by Edward VI and Lord Leycester's Hospital at Warwick was carved out of the site of the old Guild of St George within the West Gate of the town.[95] Some of these older sites strongly reflect one aim of certain medieval foundations, namely to replicate the character and rituals of the households of great late medieval domestic establishments; this is especially apparent at the Hospital of the Holy Cross, near Winchester, with its 'service' court of kitchen and stable and larger inner court with the dwellings of the brethren, rather like the lodging ranges of a conventional base court and, facing these, an ambulatory leading to the chapel.[96] The courtyard format thus became the standard for post-Reformation foundations where wealthy patrons were involved or the establishment sought to cater for more than simply a few inmates. Abbot's

55 Barnstaple, Devon.
The Penrose almshouses,
founded in 1627.

Hospital, Guildford, is one of the most famous examples, along with Whit-gift's, Croydon, the Penrose almshouses at Barnstaple in Devon of 1627 (fig. 55) and the much smaller Ford's Hospital at Coventry.[97] Some of these buildings used the plan familiar from the great courtyard country house of late medieval and early Tudor times, with gatehouse facing a great (here the communal) hall alongside the chapel; others had hall and chapel facing each other across the court. More modest examples included the type of an open court on three sides, as at the almshouses founded by the Countess of Derby at Harefield. More modest still were the single-range foundations, like that at Langley Marish, then in Buckinghamshire. This foundation is said to have been at the behest of Sir John Kederminster in 1617, though the endowment provided in his will, proved in 1631, suggests that the almshouses were still unfinished. These almshouses were essential for the support and maintenance of the fabric of Kederminster's chapel and library, recently added to the nearby parish church.[98]

The almshouse at Bray

One of the largest new foundations was that of Jesus Hospital at Bray: on the death of the merchant fishmonger William Goddard in 1609, the charge and care of the hospital was left to the Fishmongers' Company; designed to house as many as forty poor men and women, it was completed in 1628 under letters patent of 1616.[99] Goddard's statue is placed over the entrance,

56 Bray, Berkshire. Jesus Hospital, founded in 1627.

57 Bray, Berkshire, Jesus Hospital. Detail of the façade, with the statue of the founder William Goddard.

IESVS HOSPITALL
FOVNDED IN THE YEAR 1627.
OF THE SOLE FOVNDAC̃ON OF WILLIAM
GODDARD ESQ WHEREIN HE HATH
PROVIDED FOR FOR THE POORE PEOPLE
FOR EVER & LEFTE IT TO THE SOLE
CARE AND GOVERMENT OF THE RIGHTE
WOR COMPANY OF FISHMONGERS OF
THE CITTY OF LONDON OF WHICH
COMPANY HE WAS A FREE
BROTHER.
THIS NEW STONE ERECTED 1844

with a later stone tablet inscription of 1844. The great court is some 160 by 140 feet square and its uncompromising singularity suggests a very particular look at collegiate foundations for inspiration. Two particular features of this grand structure deserve further attention because they reflect issues of the long-term development of these buildings (fig. 56).

First, other than the statue, the building is sparsely decorated. These foundations were not the opportunity, obviously, for patrons to demand lavish display, other than their coats of arms; the inclusion of Goddard's statue is unusual (fig. 57). Sometimes a frontispiece to the building bears the hallmarks of classical style, though in many instances these were added somewhat later. At the almshouses of Etwall in Derbyshire, for example, a frontispiece with a scrolled pediment of 1681 was added to a house founded in 1550. An issue of decorum may be evident here, for clearly such buildings would not be the place for outright self-advertisement. Yet the urban nature of the hospital and almshouse is evident in the way that, unlike the country house of the period, whose internal courtyard ranges were often replete with ornament or increasingly classical décor, the courtyards of almshouses were discreet and highly domestic, suited to purpose, and it was the street front that betrayed both requisite expense and reference to the street itself, as in the use of colonnades at the modest Devon building at Moretonhampsted and the grander Penrose almshouses at Barnstaple, which also uses Gothic windows at each end to mark boardroom and chapel.

Jesus Hospital at Bray also eschews a large common communal space, prefiguring the decline of the use of a great hall at these buildings as time went by, acknowledging the fact that the inmates wanted communal support but also individual privacy, so long as they were able to care for themselves.[100] The major structure facing the point of entry is the chapel and there is some evidence that conventionally at almshouses the use of this facility also declined or was never provided for in the first place, as more residents used the local parish church.[101] The specificity of these foundations as communities therefore may with time have given way to the pull of the wider local community of the towns they served.

Only possibly as late as 1660 can the provision of almshouses and hospitals be said to have caught up with provisions for the poor and needy lost in the dissolution of the monasteries a century and a quarter before.[102] In a sense this was inevitable, given the highly specific endowments made for these new foundations with defined numbers, while the monasteries had a more flexible arrangement with lay infirmary halls and guesthouses and feeding and treating the poor and the traveller on a one-off, day-to-day basis. Significantly, many foundations of the post-Reformation period lived rather hand-to-mouth; many privately endowed buildings declined and faced an uncertain future when the founder's bequest ran out. Those run by corporations, usually buildings taken over from dissolved monasteries, had a better fate, perhaps because individuals were more willing to leave sums large and small to an overtly communal cause rather than to someone else's private foundation. St Giles, Norwich, as well as St Bartholomew's, Gloucester, and St John's, Cirencester, all fared well in such circumstances, and all used old infirmary halls as part of their customisation, often subdividing it to offer greater numbers accommodation.[103] Here again it was the links with the past that proved the most fruitful and stable in the formation of new urban identities in this period.

3

A Language for Architecture

How people valued the visual arts and employed them in their daily lives is measured by the language they used to engage with them, the various means through which they described visual phenomena, established ideals of appearance, enforced standards of manufacture and, when commissioning something, ensured that their intentions were carried out. It is now taken for granted that this language was the exclusive preserve of the written word on paper. Contemporaries, however, were used to seeing words on a variety of surfaces and associated the written word with all kinds of objects.[1] When a great house carries a motto or moral message, whether on its walls or along its skyline, it can be supposed that the buildings themselves carry significant messages and that there is a continuum between the structure and the messages thereon (fig. 58). It is often pointed out too that words could have particularly suggestive shapes and forms at this time, when there were no fixed standards of presenting written text; a degree of playfulness could be involved; language sometimes took its own shapes on the page in the form of lozenges, or trapped within a pattern or poem celebrating the name of a loved one.[2] Language found its way on to clothes, luxury domestic implements and furnishings. It is important not to see words as trapped within the printed book at this period, yet it is the particular preserve of documents and printed books that they share conventions and build traditions of explication and description that become part of a literate society. Documents and printed sources are studied because they reveal what society thought of buildings, how buildings were believed to be significant for society's well-being, how people monitored negotiation about the making of things and divided up areas of responsibility in seeing that buildings actually materialised. But equally words were not simply in the service of the practical, for they themselves shaped ideas about how buildings were viewed; they might evoke a world of imaginary buildings in poetry and drama that suggested ideals beyond attainment. The ways in

58 Felbrigg Hall, Norfolk, 1621-24, with the words GLORIA DEO IN EXCELSIS in the balustrade. The device is unusual but appears on contemporary building work at Castle Ashby (Northampton-shire), Temple Newsam and Skipton Castle (both Yorkshire).

which contemporaries both organised words and reacted to their stimulus to the imagination survive in a wealth of printed sources and documents, ranging from the official and legalistic (laws, contracts and accounts of payment), through the descriptive (surveys of property and inventories of personal possessions, itineraries and early county histories detailing places and monuments), to the personal (letters and diaries) and the purely imaginative (non-existent works of art in drama and poetry). Theoretical literature specifically on architecture ultimately pulled many of these diverse sources together because in making a case for itself, the language of theory made parallels with other forms of discourse. Theoretical writing therefore opens and closes this chapter on architecture and words.

The emergence of commentary on building

In this growing amount of documentation and literature, specialisation encouraged texts of very different kinds, so that particular forms of artistic production developed their own ways of literary argument. In the history of painting, for example, the specialist skill of making miniatures, known as the art of limning, became a particular branch of writing about image-making, most famously demonstrated by Nicholas Hilliard, whose *Arte of Limninge* was written about 1598 to 1603.[3] Such books dealt not only with the practice of making the work of art itself but also with the practice of living as an artist in terms of behaviour in both professional and personal life, so that issues of the social status of the practitioner came into public discourse. Reading such sources eventually became the necessary education of those with pretensions to class and status. Since all works of art of this period established their own context through a challenge to what had gone before, so it became common that each work of art made allusion to other works that it sought to copy, emulate or surpass and it might equally situate itself into a body of language which defined its genre. The art of early modern Europe invariably asked of its audience a knowledge of a body of texts that defined its intentions and meanings, a form of 'intertextuality'.[4] This 'language' of words was replicated in, or rather mirrored, a visual language emerging from the imagery itself. In England, across all the visual arts, from architecture to painting to the decoration of funeral monuments, the use of particular forms of expression that were novel and eloquent among the learned all ultimately derived from a careful blending of recognisable native traditions with those imported from continental Europe. Slowly, and in a highly individualistic way, the educated elite of England came to understand that visual or verbal reference to shared knowledge about works of art was more important and more indicative of status than commissioning a portrait that simply gave information about birth and status, however complex that depiction had traditionally been. By the time of the outbreak of the Civil War, the visual arts spoke increasingly not only through the information carried on the work (most notably through the heraldry found on the exterior of almost all early Tudor architecture and, later in the century, inscription and motto; painting and funeral monuments also used both) but by reference to modes of expression that depended on a knowledge of prototypes found in artistic traditions. This might be the *contrapposto* turn of a figure in a Van Dyck painting, the use of the classical orders on a porch to a country house or raising the awareness of the viewer to fundamental principles of proportion and order rather than detail. A drawing by Inigo Jones of a gateway for Arundel House, London, had an entirely different aim from the more pedestrian, minutely detailed drawing of the same gate by John Smythson. Patrons demonstrated their self-possession and confidence in analysing works of art by understanding such differences.[5]

Like the point raised about miniature painting above, the art of building had its own specialisms and, it can be argued, its own rather different agenda from the rest of the visual arts because of its functionality. Buildings had not only to look right but to work right. As the sixteenth century progressed military architecture in particular needed its own specialist language and discourse. Indeed it needed a particular professionalism of secrecy: while many immigrant Italians brought to England the necessary expertise for pushing the boundaries of the mechanics of defensible building, English aristocrats and government officials were careful to retain command of their employment, promotion and the secrets they were party to.[6] There is therefore a constant dialogue in writing about architecture, as well as documentation about getting buildings put up in the first place, that keeps one eye on appearance (which may potentially carry meaning) and another on practicalities.

In the history of theoretical writing on architecture of this period every treatise on building carefully engaged with previous writings, took the sense of the authority of those writings on board, but also took up the challenge of criticism based on experience. Fundamentally, books on architecture were highly practical, written by architects for other architects in the cause of sharing knowledge and they became increasingly disseminated through printed text in the sixteenth century. The impact was Europe-wide. From early beginnings in establishing ideas of decorum for different kinds of building, treatises began to provide templates for the widest possible range of structures, from the largest public buildings down to the small-scale dwellings that might be found all over the continent. There were key moves in these books to reach out to different nationalities, through the suggestion that while basic building types were everywhere applicable, the use of local building materials was to be encouraged. Treatises also developed in two other specific directions at this time. One was towards breaking the text down into books for special crafts and functions, so that practitioners of stage perspective, of carpentry or of garden design, for example, were given their own particular advice; thus the broad base of the earliest treatises, with their templates for building offered in the spirit of developing an ideal city under beneficent rule, gave way to manuals for highly specialist occupations. The second development was the burgeoning interest in the licentious, which also gave particular regions of Europe the chance to add their own particular solutions to the design, and especially the ornament, of building. This stemmed not so much from a desire to break the 'rules' of architecture as believed to have been laid down by Vitruvius but a knowing commentary on Vitruvius' advice, to which the first theorists of the modern era had adhered. The ever closer examination of classical precedents revealed that every structure adopted individual solutions that provided a range of ideas rather than a set, and ultimately stultified, vocabulary. This was an acceptance, as Christy Anderson has argued, of both buildings of the past and the texts that explored them, as *fontes* (imaginative source material) rather than *auctoritates* (unbending authorities). However, the handling of licentiousness needed skill and experience. Hence Giorgio Vasari's oft-quoted lament about Michelangelo: when he stretched the rules (as in his running ornament on the tombs in the Medici Chapel of the 1520s and 1530s) he knew what he was doing but the untutored observation of his achievement sometimes encouraged others to think that this meant there was open season on the ornament of the past and a carelessness with its principles.[7]

England, architecture and the classical past

When books on architecture, drawing upon and developing the legacy of the classical past, arrived in England from across the Channel, there was of course both acceptance and resistance, given the political and religious isolation after the Reformation. Yet England remained a Christian country and for all Christian societies, the remnants of the classical past had to be customised for the Christian world (fig. 59). Ancient Rome was pagan, so how could its buildings offer templates for Christian society? Italian theorists had done this by looking to common objectives of order and decorum between classical and Christian worlds and they had the material to hand in the remnants of Roman civilisation. For England, as for all Protestant states, the issue was one that had to reach a stage further; to suggest a national slant on this material that was contributive and not dependent on the lead from Catholic Italy. Before the foundation of the Church of Rome in the third and fourth centuries, what role did England play in the hegemony of the Roman Empire? Writing about an 'ideal' architecture has generally involved a propensity to use national characteristics, and sometimes prejudices, to make a particular point. In his *Dyetary of Helth* of 1542, for

example, Dr Andrew Boorde's advice on the planning and placing of the ideal house is determined by considerations concerning situation and orientation, though his gloss on that slips in the xenophobic. To avoid bad winds entering the house, the hall door should be angled away from, and not directly in line with, the gatehouse entry to the courtyard, in order to trap bad winds. He goes on to suggest that the builder must avoid a south-facing placing of the house because that risks the evil winds coming from France.[8] Boorde's advice is that of a medical practitioner, offering practical solutions around the idea of the house as a protective carapace. John Shute's *First and Chiefe Groundes of Architecture*, written during the reign of Edward VI but not published until 1563 (under Elizabeth), is the first attempt in English to adopt the templates and forms of Italian and French treatises; Shute acknowledges his debts to published treatises but also makes it clear that he also has first-hand experience of the best of architecture in Italy: 'that I might with so muche more perfection write of them as both the reading of the thinge and seing it in dede is more than onely bare reding of it.'[9] As Vaughan Hart has shown, however, Shute deploys the classical orders in such a way as to suggest a particularly English frame of reference, with both mythological and historical allusions. His audience is also important. The group of patrons among whom he worked in Edward's reign counted the affiliation to Protestantism as a key motif of their political stance; the allusion to generic 'order' in the use of the five orders was thus to a simplicity and clarity of organising the appearance of buildings that matched the directness of the Protestant faith which that government deliberately propagated. Language again is cleverly used to suggest the coincidence of the message on the page to the world order of the country. The use of male and female characters to embody the five orders, ranged against the proportions of the column they embody and represent, elides into an encouragement to those holding political power to act as leaders of the country in the way that the figures determine the proportions of the architecture: 'because all the members of the body have cheflye and principally a duetie to the head, as governour of the whole, and without which, al the other can not live.'[10] The dedication to Elizabeth is a means of encouraging her to lead the country as a great builder in the line of Greeks and Romans of the classical past.[11] Architectural theory came therefore to set both ideal standards of design and practical pathways of construction for practitioners. Alongside this, other forms of writing about buildings needed to offer authoritative advice and proper conduct, ultimately enforced by law.

Building by statute and proclamation

The language of regulation concerning building at this period sought both to advise and to enforce and, as with every aspect of government attempting to control its people and define the limits and responsibilities it held, preambles to government directives always stressed good intentions. Elizabeth I's proclamation of 1580 itemised three such responsibilities: the enforcement of justice, the supply of food and the maintenance of good health among her people. What were the major concerns of governing authorities to do with buildings and how were their fears and protective instincts verbalised? Governments both national and local had to deal with unforeseen events but certain patterns of such occurrence helped to build up case law and good practice. One recurrent danger of course was the incidence of fire (fig. 60). There had long been attempts to control sudden outbreaks of fire by local authorities. In his *Survey of London* John Stow makes several references to the order of Henry Fitzalwine, Mayor of London in 1189–90 (the first year of Richard I's reign), that all houses in the city should be built of stone up to a certain height and be covered with slate or baked tile; this order had been much ignored in recent times 'whereof many haue remained till our time, that for winning of ground they haue bin taken

down and in place of some one of them being low, as but two stories aboue the ground, many houses of foure or fiue stories high are placed'.[12] The next step in building regulation occurred when governments became anxious about the state of buildings, concluding that their condition revealed something important about the wider state of the country. The dilapidation of building stock was seen as indicative of a wider decay of the country's well-being and, more importantly, the social responsibility to put that right. In the 1540s Henry VIII's government issued a series of measures to re-vitalise the physical fabric of towns and cities. These were repeated later in the century, with an important concentration of laws in the 1580s, a special decade of need for compliance with all kinds of regulation given the imminent threat of invasion. Some historians have argued that these rebuilding statutes were part of a wider attempt at government control, a parcelling out of responsibility to the localities as a means of ensuring that mechanisms were in place to enforce a whole range of government directives, including social behaviour, the suppression of anti-government invective leading to potential rebellion and, most importantly, the enforcement of reformed religious practice. The careful upward effect

60 Egbert van der Poel, *A Fire at Night*, 1655–60, oil on canvas. The constant threat of fire in early modern society was reflected in building regulations which sought to enforce the use of stone and brick over wood. Kelvingrove, Glasgow Art Gallery and Museums, McLellan Bequest 111. Glasgow City Council (Museums).

of ensuring compliance sought to get first tenants themselves to take responsibility for renewal, then (failing this) their landlords and (ultimately) enforcing the passing of neglected property to the community, so that local government was landed with the task of repair and renewal.

The phenomenon of government legislation concerning the built environment during the course of the sixteenth and early seventeenth centuries demonstrates a deep concern that the state of the country's building stock was a barometer of the health of the country and also of the sense that worthy building was a measure of the wealth of the nation, thus deserving of comment and praise by foreign observers. Robert Tittler has challenged the notion that the process of government regulation begins with the Statute of 1540 and asks whether the series of acts during the century were a response to evident decline or prompts to increase the pace of what was already happening in the upturn of the physical state of England's towns and cities.[13] What exactly did the statutes identify as crucial and in what forms of language were these anxieties expressed? Further, at what point, and with what language, did anxiety pass into positive direction of building with a view to influencing not just the state of buildings but what they looked like?

Successive statutes concerning building passed in the reign of Henry VIII principally reflected the anxiety caused by the deliberate destruction of houses into plots for pasture and thus greater profit. The destruction was insidiously carried out, it was affirmed, through deliberate neglect: houses were allowed to fall into disrepair so that they could be de-commissioned. Enclosure and subsequent de-population means the decay of towns, the loss of revenues, the difficulty of finding manpower when an army needs to be raised. This deliberate decay is the theme of later statutes of the 1540s: 'divers and manye beautifull Houses of Habitacon' were left in a dangerous state, attended by 'muche oder filthe and uncleannes withe pytts, sellers and vawtes lyinge open and uncovered'.[14] The stress on the discontinuity of habitation and attached land formerly 'manured and occupied with tillage and husbandry' leads to idleness. The wording of the statutes echoes that in the Acts of Dissolution of 1536 and 1539, discussed in chapter 1, where it was impressed on new owners of properties that they were expected to continue the land use as it had long been established. Neglect and decay also threatened security, since cities and towns diminished in the realm 'whereby the power & defence thereof is enfeebled and impaired to the high displeasure of God & against his laws'.

After the middle of the century, governments sought to bring policy to bear on building not through statute but by proclamation. By Elizabeth's reign, the threat to good housing stock was perceived to come from a different pressure; now it was not de-population but overcrowding that might lead to unrest and widespread sickness. The over-populating of towns and cities led to the repeated and dangerous subdivision of properties to accom-

61 Southampton, Hampshire. The house in Bugle Street was largely built for Sir John Dawtrey in the early 16th century. Rows of jettied houses like this in towns and cities were felt to be the result of overcrowding and were the particular target of the proclamation of 1620.

modate ever growing numbers. John Stow noted how in Bucklersbury the old stone building known as the 'Old Barge', formerly a manor or great house, 'hath of long time been diuided and letten out into many tenementes'. He also noted that the house known as Coldharbour had, under the ownership of the late Earl of Shrewsbury, been demolished; in its place a great number of small tenements were now let to people of all sorts. The problem was most acute in London but was evident elsewhere also. Overcrowding led to plague and other forms of sickness.[15] The answer was to control the numbers arriving in London itself. It was therefore forbidden to divide 'any house or tenement within the precincts aforesaid into several dwellings', which should 'be kept as one house'. Furthermore, 'all sheds and shops to be plucked down that have been builded within the places and precincts aforesaid within seven years last past'.[16] Proclamations went on to forbid any new houses on plots not already containing dwellings. This policy, compared with what was to come, has been described as 'paternalistic' and it proved non-interventionist; certainly no prosecutions were brought about for some years after the two major Elizabethan proclamations of 1580 and 1602.

Under James I the policy shifted (fig. 61). After repeating the substance of the Elizabethan proclamations at his accession in 1603, in 1605 a royal proclamation sought for the first time to direct the means whereby better building could happen; it expressed a view on building materials by forbidding the use of timber in reconstruction and urging the use of brick or brick and stone. Subsequent proclamations refined this message. By a proclamation of 1620, things are taken yet further. Particular features of extension are now identified as prohibited:

> the supportation and strengthening of ruinous and old Buildings, unfit to be continued, by digging of Cellars, and bringing up new Bricke walles, by erecting new Chimneys and Staire-cases, by placing pieces of Timber, by setting on new Roofes and Rafters, and thrusting out of Dormers, knitting and fastening together the sayd new Additions unto the olde Timber by barres and crampes of Iron.[17]

Clearly this was a process of disguising decay and continuing the covert extension of existing properties for extra accommodation by other means than simple subdivision. The remedy involved new rules for building that imply a conformity of design that can be read as promoting the modishly new town houses of the day. Buildings were to have no more than two storeys, and the streets were to be rid of overhanging windows, some of the most elaborate of which were under construction in London at this time (the frontage of the house for Sir Paul Pindar, for example, survives in the Victoria and Albert Museum), but were also a feature of provincial towns and cities:

> in building of the said Houses, there shall bee no Jutties or Jutting, or Cant windowes, either upon Timber Joystes, or otherwise, but the walls to goe direct and streight upwards, and at the setting off a Water-table to be made. Also the forme of the windowes of every whole Story to be of more height then bredth, to the end the roomes may receive ayre for health, and that there bee sufficient Peeres of Brick, not less then halfe the bredth of the windowes betweene them for strength. And likewise the windowes of every halfe Story to be made square or neere thereabouts.[18]

Many historians have seen the hand and influence of Inigo Jones, four years into his post as Surveyor of the King's Works, in these regulations (fig. 62). They occurred at a time of proto-speculative building that prefigures the rebuilding after the fire of 1666 but the development can be taken further back in time; Roger H. Leech has argued that this move towards regularised rows of houses had significant precedents back in the sixteenth century.[19] A new proclamation issued under Charles I at the opening of his reign in 1625 essentially repeats these instructions.[20] Within a few years the government took unprecedented steps to enforce them.

The Court of Star Chamber had originated in medieval times as the King's Council, meeting as a court and operating as a kind of tribunal of state, offering speedy decisions to people wanting to avoid the delays of the

62   Lindsey House, on the west side of Lincoln's Inn Fields, London, 1639–41. Built of red brick, originally exposed, with the pilasters stuccoed to look like stone. Variously associated with the architect Inigo Jones and the sculptor Nicholas Stone, the house matches the ideals of early 17th-century building proclamations.

common law courts. In the 1630s it was used by the government to exercise summary and often brutal justice with the aim of raising revenue. Alongside grain-hoarders, infringers of patents of monopoly and gentry who failed to fulfil their social duties by neglecting their country seats, fourteen prosecutions were brought against builders and developers. In 1634 John Moore was imprisoned, fined £1000 and ordered to demolish this offending buildings. However, such procedures did not survive long in English building history. All prosecutions ceased during the Civil Wars of the 1640s and Star Chamber ceased to function. For the historian Thomas G. Barnes there was something of a lost opportunity for environmental planning here and this is arguably true; but what the age of statute and proclamation did for the regulation of building was to articulate for the first time a statement of preference for ways of building that privileged new materials and styles over others.[21] The emergence of new style not from an aesthetic preference but from concerns for the safety of the community underscores the often practical, rather than aesthetic or idealistic, reasons for the coming of innovation and change.

Building accounts and contracts

The other legal type of document that reflects contemporary attitudes to building ranges across the various records of particular building projects.

These fall into several categories, of which building accounts form the largest number. A few of these are in the form of books drawn up by owners and incorporate expenditure into observations on how seasonal factors and weather conditions affect building, for example the memorandum book drawn up by Sir Edward Pytts during his rebuilding of Kyre Park, Worcestershire, between 1588 and 1618.[22] Also surviving are contracts, surveys, certain minutes of official meetings and other descriptions which were the result of official tasks; these include the documents drawn up by royal commissioners in surveying the monasteries, and surveys of coastal buildings made at times of national danger such as those undertaken by Elizabeth I's government during the 1570s. It should also be noted that probate inventories, often assumed to refer only to movable goods, frequently include information about the room spaces, fittings and internal layout of houses; and, while in considerably fewer numbers, there are surviving inventories schools, shops and other forms of building. The inventory of Shrewsbury School of 1599 helps reconstruct the original layout of the building and lists all manner of non-movable items such as doors, wainscot, windows and even curtain rods.[23]

In his great survey of the documentation of buildings by contract down to 1540, L. F. Salzman noted that the sources for the fifteenth century are comparatively rich, while there are fewer from the early sixteenth. Moreover, some of the latter are concentrated around a few grand commissions since they relate to building projects such as the completion of Henry VII's Chapel at Westminster Abbey and of King's Chapel, Cambridge, both royal initiatives whose documents survive largely because of their subsequent retention in the State Papers. In addition, Salzman speculated that the introduction of paper for such documents may explain the relatively low survival rate compared with the earlier use of the more durable parchment.[24]

One of the main tests of a changing language comes at the point where patrons and builders negotiate an undertaking. How buildings were paid for has been examined by few scholars. They invariably begin with the words of Sir Christopher Wren, who advised in 1681: 'There are 3 ways of working: by the Day, by Measure, by Great.'[25] It is the last of these, covering the all-inclusive contract, or series of contracts, that proves most illuminating for the language of building, because contracted work implies forethought, negotiation and the patron's need to safeguard the outcome according to his or her wishes. The documentary evidence of construction has been well and expertly covered for the study of country houses of this period by Malcolm Airs.[26] It is likely that documentation for this species of building survives in greater quantity thanks to the continuity of certain great families with both space to keep archives and the self-interest in long-established family property. The records of urban public buildings such as town halls may have been prone to fire and the disinterest of later generations. For great houses, Airs established that there was a shift in practice over this time: the traditional form of organising the making of a house through the owner's direct employment of labour by the day, using the materials and equipment he or she had assembled, gave way to a system of contracting out each specialist task or, in special circumstances, making a contract with one man who then made his own arrangements for the supply of the various skills that brought the house into being. From this stage it was a short step towards a system of piecework, whereby craftsmen were paid by the item, controlling their output and giving an incentive to complete the task. Airs concluded that although great bodies like the Royal Works continued to employ direct labour for domestic building, thanks to the continuity of organisation and expertise, and while running repairs might also be put to direct labour, the contract system was becoming almost universal for large houses by the early seventeenth century. But did this new form of managing the building process work more generally across other types of building? And what impact did change have on the language used to specify what was required and how to get the patron's needs put into practice and subsequently verified? It seems that a different pattern emerges for other forms of building, but only certain kinds in certain regions have been researched thoroughly. In his study of building craftsmen of the towns of northern England, Donald Woodward concluded that hiring by the day for routine urban tasks on small-scale public and domestic building remained the most common practice during the long period 1450 to 1750. Contract work, however, whereby an estimate was drawn up for the whole enterprise, often did relate to large works such as the new guildhall in Hull during the 1630s and, in an especially well-documented example, the construction of the new forebuilding for Exeter Guildhall in the 1590s. At Exeter different kinds of stone were used and such items as the capitals were paid for separately.[27] Only in rather elaborate or complex buildings did public structures begin to parallel the practices of specialised commissioning that went on at great country houses.

An emerging contract system, in which the tasks were subdivided by expertise and use of materials, implies specialisation of two kinds. First, this method would suggest that the owner knew exactly what was wanted across a range of skills and had the knowledge to express this in a document that might have to stand the test of law. Second, it suggests that the craftsmen themselves had to refine their mode of self-expression to meet the owner's needs. Both owners and craftsmen needed new words to describe and put a value on such new sixteenth-century technologies as plasterwork and architectural panelling. It is unwise to be too prescriptive here or to expect that the documents will answer all the questions that might arise. Studies of the language of contract in this period in Italy have shown how difficult it is to understand fully what might be meant in every documented, written instance. There are clearly terms that were familiar to contemporary society that cannot now be fathomed, partly because the inference may be fairly non-specific but also because many instances of contract were attended by face-to-face engagement. Verbal understandings and methods of undertaking the precise inference therefore cannot be reconstructed or penetrated.[28] From English evidence, it seems, this had long been the case. In 1485/6 a carpenter was contracted to use old timbers from a demolished house to construct a new almshouse at Tattershall College, Lincolnshire, but the specification was not entirely laid out in the contract. A 'gallery' (a use of the term to describe what might be called an open arcade) at the almshouse was to be built of 'substanciall pillers of tymbre wt a goodly enhaunce clenly and workmanly wrought and made according to the com[mun]icacion in tyme past hadde'.[29] In addition, there was frequent demand for work that equalled something recently built elsewhere, perhaps preferably in excess of that, usually by such obvious one-upmanship as asking for a new church tower to be higher than its forerunner and rival perhaps just a few miles away.

Nevertheless, it might be supposed that contracting to specialist crafts-men would have sharpened the ways in which patrons defined what they wanted and encouraged a knowledge of skills that was more sophisticated in 1640 than it had been a century earlier. The evidence, however, suggests that this came into being only slowly. The terms used to contract work at Tattershall in 1485–6 are common in fifteenth-century contracts, implying known standards of production that brought into being buildings of strength ('substanciall') and good craftsmanship ('workmanly'); they often also imply a sense of fitness to purpose ('sufficiently', as used when but-tresses were to be inserted at the church of Broxbourne, Hertfordshire, and on the quality of oak to be used at Newark Bridge in 1485/6).[30] In the six-teenth century, and especially after about 1550, other terms either make their appearance or become more commonly used, but the meaning may have been intended to be elusive, borrowed from an emerging language of description, of wonder and amazement at new technology and style, rather than precisely determined by the needs of building contracts. Two terms frequently used are 'artificially' and 'cunningly'. In the 1586/7 contract for a house at Woolavington (the site of this house, long since demolished, is now known as Lavington Park), north-west of Arundel in West Sussex, very basic stonework such as the walls and the paving of the cellar use all the old terms for strength and durability. Other architectural features however are described differently; chimneys, shafts, splays, quoins, crests and espe-cially the windows are commanded to be carried out 'verie artyficiallie and conninglie'.[31] It appears that the combination of the patron's wish to put out different parts of the building and work in various materials to a range of contractors not only encouraged forms of specialised display, but also left the expected results rather imprecise. Patrons still looked to examples as a standard from which their craftsmen could copy and work, now less frequently expressed in contracts, but evident in letters and other forms of document showing payment for travelling some distance to see a useful template. The end of this chapter returns to the issues surrounding the lack of precision about changing requirements of building, and particularly aspects of visual appearance, that were only beginning to be resolved in the early seventeenth century.

The literature of 'England': topographical writing

In drawing up documents to get buildings constructed or renovated, the aim was to use language in order to specify needs and expectations. In literary production, the recording of buildings encourages a use of language that may describe a specific, unusual feature but often moves into the celebratory and ultimately into metaphor. The growth of topographical writing in sixteenth- and early seventeenth-century England stemmed from the need to justify, explain and understand the changes in the built environment that were taking place. The place of human agency, initially and most especially in the form of Tudor governments, in altering the towns, cities and surrounding landscapes in which people lived, came to be seen as something active and initiated by individuals, not simply as the working out of the will of God that had to be passively accepted. Older histories were questioned and set against extant evidence. The role of the dissolution of the monasteries in this was of fundamental importance because the beneficiaries of that process were supported, as James McVicar has argued, by a 'growing self-importance founded on the didactic history which had formed a context, and then a warrant, for the Henrician Dissolution'.[32] From this point, contemporary patrons and scholars increasingly challenged authority through historical argument and research. The language of description not only set down who owned what, but in documenting who had done what to buildings this language made apparent to the reader how recent the change had been and therefore how it might continue. This perception of recent change as driven by human action has been crucial to a sense of how, come the Civil Wars of the 1640s, revolutionaries who sought the overthrow of established government saw their role as part of a long-term process.

Matters dealing with the origin of places and their nomenclature, the knowledge of a wide range of comparative material and the setting down of the ancestry of leading inhabitants were things that only the well-travelled could offer. In the topographical descriptions of England from this period, certain foreign visitors have always been accorded a prominent place. Without the likes of Thomas Platter, for example, certain ceremonial events and appearances of the sovereign in public or at court would not be recorded; neither would some of the most unusual features of particular prominent buildings.[33] Alessandro Magno, a Venetian merchant in London for a few weeks in 1562, captures the moment immediately after the collapse of the spire of St Paul's when a wooden tower was under construction to protect the surviving stump of the edifice.[34] Yet the writings of foreign visitors were usually constrained by certain conventions of description, given that they usually had a patron to inform and flatter. Their coverage of buildings was often restricted to London and a few major buildings, dominantly the royal palaces in the environs of the city. In considering the growth of a language of description of buildings through first-hand observation, these useful but rather atomised writers, whose work was not usually published at the time, take second place, inevitably, to native writers whose published accounts of their travels are vivid and informative and were widely read by each other.

Among English texts, John Leland's *Itinerary*, albeit fragmentary and gathered together by others, remains a key document for the development of describing and categorising buildings. The sheer breadth of the geographical area that Leland covered and the attempted consistency of approach were unprecedented.[35] A fierce supporter of the regime of Henry VIII, he always regretted the loss and dispersal of monastic libraries, a regret governed by his wish to bring the nation's learning under the wing of a government wanting to promote education. Leland's knowledge of recent history comes across powerfully, learned not just from figures at court who patronised him but also from members of the educated higher gentry whom he encountered in the course of travel. While his notes towards the *Itinerary* are full of mentions of new owners of property, he often emphasises elements of continuity, even in this revolutionary period, through his recounting of the marriage of heiresses of old families to men of new wealth and power. He mentions houses that had recently been reassumed by their traditional owners, as at The Vyne in Hampshire, where William Sandys's father had taken back the old family home after its fifteenth-century tenure by the Brooke family. Leland's journeys of the early 1540s are specific to the immediate aftermath of the dissolution, when many of the buildings that he saw were in a state of transfomation. He is better informed on churches and former monasteries than he is on domestic buildings, more attentive to exteriors than to interiors. He seems able to judge the present state of unfinished work and is therefore a faithful recorder of the speed with which much happened after the dissolution. He notes at Markyate, in Hertfordshire, that Sir Humphrey Bourchier had spent much in converting the former nunnery but had not finished the task and that Fulke Greville was taking stones from Alcester Priory, Warwickshire, for his house of Beauchamp's Hall.[36] His vocabulary of description is actually quite narrow but he is able to make comparative judgements, as when he finds a manor house looking like a castle at Newton St Loe, Somerset, or at Stourton, Wiltshire, where the manor house has two courts and 'the fronte of the ynner courte is magnificent, and high embattelid castelle lyke'.[37] He is confident in separating old and new work at Rotherfield Greys, Oxfordshire (the present-day Greys Court).[38] Buildings, in his eyes, are worthy and lend status to a given place. When he comes to the town of Sleaford in Lincolnshire he states: 'the ornamentes of it is the Bishop of Lincoln's castel, and the late Lorde Hussey's house.'[39] He is aware of regional differences of building materials, so at Morley in Lancashire he sees a building 'saving the fundation of stone squarid that risith within a great moote a vi. Foote above the water, al of tymbre after the commune sort of building of houses of a[ll] the gentilmen for most of Lancastreshire'.[40] Most of all, however, it is his sense of the importance of the overall setting of a building within its urban, edge of urban, or rural landscape that is particularly powerful: 'The castelle of Notingham stondith on a rokky hille as on the west side of the towne: and hire ri[ver]et goith by the rootes of it.' Or at Stowey, Somerset: 'Heere ys a goodly maner place of the Lord Audeley's stonding exceeding pleasantly for goodly pastures, and having by it a parke of redde deere and another of falow, and a faire brooke serving al the offices of the maner place.'[41] He attempts to give the reader a sense of exact distance between places, between the centre of town and noteworthy buildings on its out-skirts, using such phrases as 'within a mile', 'half a myle', 'a mile or more'. It is as if he plots like the map-maker who has worked hard on the ground to produce an image of the physical features of the area, an idea of how long it would take to pass from one locality to another, offering, as one writer has expressed it, a sense of spatial co-ordination. Sometimes he uses a startling encapsulation of the changing use of place to remind the reader of recent, extraordinary upheaval, as in his comment on the converted monastic residence of the King's Secretary of State: 'Mr. Wriothesley hath buildid a right stately house embattled, and having a goodly gate, and a conducte castelid in the middle of the court of it, yn the very same place wher the late monasterie of Praemonstratenses stoode caullyd Tichefelde.'[42] His notes were used unashamedly and thoroughly by William Camden in the preparation of his *Britannia*, but Camden's organisation and single-mindedness takes the topographical tradition to a different stage of development, as explored below.

William Harrison has long been lauded as a faithful recorder of England in the 1570s; it is through the use of one version of his text as the intro-duction to Holinshed's *Chronicles* in 1587 that his *Description of England* has chiefly come to be known. His sections on the lives of the English, their food and diet, apparel and attire, and most especially 'Of the Manner of Building and Furniture of Our Houses' are often cited as indicators of the greater provision of comfort and luxury of the period: in particular he men-tions the proliferation of chimneys, the availability of fine tableware and the increased private space inside houses that even middle classes could now enjoy, previously a privilege only of the wealthiest class.[43] His *Description* is not strictly speaking in the topographical tradition since he covers customs and mores rather than an antiquarian history. Scholarship on Harrison has come to reaffirm his Protestantism and the biblical connotations of his *Chronological Computations from the Beginning of the World* which he began in 1565 and whose revision in 1583 heavily influenced his rewrite of the *Description* for publication in 1587.[44] In one significant instance, however, he extends the descriptive language of building: he uses new standards of comfort as a means of criticising the soft life which, as a Puritan, he suspected had undermined something of the country's strength. As he put it:

> when our houses were builded of willow, then we had oaken men; but now that our houses are come to be made of oak, our men are not only become willow but a great many, through Persian delicacy crept in amongst us, altogether of straw, which is a sore alteration. [. . .] Now we have many chimneys, and yet our tenderlings complain of rheums, catarrhs and poses [colds]. [. . .] For as the smoke in those days was supposed to be a sufficient hardening for the timber of the house, so it was reputed a far better medicine to keep the Goodman and his family from the quack [hoarseness] or pose, where with as then very few were oft acquainted.[45]

Harrison is often cited for his seemingly approving tone on higher standards of living. Behind this, however, is a sense of decline of standards which makes him part of a wider contemporary suspicion of the luxury of comfortable building.

It has long been noted how significant the local topographical tradition was in the formation of writing not just about particular localities but the country of England as a whole. William Lambarde's work on Kent is certainly the key text for the evolution of county history, and certain town histories set standards for individual places, as did Henry Manship for Great Yarmouth.[46] Lambarde's emphasis on perambulation, of seeming to walk the places under description, has been noted as of special significance for the way in which Stow went about his *Survey of London* (1598).[47]

Stow's book can be said to show more emphatically than any other text what Sir Thomas Elyot conveyed in his sense of the value of descriptive geography for the reader: 'I can nat tell what more pleasure shulde happen to a gentil witte than to beholde in his owne house euery thynge that with in all the worlde is contained.'[48] Stow's description of London is remarkably thorough. Taking all other available evidence into account, it is hard to imagine that he missed a single significant building in the City of his time, including all its churches, public buildings, bridges and gates, as well as major houses. On the great houses, many of them rebuilt many times over since the medieval period, he notes the many residents and the many changes they made. For example, he cites the Erber, in Downegate Ward, where Goffrey Scroope made changes in the reign of Edward III, going on to mention that it was 'lately new built by Sir Thomas Pullison, mayor, and was afterward inhabited by Sir Francis Drake, that famous mariner'. He specifies the materials and the methods of construction, particularly where timber has given way to stone. He chronicles changes wrought by the Reformation as some buildings ceased to be monastic and were put to public use but were later privatised, noting thereby the state of flux that the building market of London constantly showed. He points out the many injustices following the upheavals of the 1530s, such as the well-known case of his own father's loss at the hands of Thomas Cromwell: in constructing his house in Throgmorton Street at the west end of the former church of Austin Friars shortly before his fall in 1540, Cromwell robbed land from people's gardens and, in Stow's father's case, a house as well. Stow is censorious about certain modern types of luxury building and juxtaposes these with the beneficence of the citizens of earlier times, as with the fashion for

> fayre summer houses, and as in other places of the Suburbes, some of them like Midsommer Pageantes, with Towers, Turrets, and Chimney tops, not so much for vse or profite as for shew and pleasure, bewraying the vanity of mens mindes, much unlike to the disposition of the ancient Cittizens, who delighted in the building of Hospitals, and Almes houses for the poore.[49]

It is the sense of change within his own lifetime that has often been remarked upon as a particular legacy of Stow's writing; rather than simply chronicle the history of buildings, he appears to have returned, a man now in his seventieth year, to witness the passing of one use and the coming of the new, a process of coming to terms with his own life in the city in a way that has been rightly described as nostalgic.[50] It is but one moment he is recording. The churches he mentions are generally in a state of poor repair and it was not until twenty years after his publication that there were vigorous campaigns of renewal: the sum of £600 was spent on the repairs of St Botolph's, Bishopsgate, in 1617; £900 on St Antholin in 1616; and £1546 on an enlargement of St Anne's, Blackfriars, in 1613.[51] Where he can, and as much as he notes great changes to the use of individual buildings, he is keen to stress in other ways forms of continuity, particularly in the character of areas of the city, or the use of a particular street for a particular activity. He notes, for example, the use of a stone building in West Cheap on the north side of St Mary le Bow as a kind of royal viewing stand from the time of Edward III down to Henry VIII. But the impact of change is dominant: by more or less 'walking the city' Stow shows, as Lawrence Manley has put it, 'that by the measure of human experience London itself had broken from its foundations and was losing its familiar human character'.[52] Stow is the seedbed from which seventeenth-century writers such as the clergyman and historian Peter Heylyn would describe the city, in his *Cosmographie* of 1652, as an unbridled 'monster', growing continuously and out of control. In Ben Jonson's poem 'On the Famous Voyage', the poet takes a journey up the polluted Fleet Ditch from Bridewell to Holborn, along not streets of comely buildings but along the city's channels of excretion and consumption, revealing the greed and sexual degradation of its citizens along the way.[53] It is this portraying of the city in metaphorical terms that proved to enrich the recording of the built environment and ultimately found its greatest expression in contemporary drama, which revelled in disguising the city's true nature.

The quality of imaginative invention that the topographical convention brings to literature must be emphasised. It is tempting to see it as simply the pedantic listing of factual information but it remains a species of description that first had to be formulated and tested by familiar usage. As Andrew McRae has put it: 'topography was neither a figure of speech (as in rhetoric) nor a science, but a mode of invention, with its own generic rules and assumptions'; and the same writer cites a seventeenth-century source to support the idea that contemporary forms of topography were seen by contemporaries as something creative, evocative and imaginative on a par with the imagined landscapes of great literature of the past. Peter Heylyn cited as valid examples: 'Stowes Book of *The Survey of London* [. . .] the description of the Vale of Tempe in the greater Ortelius: and those of the Elysian fields, the gardens of Alcinous, and the Hesperides in the ancient poets.'[54] This topographical tradition, brought to a very full and affectionate climax in Stow's work, opened up considerably the use of the language of description. So thorough is Stow's coverage of the city and so carefully gauged his distinctions between different kinds of novelty, to be welcomed or despised, between different kinds of adaptation by private individuals and corporate bodies alike, that it results in a richer vocabulary of description thereafter. But its effect is largely additive; however much Stow's coverage is delimited by the limits of the city itself, his descriptions expand or deflate according to the depth of his knowledge about individual sites. The overall shape is indefinable and unpredictable in a way that mirrors Leland's notes towards his *Itinerary*, even though it was completed to a degree that Leland's work was not.

By contrast, as a piece of descriptive text, William Camden's *Britannia* of 1586 is organised and truly self-disciplined, closely integrated and edited from a mass of information gathered by local correspondents (his equivalent of modern-day research assistants) and directed at a professional audience of fellow antiquarians.[55] Instead of Leland's exploratory style, Camden brings to each place he describes a view on its history, to which the buildings add detail without any contradiction. Yet Leland and Camden share one crucial ambition for their writing that Stow does not. Leland's text includes the poem 'Cygnea Cantio', in which he imagines himself as a swan moving down river between Oxford and Greenwich, noting great buildings on the way. This is an imaginative leap to thinking of the built landscape as if naively, without any prejudice or preconception; Leland seems to be witnessing the country's wonders through the eyes of a different species. Camden extends this idea with the poem 'de Connubio Tamae et Isis', the thread of which runs throughout the *Britannia*. This presents a repeating poem about the heroes of the British past as a commentary on his historical narrative.[56] Turning to a poetic mode of description becomes a way of truly turning the visual experience of landscape, and the buildings within it, as a means of stressing continuities but also disjunctions in the reader's relationship to the past.

The country-house poem

Poetry and the use of buildings as barometers of the relative health of past and present have brought certain structures into the centre of contemporary debate. A series of poems explored the appearance and meaning of the English country house, demonstrating both a widening vocabulary of description and a metaphorical identity that made these great households a significant focus of the changing language of building.[57] In Elizabethan and Jacobean England, great new houses such as Wollaton and Hardwick contrasted with older ones that had been adapted over time. The fourteenth-century hall at Penshurst Place, Kent, for example, was retained as the core of the building with fifteenth- and sixteenth-century additions. By *c.* 1615, when Ben Jonson wrote the *primus inter pares* of the country-house poem, 'To Penshurst', the house had been owned by the Sidney family for just half a century. Preserving the medieval house was part of establishing a creditable justification for the family's social position. Jonson juxtaposes the house of ancient lineage, sprawling yet settled in its landscape, with the new follies of the age, built to impress rather than to serve its community:

> Thou art not, PENSHURST, built to enuious show,
> Of touch, or marble; nor canst boast a row
> Of polish'd pillars, or a roofe of gold:
> Thou hast no lantherne, whereof tales are told;
> Or stayre, or courts; but stand'st an ancient pile,
> And these grudg'd a, art reuerenc'd the while. (lines 1–6)

Jonson goes on to praise the home of the Sidneys as something locally made without exploiting local people but rather welcoming their participation in the beneficence of the lord's estate:

> And though thy walls be of the countrey stone,
> They are rear'd with no mans ruine, no mans grone,
> There's none, that dwell about them, wish them downe;
> But all come in, the farmer, and the clowne:

And no one empty-handed, to salute
Thy lord, and lady, though they haue no sute. (lines 45–50)

Here Jonson evokes a familiar theme of the period in debating the erosion of the medieval concept of hospitality, still prevalent at a house like Penshurst, at newer houses for the class of newly rich.[58] His choice of language at the close brings the reader near to contemporary discussion of the appropriate language for buildings themselves:

Now, PENSHURST, they that will proportion thee
With other edifices, when they see
Those proud, ambitious heaps, and nothing else,
May say, their lords haue built, but thy lord dwells.
    (lines 99–102)[59]

'Proportion' here is used as a verb of judgement, meaning 'set against' but also suggesting that Jonson was well aware that proportion also now conveyed a visual meaning of something applied to new architecture and that there was discussion about, and approval of, this in some circles but with which he was inclined to disagree. 'Heaps' also, and surely disparagingly, conveys a key sense of the design of some contemporary great houses, those with floors stacked one above the other, as opposed to the informal spread and casual convenience inherent in houses such as Penshurst, which had developed over a long period of time (fig. 63).[60]

The moral attributes of the owner of the great house and the sense that these buildings should ideally house small, ideal societies, remain constant themes in the series of country-house poems of the first half of the seventeenth century. The last poem of this group chronologically, Andrew Marvell's 'Upon Appleton House to my Lord Fairfax', of 1652, has been interpreted by one author as a celebration, in the Republican period, of its owner's virtuous Protestantism, expressed through the very restraint of the style of the house.[61] This style is untainted by external (i.e. continental) influences:

Within this sober Frame expect
Work of no Forrain *Architect*; (lines 1–2)

Other houses, by contrast, indulge in architectural extravagance and unnecessary size that is proud, superficial and ultimately empty of virtue ('hollow Palace [. . .] Where Winds [. . .] themselves may lose', 'Marble Crust'). Little is known about the original Appleton House but, while it appears symmetrical at least, it certainly was not in full classical dress or exhibiting expensive materials.[62] Marvell imbues it with the virtues of an early, pre-Romanised Christian church:

When larger sized Men did stoop
To enter at a narrow loop;

As practising, in doors so strait,
To strain themselves through *Heavens Gate*. (lines 29–32)[63]

63   Penshurst Place, Kent. 14th-century hall and gatehouse, with 15th- and 16th-century buildings to the left.

The plea here is for an architecture of moderation. It has been suggested that this reflects Marvell's own cautious, late time of life. Theorists of architecture also appealed for this moderation but took their formulae and structure of writing from cues in the very foreign literature that is above eschewed and dismissed.

English theory and the early seventeenth century

It has been asserted that the art of translation played a vital role in bringing the most rigorous European discourse to England.[64] It is true that certain important works concerning the visual arts were translated into English in this period, notably Francesco Colonna's *Hypnerotomachia: The Strife of Love in a Dreame*, probably by Robert Dallington in 1592; the translation of Lomazzo as *A Tracte containing the Artes of Curious Paintinge Caruinge*

& Buildinge at the hands of Richard Haydock in 1598; Hans Blum, whose Dutch original was translated as *The Booke of the Five Collumnes of Architecture* in 1601; and the first English edition of Serlio being published as *The First Booke of Architecture* in 1611.[65] But equally those who have examined the contents of the book collections of this period have noted the presence of copies of these works in the original or in other European languages; Alberti and, after 1570, Palladio were particularly strongly represented.[66] It would be easy to say that these were used simply as pattern books, but there is enough evidence among the surviving correspondence to suggest that leading court figures did indeed read them. What begins to happen therefore is a continual dialogue between the foreign terms of these books and the possibility of their translation into English. When English travellers of the first three quarters of the sixteenth century attempted to describe what they saw abroad, their words are often literal and reactive in the face of things they had no experience of in England. In his travel memoirs known as *Coryat's Crudities*, for example, Thomas Coryat describes the mosaics in St Mark's, Venice, as being made with 'little pieces and very small fragments of gilt marble, which are square, and half as broade as the nails of a man's fingers'. Crucially he concludes: 'I never saw any of this kind of picturing before I came to Venice, nor ever read or heard of it.'[67] William Thomas, in his *Historye of Italie*, described the dome of the Pantheon in Rome as 'vaulted like the half of an egg'.[68] By the end of the sixteenth century the vocabulary had widened; as books had been read, terms were now understood. Indeed some writers began to criticise the authorities from Vitruvius to modern times for their inconsistency or, in terms of the application of their rules for architecture in an English setting, their inappropriateness. What intervened was sometimes a question of building materials, but more often it was to do with a nervousness, even a censoriousness, about Catholic Italy and what was sometimes perceived as its misuse of the legacy of its classical past, as when Thomas Coryat, in his *Crudities*, censures native Italians outside the Colleoni Chapel at Bergamo for placing pagan antiquities on a Christian building.[69]

What became apparent too was the sense that the writing of theoretical literature was an exercise in educational attainment. To have appropriated the form of the treatise and be able to have dialogue with the treatises of the past was a way of showing skill and literary merit. This was the genesis of the most significant piece of sustained published writing on architecture in England in the early seventeenth century, Sir Henry Wotton's *Elements of Architecture collected [. . .] from the Best Authors and Examples*, written it seems in about two months at the end of 1623 and published early the following year, on the author's return, in his mid-fifties, from a career as diplomat at The Hague, in various German states and most notably in Venice.[70] Wotton needed a remunerated post, had his eye on the Provostship of Eton College and through his writing sought to reach the attention of George Villiers, Duke of Buckingham, an avid collector. Copies of the book were gifted to all leading courtiers. To enhance his future reputation and make it clear that writing on architecture was but the prelude to further works of discourse, he promised a future work on education. Wotton is clear about what he has read and what he accepts as authoritative writing on architecture, and is thus able to dispute the work of his distinguished predecessors. Notably he quarrels with Vitruvius' advice on entasis, the swelling of the column halfway up its height, because he cannot accept that what this might correct visually is a necessary benefit in the sacrifice of truth. He is generally brief in discussing the Orders and is particularly critical of the Corinthian. This has led one author, in an article of 1998, to suggest that here he is at odds with the use of the Order on Inigo Jones's Banqueting House, a building completed only in 1622; the usual interpretation of the connection between Jones and Wotton, that the latter somehow set down in print the theoretical ideas that Jones never published, has thus been challenged.[71] Wotton's insistence on the three principles of commodity, firmness and delight set down the true direction for the practical nature of English architecture: knowing what a building is for, understanding what it is meant to do and the uncomplicated visual pleasure it gives are primarily all that matters.

This practical outcome of what buildings are as physical entities keeps Wotton's work rooted to its key intention of advice and encouragement to build within the bounds of good sense. Inigo Jones's work is of course not explicit in words through a published discourse but through his meticulous, and ever revised, notes to the essential texts on architecture that he kept all his life; these have been re-examined by Christy Anderson.[72] Jones needed to impress a court audience, or rather, as Anderson stresses, he forms part of that essential Renaissance *topos* of the court artist who needs constantly to 'perform' to keep his job. His books are not the ends, but the means he has to think about future projects, whether they are to be realised or not. Several things emerge from the ways in which Jones separates the various roles of architecture. One is to do with the fundamental order of the classical language of architecture as he understands it, for its very nature of sequence implies chains of command. He categorises different classical modes between male and female. He parallels the styles of building with speech patterns and word usage, implying thereby the relevance of architecture to notions of class. But it is more than this, as Anderson shows. For the first time in the practices of British architects, Jones's notes set up a dialogue about architecture on paper that refers to itself; this is not a critique that is meant to be applied to building practice but to further discussion on paper for its own sake. In Jones's hands, the language of building has finally set its own rules for intellectual discourse.

4

The Role of Patrons

Patrons: building concerns in the early sixteenth century

In early Tudor England, the opportunities for patrons to extend their building activities beyond the private sphere of their own houses were governed
by long-standing conventions of setting up almshouses, hospitals and
schools under the auspices of the church. In the late Middle Ages, there was
a greater propensity than before to endow and build chantry chapels; this
was a means of enriching local churches, cathedrals or monastic establishments while also ensuring prayers would be said after the donor's death.[1]
Good works were therefore quite specifically meant to succour the individual during time in Purgatory. In his will, drawn up on 3 December 1540,
William Sandys, 1st Baron Sandys of The Vyne and Lord Chamberlain to
Henry VIII, left the bulk of his estate to his son Thomas.[2] Pre-eminent in
this estate were two great houses. One was the house of The Vyne, some 4
miles from the town of Basingstoke in Hampshire, a property that William
Sandys's father had reacquired in the late fifteenth century after a long
leasing out; here William had built, in a determined building campaign
between 1524 and 1526, a new and sprawling multi-courtyard house, of
fashionable brick and with fittings and furnishings of extraordinary quality,
purchased through his agents in the Low Countries and facilitated through
his own governmental posts in the pas-de-Calais (fig. 65). At The Vyne was
a chantry chapel, a space that survives with probably more of its original
structure and fittings of the early sixteenth century than any comparable
chapel in a private house in England. Sandys's other house had been
acquired through an exchange with the Crown in 1536, for it was the newly
suppressed Augustinian monastery of Mottisfont, also in Hampshire but
west of Winchester and some 30 miles distant from The Vyne.[3] The latter
was clearly intended to become Sandys's main residence but the work of
transformation there was still under way in 1540 and the house was only

64 St Mary's, Thame,
Oxfordshire. The tomb of
John Williams in the
chancel. Having died in
Ludlow on 14 October, he
was buried here on 15
November 1559.

65 The Vyne, Hampshire. A detail of the east end of the house from the north, showing William Sandys's chapel and private tower of the 1520s.

beginning to be furnished, though already Sandys had installed here his latest and most valuable set of tapestries of the history of King David.[4] 1536 must have been a decisive year for Sandys in terms of financial commitment for as well as taking on the conversion of a monastery, he ordered tombs for himself and his wife Margery (she was to predecease him in 1539) from a Netherlandish tomb-maker. These raised tomb chests, to be made of dark marble from Tournai, were to be placed in the Holy Trinity Chapel at the Church of the Holy Ghost on the northern edge of Basingstoke.[5] The chapel had been built by Sandys in the early 1520s and fitted out with the finest Flemish stained glass, so it was appropriate that he would be commemorated and prayers would be said for him in the devotional setting he had created (fig. 66). The Holy Trinity Chapel was clearly his major ecclesiastical commission, for there is little evidence that he ever did much for the parish church of Sherborne St John immediately proximate to the old family home of The Vyne, save for leaving it 40 shillings in his will. Sandys's building at The Vyne followed his elevation to the peerage in 1523 and the final, splendid, fitting-out of the house probably coincided with his assuming the post of Lord Chamberlain in 1526; royal visits to the house both preceded and followed this event. Taking on Mottisfont ten years later and ordering the tombs were doubtless prompted by his wish to join everyone else at court in benefiting from the dissolution of the smaller monasteries, despite his essentially conservative religious outlook; perhaps the fact that it formed part of an exchange salved any twinges of conscience. Providing for his tomb may have been part of his need to settle the disposal of his mortal remains in a satisfactory and traditional way following three momentous years of parliamentary activity that had dis-established the church from its

66 The ruins of the Holy Trinity Chapel, Basingstoke, built for William Sandys in the early 1520s. The remnants of his tomb in Tournai marble, commissioned in 1536, are placed against the south wall.

anchor of allegiance to Rome. How Sandys squared his spending with his income is in any detail a closed book, but he must have thought carefully about balancing his need to maintain a good household in keeping with his status, providing a significant endowment for a magnificent chapel and securing a fairly expensive but unpretentious funeral monument, all at different times as the political and religious situation shifted around him.

There is, however, another side to Sandys's building activities that does not normally feature in the consideration of such a courtier's patronage. This was the considerable responsibility he had for building works to do with his official posts. Some courtiers were responsible for domestic buildings; many at Henry VIII's court held keeperships of great royal houses and there is some evidence that they lived there semi-permanently, attending to the buildings' upkeep and repair.[6] For Sandys the duties were principally for fortified structures, for example as Treasurer of Calais between 1517 and 1526 he was in charge of supplies, repairs and changes to the fortifications. In 1526, when he became Lord Chamberlain to the royal household, he switched jobs in the pas-de-Calais and took on the post of

Lieutenant of Guines. This was a large moated castle and the site of both defence and royal diplomatic events; nearby in 1520 the Field of Cloth of Gold had taken place, the meeting between Henry VIII and Francis I of France that Sandys had played a significant part in organising. In 1537 Sandys wrote to Cromwell to ask that the Surveyor of Calais be authorised to build him a new kitchen because the old one had been taken down and there was no place to dress meat save under a wall. In the late 1530s he was also responsible for overseeing the drawing up of a long report on the fortification of Newneham Bridge, a critical crossing point in the English territory. Such duties carried therefore the need for continuous in-service training, a familiarity with the latest in military engineering and the increasingly sophisticated way in which ideas were transmitted on paper. A letter from Sandys and other commissioners devising the temporary palace for the events of 1520 mentions a 'platt' (or plan) being passed from them to the king for final approval.[7] The development of the patron as 'expert' became distinctive among later sixteenth-century patrons: William Cecil was to become famous in this respect, especially at a period when care for the nation's defences was once more a primary call on the politician's time.

It was not only leading courtiers who were able to spend on a range of building schemes on the eve of the Reformation. Gentry and merchant classes did so too. From a similar generation to Sandys was the draper George Monoux, Lord Mayor of London in 1514–15; born in or before 1465, he died in 1544. He features in John Stow's long list of sixteenth-century mayors and their generosity to the community of London and beyond the city; in Monoux's case this generosity was at the church of St Mary, Walthamstow, then in the county of Essex. Here he shared the cost of extending the church with the bequest of another Lord Mayor, Robert Thorne, who predeceased him by twelve years. According to Stow, Monoux 'reedified the decayed Parish Church of Waltomstow or Walthamstow, in Essex: hee founded there a free schoole, and almes houses for 13 almes people, made a Cawsey of timber ouer the marshes from Walthamstow to Locke bridge, &c.'[8] Monoux certainly paid for the new upper parts of the north aisle and probably also for the raising of the brick tower, attributed to his generosity as early as John Weever in his *Ancient Funeral Monuments* of 1631.[9] The Monoux chapel survives at the east end, as does the brass from his tomb chest, which originally stood between the chancel and the north chapel. The almshouse and grammar school also survive to the north of the church, though partly reconstructed in the 1950s after war damage. The maintenance of the aisle and tower became the responsibility of trustees after Monoux's death, and this led to problems a century later when the church was found to be in disrepair.[10] The fragile nature of long-term provision for churches, schools and almshouses were to prove a running sore throughout this period, leading to many disagreements between parishes and the heirs of benefactors.

Patrons therefore made decisions about where they lived and built anew, where they chose to endow buildings for public benefit, how much money they spent on buildings relative to other major enterprises in the visual arts such as great funeral monuments or, from some point in the later sixteenth century onwards, more rarefied and specialised activities such as picture collecting. They had to decide at what stage in their careers to do these things. Taking account of such activities in patrons' lives opens up useful windows on the changing circumstances in which the patronage of building took place; questions about the means and the timing of such enterprises arise. A journey through the following century and an examination of a range of patrons, male and female, shows how certain courtiers who, like Sandys, became prominent at Henry VIII's court lived beyond that time to create great houses and newly endowed charities; next there is the issue of great churchmen whose patronage marked a shift from their pre-Reformation predecessors. A new generation arrives with prominent Elizabethan and Jacobean figures at court who sometimes spent extravagantly. And finally there are gentry patrons, whose works proved the true foundation of a lasting local presence and patrimony for their descendants. Just as the pattern of the Tudor and Stuart sovereigns' spending on royal palaces has been closely investigated with respect to where the king or queen lodged and how much time they spent at each property, it is important to be aware of the range of these patrons' houses and how their attention and resources were divided between them. Attached to many of these properties were other buildings for the community that they endowed. How did this balance of interests affect their financial thinking? An argument about lavish spending on personal pleasure through building resounds through the commentaries of this time.[11] Expenditure on private as opposed to public enterprise was clearly a live issue for contemporaries, as is evident from Stow's comment on pleasure buildings in London, quoted above. The wealthy of the post-Reformation world had constantly to think about the setting of private luxury against civic responsibility.

Two Henrician survivors: Richard Rich and John Williams

William Sandys is usually characterised as a courtier of the old school, a man of a generation loyal to the new Tudor dynasty (he was in his mid-teens when Henry VII seized the throne in 1485), probably conservative in religion against the background of the Reformation of the 1530s, yet in the patronage of building somewhat daringly fashionable, at least in the surface ornament of a great house and the luxury goods within. On learning of Sandys's death in December 1540, Charles de Marillac, the French ambassador to the English court, wrote back to France that 'lord Sens, Great Chamberlain, died four days ago, who was much esteemed here and was

67 Hans Holbein, *Richard Rich*, black and coloured chalks on pink prepared paper, *c.* 1540. Royal Library, Windsor. The Royal Collection, Copyright 2006 Her Majesty Queen Elizabeth II.

one of the few ancient captains left'; the remaining members of this group included Sir Richard Weston (died 1542), Henry Lord Marney (died 1523) and Charles Brandon, Duke of Suffolk (died 1545), all builders of great courtyard houses.[12] Some also endowed the local church, particularly if they intended their own burial there, so that the church at Layer Marney, in Essex, is very much all of a piece with the great gatehouse and adjoining ranges built by Henry Marney and his son John as the beginning of a grand courtyard house. They are both buried in tombs covered with terracotta in the church nearby. All these men served in traditional capacities at the royal court. However, two other courtiers, some ten to fifteen years younger than

Brandon (probably the youngest of these four) found their moment of opportunity in the 1530s and then lived beyond Henry VIII's reign into the earliest years of Elizabeth I. Richard Rich, 1st Baron Rich (1496/7–1567), and John Williams, Baron Williams of Thame (c. 1500–1559), both took up administrative roles that were the outcome of a new order of central government organisation brought about by the dissolution. They both benefited from grants and sales of ex-monastic property, notably in London and also in new power bases that they built up within reach of the capital. Not only their endowments but the buildings that grew from these around a clearly identified new country seat and its adjacent town were to dominate these local communities for generations to come.

Rich came to prominence as a lawyer and achieved his first major post as well as a knighthood in 1533 when, under the auspices of his patron Thomas Audley, the new Lord Chancellor, he became Solicitor-General (fig. 67).[13] He was responsible for the drafting of some of the major bills of the Reformation Parliament in the 1530s. The most popular conception of him also belongs to this time for his part in the examination and trial of Thomas More and John Fisher led to condemnation down the years from a contemporary, the above-mentioned Marillac, to its twentieth-century version by Robert Bolt in *A Man for All Seasons*, first written for radio (1954), then adapted for the stage (1960) and twice filmed (1966, 1988). Rich was a man created by the Henrician regime with a natural adherence to traditional religious practices. He remained faithful to Catholicism until his death, even though he proved able to trim his sails towards more radical reform under Edward VI. His pursuit of heretics was led by the needs of government and good order. From 1536 he was Chancellor of the Court of Augmentations, overseeing the process of dissolution and thereby also setting a reputation for ruthlessness and opportunism in the historical appraisal of this period. Under Edward VI he was raised to the peerage and became Lord Chancellor, a post he lost in the struggle between the Protector Somerset and John Dudley, who became Duke of Northumberland in 1551. Thereafter under Mary and Elizabeth he served only as a Privy Councillor, retaining the title but never actually being summoned to Council after 1558. His presence, albeit under instruction, at the burning of Protestants in the previous reign may also have rendered him vulnerable to criticism.

Rich surrendered his seal as Lord Chancellor to John Dudley at his house of St Bartholomew's, Smithfield, on the last day of 1551. This was his major London house and one of his chief spoils from the dissolution, for he lived in the suppressed Augustinian house from 1540 and purchased it for £1064 in 1544.[14] The nave of the church was demolished and the choir retained for parochial services and it seems that Rich lived east of the chapter house range in the prior's lodging, newly built for the last prior, William Bolton, in the years before the Reformation; one fragment of Bolton's work remains, the famous oriel looking into the south side of the church, the climax of his walk from his upper-floor lodgings to witness the service below in the chancel.[15] Rich's assumption of this property marks a sea-change in the accommodation of leading courtiers in London from similar, undistinguished origins who had often sought temporary lodgings when business called them to London. Former monasteries provided the first wave of substantial houses, followed by newly built houses, especially along the Strand, forming the second wave, precipitated by the Duke of Somerset's own Somerset House, begun under his Protectorate of 1547–51.[16] Though part of the eastern range of the monastic cloister remains at St Bartholomew's, nothing now survives of the buildings to the east where the prior's lodging and thus Rich's house was. A survey of 1616 and excavation of 1912 have helped to reconstruct the building. He was forced to surrender the house in 1555 when Queen Mary set up a new Dominican house here, but he recovered the property under Queen Elizabeth; it was there that his wife, Elizabeth (née Gynkes or Jenks), was later to die.

However, the burial of Elizabeth, Lady Rich, was not in London but at the heart of one of Rich's great estates in Essex, a county in which it has been estimated that he spent more than £5500 on property.[17] She was buried in the church of Rochford, where Rich had a grand new house, on a site acquired from Henry Cary, son of Mary Boleyn, whose father Thomas had owned it at his death in 1538. Rich almost certainly commanded the building of the new brick west tower of the church and, during the 1540s, the great house itself, large if much-altered ranges of which survive.[18] He died at Rochford in June 1567, a month after drawing up his will. This document is crucial in seeing where and how he really wished to be remembered for in a codicil drawn up just two days before his death he makes extra provision for local almshouses and their very site: 'also as much ground within the clap gate leading to Rochford town as shall serve for the site, garden and orchard where the almshouse shall be builded as is now staked out.' This almshouse was still unbuilt in 1581 at the time of the death of his son Robert, 2nd Lord Rich.[19]

Elsewhere in Essex, however, Rich was successful in founding and building charitable endowments on another major estate. In 1536 he acquired the former Augustinian house of Leighs (or Leez) Priory, some 10 miles north of Chelmsford (fig. 68).[20] He is likely to have pre-planned his ownership here before the grant was awarded since he purchased some monastic furniture and utensils at the dispersal of the house's goods earlier that year.[21] In the following two years he built up his estates in the area with lands granted by Syon Abbey, the Bridgettine house doubtless hoping for his support in the uncertain time between the dissolutions of the lesser and greater houses.[22] The great house he constructed at Leighs, based on the monastic remains, is one of the most extraordinary of such conversions: he appears to have retained the nave of the church as his hall and essentially preserved the outer court, yet he partly encased much of the entire stone

68   Leighs (or Leez) Priory, Essex. The inner gatehouse, rebuilt in brick by Richard Rich after the dissolution.

structure in brick. The surviving inner gatehouse is one of eastern England's most spectacular early Tudor examples. The plan of Rich's house was also unusual in that anyone penetrating the outer gatehouse turned 90 degrees to access the great hall, quite opposing the usual practice of having the hall facing the entrance. The house's original full extent is shown in Nathaniel and Samuel Buck's print of 1738, some fifteen years before extensive demolition took place.[23] It is often suggested that the plan with its 90-degree turn deliberately echoes that of the great royal house of New Hall at Boreham, near Chelmsford, and though this was a royal property at some distance, Henry VIII did visit the house in 1539.[24] This house was Rich's 'capital mansion house' left to his son Sir Robert in his will and it marks the particular significance of this site to Rich's sense of self-esteem.

Near to Leighs is the small town of Felsted and it is clear that Rich always intended burial here after securing the most significant properties in the

69 This effigy of Richard Rich is on the tomb of his descendant, the 1st Earl of Warwick. Attributed to Epiphanius Evesham, Felsted church, Essex, *c.* 1620–21. Here, as opposed to Holbein's portrait of him, Rich is shown as an Elizabethan potentate, his political success and charitable foundations having established the family's local reputation.

area, though it took the initiative of his grandson's will to get his monument erected about 1620–21. This has been attributed to Epiphanius Evesham and shows scenes from Rich's life, his actions supported by the virtues of fortitude, hope and charity, very much to underline the fact that family honour and prosperity derived from his high office under the Tudors (fig. 69).[25] Church and charity are yoked together here: Rich was responsible for the founding of a school at the edge of the churchyard, adjacent to the parish church, using older buildings (fig. 70). During the Marian reaction he had founded a new chantry at Felsted to replace the dissolved Trinity Guild, with a chaplain and a Lenten dole of herrings for the parishioners of this and two adjoining parishes. A modest house at Felsted, called Ingram's, was to serve as the chaplain's residence.[26] With the re-suppression of these new foundations after the accession of Elizabeth, Rich turned the endowment to educational purposes by founding the school in 1564, with the chaplain as the first schoolmaster. The aim was to take in eighty scholars, preference being given to boys from Rich's Essex lands; it became one of the leading schools of the eastern counties during the following century, taking in over a hundred pupils.[27] There has been some debate as to whether the surviving simple, timber-framed school building may predate the sixteenth century; it was certainly re-tiled at the time of foundation and again in the last year of Rich's life. Schoolroom and usher's chamber filled the upper floor; beneath these were a dwelling and shops. In 1564 Rich also

provided for an almshouse at Felsted for six people, endowed with rectory lands at Braintree and certain other tithes.[28] Rich's 'commemoration' at Felsted, a short distance from the house that most significantly expressed his stake in the post-Reformation regime, was therefore multi-faceted; a planned tomb, a school, an almshouse, all together in one sense replacing the chantry that could no longer be endowed.

Rich was originally from Hampshire but became principally associated with Essex. Similarly, John Williams was to install himself in a town and a part of the country with which he had no previous family ties (fig. 64). He had minor offices at court in the 1520s but the crucial link to his eventual power base in Oxfordshire took place in 1535 when, at the age of thirty-five or so, he became the receiver of Thame Abbey, whose abbot Robert King was brother-in-law to Williams's sister, Anne. In the same year he was appointed Master of the King's Jewels jointly with Thomas Cromwell, keeping the post for himself at Cromwell's fall in 1540.[29] Like Rich, he enjoyed former monastic property as his London house, the priory of Elsing Spittle, Cripplegate, for which he paid £530 and which also served as his office to the royal post. Stow gives a vivid description of a disastrous event there:

> In the yeare 1541. Sir Iohn Williams maister of the kinges Iewels, dwelling in this house on Christmas euen at night, about seuen of the clocke, a great fire began in the gallery thereof, which burned so sore, that the

flame fiering the whole house, and consuming it, was seene all the Cittie ouer, and was hardly quenched, whereby manie of the kings Iewels were burned, and more imbeseled (as was said).[30]

In 1544 he became Treasurer of the Court of Augmentations at a salary of £320 per year, a post he retained until the court ceased to function ten years later.

By this date Williams was well established in Thame and its vicinity. At the beginning of Edward VI's reign he was to buy the abbeys of Thame and Notley, but he already had a major house. He is likely to have been responsible for the great house of Rycote, the stable building of which now survives only as a fragment.[31] Williams is usually credited with taking over ownership here only in 1542, but he was evidently in residence some years before that: a letter of 1535 written from Rycote by Gregory Cromwell to his father Thomas mentions the hospitality he had received from Williams.[32] The great courtyard house, known in its fullest extent from the view by Henry Winstanley of 1688 and that of Jan Kip of 1707, was of the familiar, early Tudor, multi-courtyard type in broad shape, with corner turrets and battlements, though Winstanley and Kip differ in their depiction of the window openings, one arched, the other with straight heads to the lights. The great row of windows of the hall range would indeed be unusual for a house of the 1530s, suggesting that window openings were updated after Williams's lifetime.[33]

The late years of Edward VI's reign were troubled ones for Williams. Accounts from his years at the Jewel House took many years to audit and there was a similarly lengthy scrutiny of those he had drawn up for the Court of Augmentations in the reign of Mary. According to Edward VI's journal Williams had disobeyed an order not to pay pensions without the Privy Council's knowledge and this led to his imprisonment in the Fleet for six weeks in April–May 1552.[34] But the period of troubles had begun earlier when in 1549 his unpopularity as a landlord led the Oxford rebels as part of their uprising to invade his park and kill all the deer. This may have led Williams to ensure that local memory of him after his death was to be something different (fig. 71). His benefactions to almshouses and to the foundation of a grammar school in Thame form one of the most telling groups of endowed buildings of this period. They were certainly envisaged as belonging together, for in the School Statutes the final securing of the future of the almshouses was made by Williams's executors as 'a kind of necessary appendix to crown and complete the whole undertaking'.[35] The timber-framed almshouses at a right angle to the High Street were built, it would seem, in the 1550s, and originally provided six dwellings of two rooms each. The grammar school, of rubble with dressed stone copings, was constructed only after his death in 1569, but his coat of arms was placed over the main entrance to remind everyone whose wealth had paid for it; he willed four rectories and parsonages to his executors 'to fynde and sustaine with the proffitts thereof a Schoolmaster and an Usher for ev'r in such sorte and tyme as my said executors shall think most conveniente for the maintenance of the said Schoole for ev'r'.[36] The school officers, master and usher, lived in the range facing on to Church Row with the boys in the attics. Behind, at right angles, is the schoolroom (fig. 72).

Williams's last years were politically successful. Queen Mary raised him to the peerage in 1554 at the end of his post at the Court of Augmentations and perhaps too in reward for his raising 6000 troops on her behalf in Oxfordshire at her troubled accession the year before. He was known to be basically sympathetic to Protestantism and he enjoyed the favour of Elizabeth. He died in October 1559 at Ludlow, Shropshire, barely a year into his new job as President of the Marches of Wales. But it was back to Oxfordshire that his body was taken two weeks after his death. An elaborate ritual between house, town and church followed. The body lay in state in the Great Chamber at Rycote for seventeen days under a great pall of 24 yards of black velvet with a cross of white satin upon it, lined with black buckram garnished with the escutcheons of Williams and his two wives. On 14 November it was taken to William Dormer's house at Thame, where it lay in the hall there overnight before burial in the church the next day. After the ceremony twelve of his yeoman who waited on the body as well as other mourners and attendants went back to Rycote for dinner. A dole of 2 pence was given to all the poor who were present. The heralds set up his hatchment on the walls of the chancel and they were rewarded with 40 marks, the furniture of the hearse as well as their black gowns and coats. The hatchment stood until after Christmas. Afterwards the great tomb chest of Chellaston marble was made in the chancel to commemorate him permanently. His executors were instructed to sell his manor, lands and tenements of Leistrop for the funeral, his tomb and the payment of debts. The warden and scholars of the school, by the indenture of the school's foundation drawn up in 1574–5, were to pay a yearly stipend to the parish clerk of Thame for dressing the tomb and keeping it clean.[37]

Rich and Williams are therefore exemplars of the courtier class of new professionals made by the Reformation and wanting to perpetuate the memory of themselves by conventional means, yet without the possibility of the chantry foundations that were open to their predecessors. Nevertheless they endeavoured, in their rural power bases, to set up a series of buildings that in their association with each other gave the semblance of continuity and beneficence to their communities. Their investment in buildings raises issues that were to continue in the century that followed: London establishments that firstly served attendance at court were increasingly to be used as houses in which to entertain and, in some cases, to showcase collections; outside London, there was a concern that the patron become identified with a significant place, an important consideration since so many of the mid-century generation found themselves newly powerful and seeking new landed estates in the wake of the dissolution. Furthermore, the courtier professionals were increasingly aware that their personal religious affiliations had a bearing on the kinds of building they endowed; they shared an interest in education; and, prone as their descendants might be to unbridled household spending or disinterest in the good intentions of their predecessors, the uncertainties of both houses and benefactions in the long term were to continue.

Churchmen after the Reformation: the case of Whitgift

As far as the redistribution of church property was concerned, courtiers such as Rich and Williams did not benefit only from the dissolution of the monasteries; the depletion of the lands and houses of the bishops in the period after the Reformation was yet another arm of the government's control of Church resources.[38] It has been estimated that slightly more than a third of episcopal residences, some 67 out of 177, had been alienated by grant or permanent lease between the later years of Henry VIII and the end of Elizabeth's reign.[39] The major and most celebrated losses were in London, where many of the palaces or 'inns' of the bishops became the site of the new urban residences of the courtier class. But many were lost outside London as well; the Crown was especially voracious of the residences of the Archbishop of Canterbury because some of these, for example Otford and Knole, commanded the route between Dover and London and Henry VIII envisaged many journeys to Dover in pursuit of his wars against France in what proved to be his last years.[40] Richard Rich gained former bishops' houses at Braintree and Chelmsford, within easy reach of Leighs.[41] The situation was somewhat stabilised during Elizabeth's reign when the bishops took to long spells of residence in their dioceses to undertake the serious responsibility of establishing the Elizabethan settlement. The provision for their financial support and appropriate housing was made through an Act of Parliament: the Crown was enabled to take episcopal manors during a vacancy, but houses commonly used as dwellings by the bishops and demesne lands held with these for the maintenance of hospitality were exempted. After a period of disruption therefore from the 1530s until about 1560, some of the bishops settled in to repair and extend their houses, though it could never be on the lavish scale that their late medieval predecessors had enjoyed. Many of them complained that resources were too tight for such building enterprise, though their grievances centred on what was left of their manor house provision rather than the palace in the cathedral city. Bishop Barnes, for example, complained about the house at Stockton when he took over Durham in 1577; and at the state of Somersham there was a long vacancy following the death of Bishop Cox of Ely in 1601. Archbishop Sandys of York managed a new personal house for himself at

73　St Michael and All Angels, Croydon, South London. The tomb of Archbishop Whitgift, who died in 1604.

Woodham Ferrers, Essex, in the 1570s, but such completely new building was rare.[42] Bishops of the reformed faith, or most of them, had families to support and in a sense their reconstituted palaces and houses took on the nature and workings of secular houses in a more direct sense. Similarly, as several formal rituals of Catholicism had been abandoned, certain religious observances and the need for consecrated spaces of the great late medieval episcopal palaces had also disappeared.

Spending money on buildings to support the future of the see was one way of dispensing reduced income. Another was through charity. It is generally argued that in their individual areas of responsibility bishops were unable to do very much, and only a small number of bequests and foundations stand out. The bishops in fact came in for frequent criticism for being over-generous to their families in their wills. There was also a sense that over-generosity from such a public position was somehow inappropriate. And in this respect, as in many others, there remained the shadow cast by the extravagance of Thomas Wolsey: his foundation of a school at Ipswich did not survive his fall in 1529; and his great collegiate foundation, Cardinal College, Oxford, though it was re-founded by Henry VIII in

1532, dwindled initially to being an ecclesiastical college of secular canons and not the great centre of university education for those from humble backgrounds like Wolsey's.[43] In Elizabethan times, one generous bequest to the poor was the £600 left by John Scory, Bishop of Hereford, but he had only one daughter and an estranged son to consider.[44] Another was the foundation of a large school and almshouse at Croydon by John Whitgift, Archbishop of Canterbury from 1583 to 1604, who famously remained unmarried, earning the admiration of Queen Elizabeth, fiercely opposed to the marriage of bishops, who called him her 'little black husband' (figs 73 and 74).[45]

Whitgift's foundation was based on some years of harbouring his resources. Just after he was raised to the archbishopric of Canterbury from the see of Worcester, leases fell due which enabled him to raise £1000 per annum in 1584–5 beyond his normal rental income on his estates. Though unmarried, he kept a substantial household which served the queen both on her many visits to him and in times of heightened security; it was captains from Whitgift's household leading a force of forty horsemen and forty footmen, who secured the arrest of Robert Devereux, 2nd Earl of Essex, in the abortive rebellion of 1601. From his earliest years as archbishop he supported young scholars and entertained them, to the extent that his first biographer George Paule described his house as a 'little academy'.[46] Whitgift kept the archbishop's palace at Croydon in good repair, as is evident in the surviving spaces of hall, guardroom and chapel from the work of his fourteenth- and fifteenth-century predecessors William Courtney, Thomas Arundel, John Stafford and William Bourchier.[47] He kept the palace at Canterbury and the manor house of Bekesbourne in order and tried unsuccessfully to wrest back from the Crown the palace at Otford, pleading that he had 'never a house in Kent fit for him' by pressing for its keepership.[48] In 1584 he initiated a bill in Parliament for the recovery of Eastbridge Hospital at Canterbury, a foundation of the archbishops in the twelfth century which had fallen into a ruinous state and retained no master or brethren.[49]

It was in November 1595 that Whitgift secured the licence to found an almshouse dedicated to the Holy Trinity at Croydon. In the foundation deed dated 25 June 1599 he states that 'being seised of an estate of fee simple of and in one building of brick, or brick house, newly and lately by him built and erected in Croydon' and other property he established the site

> to be an hospitall or abiding place for the finding, sustentation and reliefe of certain maimed, poore, needie or impotent people to have continuance for ever [. . .] to consist of one Wardeine which shall be the head of the said Hospitall, and of maymed poore or impotent persons not exceeding in all the number of forty, which shall be the bodye and members of the said Hospitall.

In the statutes another purpose is revealed, the foundation of a school:

> First I do ordeine that the number of the bretheren and sisters of the saide Hospitall shalbe ever thirtie at the least and so many more, under xl. in all, as the revenues may beare; Of the whiche number of bretheren one shall teach a common school in Croydon in the schoole house there by me builded.[50]

In a document of September 1602 the cost of hospital and school thus far is recorded as £2716 11s.

The quadrangle of the hospital is very simple in plan and has been compared with conservative collegiate building in brick at the universities at this period. The west (entrance), north and south sides contain the originally four-room houses, with single-room dwellings for the inhabitants much as a contemporary Oxbridge college would have had rooms for scholars. The east range contained the chapel at the south end and the usual, domestic arrangement, familiar from both colleges and courtyard houses, of hall with kitchen at the low end in the northern half of this range. Also in this range in 'that chamber over the hall, and the two chambers over the inner gatehouse' were provided by the statutes to be 'reserved to myself and my own use during my life' and here Whitgift spent much time in his last years until his death in 1604, probably the sole example of a benefactor of such high status living amidst his charitable foundation. In Sir George Paule's *Life of John Whitgift* of 1612 the author records how

> the Archbishop had ever a great affection to lie at his Mansion house at Croydon, or the sweetness of the place, especially in Summer time. [. . .] yet, after he had builded his Hospital, and his School, he was further in love with the Place than before. The chief comfort of repose or solace that he took, was in often dining at the Hospital among his poor Brethren, as he called them. There he as often visited by his entire and honourable friends, the Earls of Shrewsbury, Worcester, and Cumberland, the Lord Zouch, the Bishop of London, and others of near place about her Majesty, in whose company he chiefly delighted.[51]

For bishops who had held more than one see, it was felt inappropriate to be buried at one cathedral rather than another. So Whitgift was duly interred in the church of St John the Baptist at Croydon, next to the Old Palace. His tomb, restored after a fire that destroyed the old church in 1867, was commented on by Henry Holland in 1620: 'a monument has been erected to (Archbishop Whitgift's) memory by his heirs, beautiful but nevertheless fitting in its moderation to the virtues of such a man, for to such a man a splendid monument is not unbecoming.'[52]

Patrons: debts and income

Apportioning revenues to building alongside the courtiers' other outgoings became a necessary skill to develop as the century progressed. In general terms, historians have judged some Elizabethan and Jacobean courtiers harshly in this regard; certainly the ambition of some of their enterprises proved a step beyond their early Tudor predecessors. During the first half of the century any possible matching of income to expenditure on houses usually worked in favour of the courtier ending up in credit. Revenue from lands probably averaged between £2000 and £3000 per annum for courtiers of the 1540s, for example Charles Brandon, Duke of Suffolk and brother-in-law to the king on the one hand and Ralph Sadleir and William Petre, both Secretaries of State and not yet ennobled on the other.[53] Only a few all-inclusive sums for the building of a great house are available for this period, but those available often come in at under £2000. By some way the most expensive for which there are records is Hengrave, Suffolk, on which the wealthy merchant Sir Thomas Kytson spent some £3500 between 1525 and 1538.[54] In addition these were the type of men who bought former monastic properties at low prices, acquiring a house to live in which could tolerate only minimal conversion costs for between about £800 and £1500, a price that was to rise significantly as the source dried up in the reign of Edward VI. Compared with these sums, those from later in the century reach phenomenal proportions compared with income. Such restructuring commanded the best expertise; building often took place slowly, in expensive stone rather than brick; some of the owners demanded entirely new sites and thus put up foundation costs which their predecessors did not pay, the vast majority of them modifying and extending older country houses. The cost of building in London and then maintaining that level of investment through an annual presence in the city with a substantial household clearly was a significant drain on resources, and the crisis years for many were during the reign of James I.[55]

Historians have tended to consider the financial fortunes of great Elizabethan and Jacobean families over several generations, emphasising the fact that there was the genuine establishing of a dynasty going on by this time, yet always prone to the aberrant family member who put everything at risk. In his book *Family and Fortune*, Lawrence Stone analyses a wide range of sixteenth- and seventeenth-century aristocratic experience. The line of Manners, Earls of Rutland, did not build extravagantly and kept finances afloat through successive marriages to wealthy heiresses but suffered a depletion of manorial income over the century after 1560 due to the lack of male heirs and thus a dispersal of lands through female marriage. The Wriothesleys, Earls of Southampton, rose to prominence through Thomas Wriothesley's garnering of monastic estates in the 1530s and 1540s, but the family then declined in fortune in the later years of Elizabeth's reign and throughout James I's; subsequent recovery was brought about through the development of the family's London properties as speculative building development (fig. 75). But it is always the single example of Robert Cecil that commands the financially disastrous end of the spectrum; the period 1608–12, during the building of Hatfield House, has been more scrutinised than any other. The balance between income and expenditure in the case of this courtier has changed dramatically. Robert Cecil's income from land was perhaps £6000 per annum, so predictably double that of someone in a comparable position seventy years earlier.[56] If the total cost of Hatfield was indeed £40,000 during these four years, the country house *de novo* has moved from being about the equivalent of a year's regular income in the 1530s and 1540s to more than six times that sum seventy years later. Cecil was able to do this, build at Salisbury House in the Strand, Cranborne in Dorset and endow London's New Exchange through raising huge loans, taking both legal and illicit revenues from his three major offices of state and land sales. In this pattern of spending, giving to charity and building for charitable purposes necessarily took a back seat and yielded only short-term benefit. He gave £60 per annum in regular alms to the poor, though he showed a willingness to spend when things were particularly bad; after

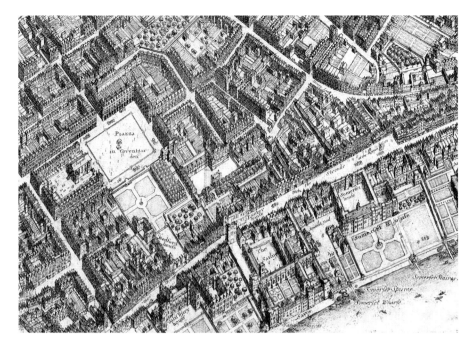

75 Wenceslaus Hollar, *View of Westminster*, engraving, 1658. This detail shows the development of the Wriothesley estates in Holborn at the left, with mansions on the north and south sides of the Strand including William Cecil's house ('Exeter House'). Copyright The Trustees of the British Museum.

the harvest of 1608, for example, he heavily subsidised the provision of wheat and rye to those near his houses at Westminster and at Hatfield. He settled £40 a year on the almshouse at Cheshunt, Hertfordshire, in 1605 and in the same year contracted to set up and maintain a house for teaching forty poor boys in pin-making. A factory was set up at Hatfield in 1609 for new draperies. But as with many schemes initiated at this period, long-term prospects were not good beyond the patron's death and the latter project fell through in the early 1620s.[57]

William Cecil: 'no new feathered gentleman'

The timing of benefaction and secure provision for its future were clearly important as was the choice of place. Three prominent Elizabethan and Jacobean courtiers, all raised to the peerage, William Cecil, Robert Dudley and Henry Howard, between them show a range of problems and solutions to benefactions which then took their place in the context of their wider building activity. These were the political heirs of Richard Rich and John Williams, discussed above, and were acknowledged as such by these men; Williams left two nags to Cecil in his will and to Dudley he left a black mare and a colt 'which mare I take to be the best in England'.[58] William Cecil, Lord Burghley, father of the high-spending Robert, was one of the great builders of the age and his career both as courtier and as architectural patron spans the early and late Tudor periods like no other (fig. 76). He was a key member of the Protestant circle around the Protector Somerset, their power and influence growing in Henry VIII's reign in opposition to the dominant conservative faction of those years. The reign of Edward VI formed their moment in power, their brief ascendancy. Cecil's London base begins in the 1540s with the familiar early Tudor pattern of a modest house barely above the level of rented lodgings, in Cannon Row, Westminster, where his father died in 1553.[59] Later he acquired the London house on the north side of the Strand of Sir Thomas Palmer, a fellow courtier who was executed in the wake of the abortive attempt to install Lady Jane Grey on the throne in 1553. Palmer's brick and timber house gave way to the grand courtyard house of Cecil's later years. The plan of this house was discovered in 1999 and is likely to date from the mid-1560s, though the fact that the 1580s has also been discussed as a possible date demonstrates the difficulties of dating the completion of this building.[60] Cecil also fulfils the pattern of the acquisition of a commuter house that enabled him to keep a young family in proximity to Westminster. From

76 Anglo-Netherlandish School, *William Cecil*, oil on panel, *c.* 1571. The Collection at Parham House, West Sussex.

1549 until 1564 he used the old parsonage house at Wimbledon, the main character of which of this period is recorded in the 1649 Parliamentary Survey.[61] The pressures on the courtier increasingly as the century wore on to entertain at least his peer group if not actually the sovereign led Cecil to building the most significant house of the Elizabethan period, his great house at Theobalds in Hertfordshire, some 10 miles north of the city of London, a house visited often by Elizabeth and so insistently by James I that in 1607 it was exchanged for the royal palace of Hatfield, soon thereafter the site of Robert Cecil's expensive rebuilding discussed above. The replacement of a modest moated house, the venue for Elizabeth's first visit in 1564, happened in the year after Cecil's purchase. Within the following year Cecil began the great enlargement and the original courtyard, the north and south wings to the middle court and his new hall and loggia were in place by 1571. The next fifteen years, however, were spent in considerable aggrandisement. Probably no other great non-royal house stood so close to the centre of London at this period.[62]

Cecil's most substantial attention to place and benefaction was focused on the next outer ring of his national interests, the building of his great country house on the outskirts of Stamford, always known since as Burghley House, after the title of nobility he acquired in 1571. Work here was allied to his involvement in the town itself (fig. 77). At Burghley Cecil was building not on lands and properties acquired directly through his position as courtier, but on his old family inheritance. Construction at his new Elizabethan mansion began as early as 1553 and continued, after considerable breaks, at least as late as 1580. The building history of the house been expertly investigated. It is generally agreed that the core of the most stylistically advanced part of the house, containing the originally arcaded inner court and the grand stair in the French style of *rampe-sur-rampe* dates from the 1560s, showing how concerned Cecil was with the construction of a modern house. Then there were considerable changes in the 1570s, with the relocation of the chapel and the final redesign of the Great Hall, leading to the completion of the west front and the completion of the long gallery in the entrance range by 1578. Commentators have noted how the external appearance of the west front shows the house at its most conservative, since this range harks back to the entrance ranges of early Tudor houses, with a turreted gatehouse at the centre. It is as if Cecil were deliberately evoking something in the style of fifty years earlier and in a sense thereby linking himself to the broader achievement and stability of the Tudor dynasty itself. The symbolic aspect of Burghley is undeniable since when Cecil described it as his principal house in 1586 he had not lived there for any length of time for twenty years, and an aborted visit by Elizabeth proved the only time she came near to staying at the house.[63]

Cecil's key role in architectural innovation at this period has been much discussed, not only in the sense of his active patronage of the process of building but also in his knowledge of the making of buildings through enquiry into and support for maps and plans, both in his governmental and private concerns.[64] His grasp of the need for economic enterprise to support the country reached as far as his home town.[65] In the 1560s he supported a scheme for the setting up of a canvas-weaving industry at Stamford; this met with only modest success but in the same decade he was active in helping Dutch immigrants to settle in the town, gave a house for the lodging of ten families and by 1572 was involved in correspondence to endow a German church.[66] This was in keeping with Cecil's support of alien communities in England. His final act of benefaction to the town was modest but clearly one he had intended for a long time. As early as 1549 he had acquired the hospital of St John the Baptist and St Thomas the Martyr in High Street, St Martin's, founded originally in the twelfth century to help travellers and the local poor (fig. 78). While the chapel of the foundation had continued in use, the hospital had ceased to function some time before Cecil's acquisition. The earliest certain date that records its use as an almshouse is 1595. It was fully endowed by Cecil in 1597 as an almshouse for thirteen old men, and the surviving L-shaped block next to the river dates from the following years. Modest in scope, the foundation proved an unusual survivor as a private endowment: around 1616 the east–west range was extended to more than triple its length; and it re-used medieval material, as the building of the 1590s had done.[67]

The Ordinances for the hospital are some of the most illuminating that survive concerning the patron's wishes about the people to be supported.

There are the predictable controls on the morals, the medical history (no lepers or sufferers of the French pox) and behaviour of the inmates (no lunatics). They give a sense of how such places were lived in: unmarried men should lodge every night in the house; married men could live beyond it within St Martin's parish or in the borough of Stamford but had to lodge one night a month under its roof. They also hint at the kinds of men Cecil wished to reward in their old age, probably those who had worked for him:

> the sayd poore men shall be (as near as may be) chosen out of such as have bene either honest souldiers or workemen, as Masons, Carpenters, or other Artisans of handy crafts, or Labourers in any work or in Husbandry, or servants that are by sickness, age or other impediment, unable to get their living by their handy worke or by daily service.

The Ordinances require that the men go in their livery gowns to St Martin's church to common prayer three days a week and all holy days 'and shall sit or kneele in some place appointed by the churchwardens'. In view of Cecil's burial in the church there would have been a sense that they were continuing to pray for their founder, albeit in a way that was differently handled, yet offering thanks to the benefactor in the pre-Reformation world. The memory of Cecil was kept alive too by the presence of his successors:

if at any time he that shalbe mine heire of my house at Theobalds in Hartfordshire, shal come to Burghley, or Stanford, the said poore men shall present themselves dutifully unto him, and shall offer any service they can do to him, in memories of the founder William Lord Burghley, Ancestor of the said owner of Theobalds.

The hospital was also directly linked to the local great house itself:

> they shall every first Sunday in every quarter goe to Burghley house (if the Lord of Burghley, or the Ladye his wife shall there keepe houshold) and there shall dine at one table together in the hall, where they shall have two meale of meate, every meal of two dishes, one with pottage and boiled meate, the other roste (if it bee a fasting day) and if it be a fish day, then they shall have two like meales of white meat and fish.[68]

This sense of preserving his memory in his home town, linking the great house with a charitable foundation and the site of his burial brings buildings together in a celebration of William Cecil's achievement and legacy.

Robert Dudley in London and the West Midlands

Unlike William Cecil's inheritance of lands at Stamford, other courtiers had no such obvious place to which they could attach themselves. The other two courtiers under scrutiny here both suffered initially from their fathers' attainder. Robert Dudley was the fifth son of a disgraced and fallen mighty courtier, John Dudley, Duke of Northumberland. All his father's great building projects were forfeit to the Crown in 1553; his earlier assumption of the Duke of Somerset's house at Syon on the Thames near London, his London house at Ely Place and the vast new range of buildings at Dudley Castle in the west midlands, intended as the centrepiece of his great landed estate. Before the catastrophe of 1553 the young Robert Dudley was intended by his father to 'keep a good house in Norfolk' by the endowment on him of manors there, based on Robert's marriage in 1550 to Amy Robsart, who came from a Norfolk family. He got the taste for his own London establishment when he lived for the last few months of Edward VI's reign at Somerset Place, the unfinished great house of the Duke of Somerset. He was appointed the house's keeper, providing a link between royal patrons since he remained in office after Princess Elizabeth exchanged Durham Place for Somerset House shortly before Edward VI's death. After attainder, escape from execution and a spell in the Tower during the reign of Mary, Dudley was nominated Master of the Horse at Elizabeth's accession in 1558 and granted Kew House, which he used for several years; it was thence he retreated at the shock of his wife's sudden death in 1560, an event whose suspicious circumstances were to haunt his career and some people's opinion of him. His remarriage in 1578 to Lettice Knollys Devereux, the dowager countess of Essex, made him the stepfather of his godson, Robert Devereux, Earl of Essex, who was seen by many as his possible heir. Dudley's lack of a legitimate heir (a son of the second marriage died at three years old in 1584) certainly influenced the pattern of his buildings and bequests.[69]

It was the years 1563–4 that proved the foundation not only of Dudley's prime position among the queen's favourite courtiers but also his landed estate. He gained the Lordships of Kenilworth, Denbigh and Chirk in 1563 and the Earldom of Leicester the following year. These honours and grants, along with the elevation of his brother Ambrose to the Earldom of Warwick, marked something of a return to his father's power base of the west midlands with a landed interest now also reaching into north Wales. Dudley has often been described as 'not a compulsive builder'; he certainly was not responsible for entirely new, grand domestic structures on a par with those of Cecil or Sir Christopher Hatton.[70] This, however, underlines the understandable bias towards reading new, large country houses as the sole barometer of building enterprise. Dudley's pattern of buildings reveals wider political and religious considerations. In London he moved into Durham Place after the sale of Kew and in 1570 he bought Paget Place near Temple Bar. This became the house known as Leicester House, which when it was inventoried at his death in 1588 showed the extent of his family responsibilities. As one of the few great palaces of Elizabethan London, it may have paralleled the divided use between brothers of the same family and of similar rank, common to the palaces of Italian Renaissance cities. Rooms were appointed for his brother the Earl of Warwick and his stepson the Earl of Essex, though the comfortable furnishings were modest and old. His great house in the immediate environs of London was at Wanstead, where he undertook building from 1577. Queen Elizabeth is known to have visited Leicester House seven times and Wanstead eight.[71]

Dudley first went to Kenilworth in 1566, at the time of Elizabeth's initial visit there (fig. 79). The work he began at the castle, refurbishing the medieval buildings and constructing a new gatehouse and range of lodgings, formed the setting for a series of visits by the queen, culminating in the last and most famous of them in 1575. Entertaining Elizabeth has been the focus of much scholarship and debate; the iconography of the Kenilworth entertainment of 1575 with its focus on the legend of Arthur has been much analysed, and sometimes argued as one of Dudley's boldest attempts to persuade the queen to marry him.[72] What is important here is that the last phase of his work at Kenilworth in the early 1570s coincides with much other attention to his regional influence as a means of underpinning Dudley's eminence and patronage, but also fulfilling his religious convictions.

As discussed in chapter 2, the building of a new church at Denbigh was a rare example of a planned space for Puritan preaching. Its physical and

79 Kenilworth Castle, Warwickshire. The gatehouse originally built for Robert Dudley in the late 1560s.

political context is equally important. The town needed a new church because its centre of population had shifted during the fifteenth century. Dudley endowed the building in the purlieus of his own castle with the approval of the diocesan bishop, William Hughes of St Asaph, though it has been suggested that Dudley may have hoped that Denbigh would replace St Asaph as a new cathedral in the region. The key event to prompt its beginning in 1578 was the appointment two years earlier of Edmund Grindal to the see of Canterbury: in this Dudley had a supporter in his effort to protect – or, some have argued, even promote – Puritanism as a way of countering the growing Catholic threat. In 1579 an appeal for funds for the church was made by the Privy Council. It appears that the building was complete up to the roof by 1584, but at this point Dudley had to abandon the scheme: 'to leave of his buildyng begonne at Denbighe as I heare saye he hath donne', as an antagonistic papist tract recorded in that year. Whitgift's appointment to Canterbury in 1583, given the new archbishop's record in rigorously and successfully defending the position of the established church against the reformers, may also have discouraged Dudley's active support of the Puritan cause.[73]

It was in September 1571 that Dudley paid his second recorded visit to Warwick, the details of which are fully recounted in a document known as the 'Black Book', by the town clerk and recently elected Member of Parliament, John Fisher.[74] The picture he gives of a great lord entering his own territory is very vivid: on 29 September, the Feast of St Michael, Dudley went to the collegiate church of St Mary in full robes of state to sit beneath a cloth of estate; this was an important symbolic gesture since Dudley prized his descent from Richard Beauchamp, Earl of Warwick, buried in the church where he too was later to be interred. Fisher goes on to describe how he travelled to see Dudley at Greenwich two months later. At this meeting Dudley expressed his wish to support the town:

> And therefore many such poore as I perceve you have, I woold to God you woold some wayes devise that they may in sort be relieved an yor comonwealth profitted. And because I am of that countrye & mynde to plant myself there I woold be glad to further any good device with all my hart.

Dudley had already secured the passing of an Act of Parliament earlier that year, the only private one he ever secured, for the foundation of a hospital in his name either at Kenilworth or at Warwick, thus envisaging the foundation that came to be known as Lord Leycester's Hospital. On the September visit Fisher records how Dudley first looked at a site in the churchyard for this purpose but the dignitaries of the town had already considered how they might 'move his honor to found his said hospitall in the said borowe as a place convenient And whither the towne woold offer unto his L. any part of their burges hall & buildings there towards the pformance of so good a woork'. The guildhall was originally the property of the combined guilds of St George the Martyr and of the Holy Trinity and St Mary, adapted for town government after the Reformation.[75] A chapel survived over the west gate. Dudley was shown the building and employed his mason, William Spicer, currently employed on his work at Kenilworth, to survey the place:

> insomuch that his Lordship apointed one Spicer being his srveyor of his woorks to survey the same wth spede & to signifie him of his opinion so the said Spicer wtn two or three days after was by the said Butler brought to the place & was shewed all wch he thought very convenient so as the said Earle might have all aswell the chapell as skolehouse Burgers hall & all other prmes garden & buildings.

In return, the town hoped that this generosity would be matched by things in kind, namely that Dudley's brother the Earl of Warwick would give some otherwise unused waste ground to build houses and that Dudley would give timber from his estates for their construction. The brothers did indeed help the town by surrendering properties for public use. By indenture of 1576

80 Lord Leycester's
Hospital, Warwick. The
courtyard with the range
on the right was a 16th-
century adaptation of a
15th-century range. The
master's house on the left
was much restored in the
19th century.

they granted to the bailiff and burgesses of Warwick St Peter's Chapel, the
Shire Hall and Cross Tavern; the last of these certainly served as the guildhall thereafter.[76]

It is not known when the buildings for Lord Leycester's Hospital came
into use (fig. 80). Deeds of 1585 laid down Ordinances for government and
specified that priority at the hospital be given to 'the finding, sustentation,
and relief of poor, needy, impotent men, and especially as such as shall be
hereafter wounded, maimed, or hurt in the wars in the service of her
Majesty, her heirs or successors.'[77] Every brother was expected to 'keep his
Chamber Sweete, without wilfull anoyenge any of his Brethren in any fylthie
or unseemlye maner'.[78] In view of Dudley's imminent departure for war in
the Netherlands, the shift towards the war-wounded is significant, as is the
stated preference given to men who originated from Dudley's own west midlands power base. Dudley made provision in his will for the upkeep of the
hospital, considering that he believed it needed £200 per annum of income
to survive. It was endowed with a considerable estate with income from
manors all over the county and this was to be further topped up if necessary. After Dudley's death in 1588, the good faith expressed in his will was
kept with the hospital for two years, but Ambrose's death in 1590 brought

great uncertainty, emphasising the fragility of such foundations. Robert Dudley's widow claimed the estates as dower and withheld income so that Thomas Cartwright, Dudley's Puritan appointment to the post of master in 1585, had to appeal to Cecil to save the bequest and an Act of Parliament had to certify Dudley's wishes.[79]

The hospital was made up of a group of buildings, largely dating from the late fifteenth century and intended for various purposes. The main quadrangle at the core of the property was adapted to make a master's house facing the gateway; this was heavily restored and faced with imitation timbering in the mid-nineteenth century. The east range, however, with timber galleries, open on the ground floor and partly closed above, facing on to the court, has a framing different from other parts of the complex. This evidence and that of the roof suggest an original date for the east range possibly from the early fifteenth century, yet it also bears the most evidence of surviving work from the sixteenth century and thus the transformation of the former guildhall and school into Lord Leycester's Hospital. A large stone chimney on the east front may well date from the time of the hospital's beginnings, and internal nineteenth-century plasterwork here may be recording a lost date of '1571'. The stair in the south-east corner of the court is certainly Elizabethan.[80] Dudley had got a good deal from his transactions at Warwick, including approbation in the town which he seemed to want as a base for his interests in the west midlands, 'Because I am of that countrye & mynde to plant myself there', as he said in the interview with Fisher at Greenwich two months after his visit.[81] His association with a particular place was not at the outset of his career as obvious as that of William Cecil, Lord Burghley, with his landed inheritance, but Dudley's affiliation with the west midlands formed his power base and his sphere of patronage.

Henry Howard, Earl of Northampton and three almshouses

Henry Howard, who was born in 1540, was, like Dudley, the son of a fallen nobleman, being the second son of Henry Howard, Earl of Surrey, executed in the last days of Henry VIII's reign. He was educated at Cambridge and was the only man of such a high aristocratic family known to have taught at the university during this period; he stayed as Reader in Rhetoric until 1569. While he remained always loyal to Elizabeth and is believed to have been received secretly into the Catholic Church only shortly before his death in 1614, his life was determined by the suspicion surrounding the Catholic Howards, especially after the execution of the Duke of Norfolk in 1571 and during the plots of the 1580s; indeed, he endured imprisonment in the Fleet for a spell in 1583. He was in his late fifties when Robert Devereux,

81 Nicholas Stone and Isaac James, a fragment of the kneeling figure of Henry Howard, Earl of Northampton, from the tomb originally at St Mary-in-the Castle, Dover, transferred to the chapel of Holy Trinity Almshouse, Greenwich, National Monuments Record.

Earl of Essex, brought him to court and Elizabeth granted him a pension of £200. Things took an even more favourable turn in 1603 because his vital contribution to securing the succession of James led to his appointment to several posts, including that of Warden of the Cinque Ports, a role of which he was proud; he was to be buried in Dover Castle, where he had been constable. In 1604 he became Earl of Northampton and was central in the negotiations for peace with Spain that year. He gained the somewhat nominal post of Lord Privy Seal in 1608 and it was only after Robert Cecil's death in 1612 that he became the most powerful Privy Councillor (fig. 81).[82]

As far as great houses were concerned, Northampton's building work focused mainly on two places, his new London house at the western end of the Strand and, like many courtiers before him, the refurbishment of a property he held by virtue of royal office. As Keeper of Greenwich Park he used the lodge built in Henry VIII's time, which once stood on the site of the present observatory. In his last years Northampton was to recall that he had been brought up at the lodge.[83] In 1611 Simon Basil, Surveyor of the King's Works, complained to Robert Cecil that at Northampton's behest he had taken down the upper garret and second storey of his house, resulting in the loss of two good rooms, and added that Northampton now wished to remove other parts of the house. In 1613 Northampton survived a struggle with James's consort, Queen Anne, over the Keepership of the Park, which she claimed as rightfully hers. To emphasise what he saw as an unselfish devotion to public duty, he denied all profit from the office: 'With the park there goes no other benefit than the fee of three pence a day. [. . .] My charge is treble to the gain and to enjoy the lodge without the care of the park would make me ridiculous.'[84] The inventory taken at Northampton's death reveals something of the layout of the house, still, it seems (despite Basil's comments of 1611), of three storeys.[85]

Northampton's house at the west end of the Strand was a large court-yard building, its garden leading on a sloping site down to the Thames. It was to become celebrated in the seventeenth century as Northumberland House after it passed to the Percy family in 1642.[86] As Northampton House it was recorded by both Robert Smythson and John Thorpe in their draw-ings, Smythson's executed probably on his visit to London in 1609 and Thorpe at a time when changes were envisaged since his plans of both ground and upper floors show annotations in different hands. Thorpe's indi-cation of an upper floor long gallery, on the west side, of 160 feet, gives a sense of the scale of the house. The inventory of the house taken in 1614 shows that this huge room contained large and deep tapestries of seven nar-ratives of the life of Christ valued at £107 5s. The sloping site also meant that the south side, looking over the garden to the river, was single-storeyed

82 Castle Rising, Norfolk. The brick almshouses founded by Henry Howard in 1608.

with a terrace above. According to George Vertue, Flemish craftsmen were employed for the overall design and the frontispiece in the centre of the Strand front.[87]

It has often been claimed that Northampton was exceptional in his charitable gifts. He founded three almshouses, about which it is notable that they are situated in quite different parts of the country. Near London, close to his house at Greenwich, he founded the Holy Trinity Almshouse in 1613, which was to care for twelve poor men from East Greenwich, and a further eight from his birthplace in Shotesham, Norfolk. The capital value of endowed lands was £3833 and the Mercers' Company was named as administrator. At Castle Rising, Norfolk, he founded an almshouse for twelve poor women in 1608, spending £451 14s. 2d. on the building and endowing it with £100 per year from his Norfolk lands (fig. 82). The original book of statutes signed by Northampton's executors lays down the apparel of the women, including a livery gown of blue broad cloth lined with baize, with the founder's badge with a lion rampant embroidered on the breast; a hat to match the gown is also listed. These were given out and collected in by the governess each Sunday. The governess rang the bell and shut the gates at prayers twice daily, at 9 a.m. and 3 p.m.; she had to look to the repairs of the house that not so much as one stone be missing in any of its walls and to keep a garden.[88] Finally at Clun, in Shropshire, he founded in 1607 the almshouses of the Holy and Undivided Trinity, though

83   Clun, Shropshire. The stone almshouses of the Holy and Undivided Trinity, founded by Henry Howard, Earl of Northampton, in 1607 and constructed in 1618.

this was not constructed until 1618 (fig. 83). One of the most notable passages of his will attempts to ensure that his executors finish the building of the three hospitals:

> And I chardge them especiallie to have a care that they procure the Hospitalls at Rysing and Greenewich which I have begunne to be founded and incorporated. And those twoe and the Hospitall at Clun to be finished and endowed, that is to saye, the Hospitall of Clunn to be endowed with the free Rentes of the Rectoryes of Clunn and Bishops Castle, beyng Fee-farm Rentes, and with the Rectories of Knighton and Church Stow, which I will shalbe conveyed to that Hospitall by myne heire.

Any excess funds after ten years were to 'be put as a stocke into the treasurye of every of the saide three Hospitalls'.[89]

All three buildings remain, though they have all been altered and their chapels rebuilt in the nineteenth century. Greenwich has a largely nineteenth-century entrance range to the north, facing the river, probably of the same period as the rebuilding of the chapel in 1812. Greenwich and Castle Rising share a similar basic plan of entrance range with hall and chapel opposite. Castle Rising is of brick and carstone and preserves some of its original panelling in the upper room over the two-storeyed entrance. It also has some Jacobean furniture, including the original treasury chest; some of the rooms contain a bedstead, chair and stool-table.[90]

Women as builders, as managers of buildings

The lives of women and their positive agency in initiating enterprises such as building and estate management have come into increasing scholarly prominence. It is still important to consider and place in context those women patrons of building who have always seemed exceptional: Elizabeth, Countess of Shrewsbury, and Lady Anne Clifford have received more attention than the others, but it is also the case that interest in buildings and responsibility for the maintenance of their fabric have become significant areas of study.[91] It is not just the extraordinary design that commands attention but the evolution of buildings in the hands of those who had a care for their range of purposes. In this sense, while powerful men can be said to have been understood through their patronage of great buildings as symbols of status and power, far more structures were maintained by those responsible for the day-to-day running of a household, usually women, or indeed, men and women working together. Understanding the workings of a house is certainly enriched by considering the way that women used the internal spaces flexibly, how they resorted one to another between houses, at all class levels. It is important to stress the positive aspects of female control and their management of the key aspect of hospitality at all houses of some size or significance, which oiled the wheels of social intercourse both across the same class and between the classes. As the sixteenth century progressed, it becomes increasingly clear that the further up the class ladder one looks, the more one finds that women were restricted in their movements; they were seldom allowed to invade male physical or psychological space.

More than this, the immense social resonance of what one might call the 'passive voice' in architecture has come to be explored and appreciated; that absence of activity nevertheless implies a presence without which certain buildings would not look, and certainly not have operated, in the way that they did. This begins at the very top of society.[92] While it is true that Queen Elizabeth undertook no truly major building commissions compared with her father or grandfather, several factors build an undeniable picture of the sovereign as 'active' in architecture: the consolidation of the stock of royal palaces into a group of 'standing' palaces in any one of which the court could always live; the steady maintenance of the core group through redecoration; the responsibility of her government for coastal and border defences; and her initiative in supporting those towns damaged by fire. Yet it is more than this. Historians recount how courtiers built to entertain the queen and how they identified patterns of iconography in fittings and decoration that flattered her in their country houses. So, by a transfer of responsibility, Elizabeth was 'responsible' for some of the greatest buildings of the age, notwithstanding the fact that the Crown did not own or initiate them.

Both in terms of land ownership and the realisation of significant buildings, Lady Anne Clifford (1590–1676) was among the most powerful women of the period. Her tenacity in the retrieval of her father's estates in her later years and her projects for building on her northern lands have been celebrated, along with all the complex signals of tradition and lineage that meant so much to her. Yet it is also those 'lost' years recorded in her diary, living the lonely life, in the frequent absence of her husbands, as mistress of the large houses of Knole and Wilton as the countess wife of two earls in succession that makes her presence at those houses part of their history, even though the visual impact she made was slight.[93] Elizabeth Talbot, née Hardwick, Countess of Shrewsbury (1520–1608), often called 'Bess of Hardwick', is primarily associated with the building in the 1580s and 1590s of two great houses alongside each other on her family lands at Hardwick, Derbyshire, after her fourth marriage to the Earl of Shrewsbury had broken down (fig. 84). The design of these buildings and their place in the history of English domestic architecture are highly significant, but so too are the internal arrangements at the house. These seem to encompass the particular domestic arrangements of a matriarch with children from earlier marriages to house and marry off. Although the building accounts are incomplete, they provide evidence that she managed to keep the house within reasonable spending limits through the exploitation of her own

estate resources, in building stone, glass-making and indeed manpower.[94] Moreover, Gillian White's research has brought out how Bess's decoration of Hardwick New Hall, and indeed the collection of objects there, do not belong entirely of a piece to the 1590s, a position that had long been an unstated implication of the making of this house; generations of historians have leant on this belief in order to stress the house's novelty and to let it serve as the exemplar of its age. There are certainly influences from the latest print sources of the period in many movable objects and decorative schemes from her last years, for example the image of Cybele for the over-mantel of her 'little dyning chamber' taken from a print of 1586 after Hendrik Goltzius. Such references show that she was indeed patron of modern and fashionable luxuries, but many things were also brought in from her earlier houses, and in particular the great house of Chatsworth, whose contents she built up alongside her second husband, William Cavendish, who had died as long ago as 1557.[95] Bess of Hardwick lived with the past just as much as she encouraged new building and innovative design.

It is often assumed that in the establishment of the norm of strong patri-archal inheritance after the Reformation, wealthy men were fixated on the notion of leaving the bulk of their property, and especially the best house with all its seigniorial and territorial associations, to the eldest son. The facts suggest a more complex picture than this. Women clearly ran prop-erties on a sound financial basis and took charge of day-to-day manage-ment. The evidence here is from the rich studies of the lives of widows, where for the years 1450–1550 the work of Barbara Harris has shown that widows of gentry and aristocratic classes were conventionally left property above their dowries and jointures, and that this often included houses. In a small proportion of her sample of 523 wills of male testators, some 21 per cent of men left houses, often in London, or manors to their wives; about half of these men gave their wives the chief mansion house, by-passing the male heir. It is likely that a majority of male testators overall left some house for their widows to live in during the remainder of their lives.[96]

It was rare for high-born men and women of early modern England not to marry, but those who left no children had particular responsibilities towards their estate. Generous public benefaction was often the result. Part of the reason for Henry Howard's foundations was of course his having no heir of his body; his great-nephew the Earl of Arundel got the bulk of his estate, including use of the lodge in Greenwich Park, while his nephew the Earl of Suffolk got the Strand house. Frances Sidney (1531–89), whose family moved in high court circles, was also childless and chose to put her resources into a huge educational bequest. She married Thomas Radcliffe, Lord Fitzwalter, in 1555. In 1557 he became Earl of Sussex. She lived with her husband during his postings as Lord Deputy of Ireland (1556–64) and Lord President of the North in the 1570s (his death in 1583 left her wealthy). By the late 1570s she was certainly one of Elizabeth's women of the bedchamber and is duly one of the group of powerful noblewomen and servants of the queen who are commemorated in the side chapels of the east end of Westminster Abbey.

Alongside bequests to poor preachers of London and a lectureship at the abbey Frances Sidney had annually set aside revenues towards the founding of a college at Cambridge to the sum of £5000, to be supplemented by the sale of certain goods.[97] Her executors had difficulty in procuring the site of the former Greyfriars, which had been systematically robbed of stone since its conveyance to Trinity College in 1546. Building was begun in May 1596 and the three ranges that make up Hall Court of Sidney Sussex College were completed by 1600 (fig. 85). Frances Sidney was very much therefore the enabler; though she wished the college to be a 'good and godly monument for the mayntenance of good learning', there is no evidence of her wishes as architectural patron.[98] The sequence of events here thus echoes that concerning another female patron from the beginning of the century at St John's College, where the foundress, Lady Margaret Beaufort, died in 1509 during preliminary arrangements; the adaptation of the former hospital of St John the Evangelist on the site and the building of the first court were begun in 1511. However, knowledge of Lady Margaret's wishes would have been understood through her previous benefaction, the re-foundation of the Grammar-College of God's House as Christ's College. This was begun in 1505 and was well under way at her death; progress was reported in her household books, now preserved at St John's.[99]

85 Sidney Sussex College, Cambridge, completed by 1600. The college's two courts are separated from the street by a wall, with some original late Elizabethan brickwork on the north side of the north range of Hall Court at the left.

The examples of women patrons of the early seventeenth century who do seem to be commissioning, of their own volition and from their own decisions on taste, buildings at the forefront of innovative architectural design, appear to have evolved naturally from what had gone before. Two of the most celebrated came to commission their astonishing buildings late in their lives. Both enjoyed the benefits of an education superior to most of their elite female generation and, while they were certainly inspired by the activities of their husbands, it was probably the unusual nature of the husband as the aristocratic outsider that encouraged innovation. Notwithstanding their friendship, one very important thing separated Mary Herbert, née Sidney, Countess of Pembroke (1561–1621), and Aletheia Howard, née Talbot, Countess of Arundel (after 1582–1654) – their religious affiliation. Mary Herbert's brother Philip Sidney, whose life, early death and poetry used to inspire a glamorous image of the Renaissance polymath, has come to be seen as difficult and restless and governed by political opportunism; in this narrative the role of his sisters as keepers of his posthumous iden-

86 Houghton House, Bedfordshire. The remains of the house begun for Mary Sidney in 1615.

tity has been frequently told.[100] Like her mother Mary Dudley, eldest daughter of the Duke of Northumberland, and the sisters Anne Bacon and Mildred Cecil, daughters of Sir Anthony Cooke, Mary Herbert was educated in a range of languages and a peripatetic upbringing during her father's spells as President of the Marches of Wales and as Deputy of Ireland. Her Protestant convictions were less doctrinal within an English context but she was fierce in her support of French and Dutch Calvinism and she steered her efforts to edit her dead brother's poetry and gild his fame in that cause.[101] The small house she commissioned in her widowhood at Houghton, near Ampthill in Bedfordshire, is in many respects a conventional small Jacobean house but contains on north and west fronts remarkable classical loggias that have conventionally been associated with the name of Inigo Jones (fig. 86). They certainly echo the language of several designs he made at this time, which implanted classical doorways into older or more conservative buildings, and recall the sketch that he made of the loggia of Palladio's Villa Thiene in his copy of the architect's *Quattro libri*.[102]

Aletheia Howard's patronage of building can be said to reflect the twin aspects of female patron as devisor of her husband's wishes, and thus probably equally responsible for the structure's appearance and use; in her case, acquiring a personal identity through a building project was reflected in a scheme undertaken late in her life. Between her coming back to England from Italy in 1614 and her return there in 1620 she appears to have been site manager for many of their joint projects, a house in Highgate, the building of Arundel House on the Strand and the improvement, from the plans of Inigo Jones, of the interiors of the lodge in Greenwich Park which was inherited in 1614 from Arundel's uncle, the Earl of Northampton. Arundel's letters to her point to her role as managing his bidding but also playing some intervening role:

> I pray take order that the mattes, and all the stuffe, be taken out of the roomes towards the water, at Arundell House, for on Monday I have given order they go in hand, to deal with the windows; and I pray bid Wilson make very great haste, for now is the only spare time, and I desire exceedingly to see things done.[103]

Much later however, in the 1630s, Lady Arundel played a more decisive role on her own behalf in the adaptation of Tart Hall, the Arundels' new house in St James's Park. The Catholic priest George Gage seems to have been responsible for advising Lady Arundel on the initial phase of work here in the 1630s, but it was Nicholas Stone who did further work in 1639; both these advisers played a role in creating something that has been characterised as a rival house, or *casino*, for Lady Arundel, which paralleled the contemporary use of the Queen's House at Greenwich as a place of retreat rather than fit for a large, working household. It has been convincingly argued that the building in the background of *Spring* from the series of prints of the seasons by Wenceslaus Hollar of 1641–4 is the hall itself and that parallels can be drawn with villas in the Veneto and palaces in Venice that Lady Arundel would have seen. Here Lady Arundel entertained Catholic friends and built a collection distinct from the famous one gathered by her husband.[104]

As daughters and subsequently wives, often of more than one person, all the women discussed above lived through their lives in a variety of houses, some of old building, some of new. Sometimes the character of the female patron's own choice comes to the fore, often once she had become widowed; but it also seems that a wife would serve as interlocutor between husband and his peer group, or across different generations and connections of her family. Aristocratic women in particular had extraordinarily long lines of responsibility across their offspring and the connections of their relatives. The gentry class also shows these patterns. Dorothy Hopton (*c.* 1570–1629) came from a family with lands in Somerset and Suffolk.[105] It is likely that she spent most of her early years at Witham Priory in Somerset, probably in a house only moderately adapted from the previous monastic house on the site; it is not known what this looked like on account of an extensive eighteenth-century remodelling.[106] During her first marriage to William Smith she probably lived at a house in the parish of Great Cressingham, Norfolk, and she was to be buried with her first husband in the church there.[107] She subsequently married Nathaniel Bacon in 1597, held a house in Norwich thanks to his settlement on her, and lived with her husband at Stiffkey, Norfolk, in the extraordinary house built by her father-in-law, Sir Nicholas Bacon, Keeper of the Great Seal, for his son Nathaniel between 1576 and 1581 (fig. 87).[108] Then about 1607 Lady Dorothy convinced her husband that they should build a new house at Irmingland, about 10 miles from Stiffkey, and they divided their time between the two houses thereafter. An inscription was placed over the door which underlines her involvement: *Nathanael Bacon miles, anno aetatis suae 63, pro Dorothea uxore, et Gilielmo-Roberds Smith, filio ejusdem Dorotheae, has aedes erexit ano 1609* (fig. 88). Among a handful of surviving letters are those she wrote to her step-grandson, Sir Roger Townshend, later to become the builder of Raynham Hall, Norfolk, whose advice she sought on many practical matters. Thus Lady Dorothy's domestic life spans the whole gamut of the kinds of houses that formed the century. She began life in a converted monastery, went on to live in a Norfolk house probably built early in the sixteenth century, then in a house of the 1570s but with a distinctive U-shaped plan common in great East Anglian houses of the 1550s; when it

87 Stiffkey Hall, Norfolk. Built between 1576 and 1581.

IRMINGLAND HALL in NORFOLK.

A House belonging to Edm.d Craddock Hartopp, of Pines in the County of Devon Esq.r to whom this Plate is inscribed.

Publish'd as the Act directs, Feb.y 21.st 1780, by M. Booth, Norwich.

came to her own choice and devising, however, she inspired a modern, if modest, gabled, brick, Jacobean house. Her unremarkable life does not take one into the great spaces and buildings of her period but her experience of domestic life would have encompassed the entire span of change of surroundings covered in this book and the cautious steps towards new forms and styles embraced over a long period of time.

88 Irmingland, Norfolk. From a print of 1780. Courtesy of Norfolk County Council.

5

Representing Buildings

As explored in chapter 3 above, a great change in verbal description of the built environment took place during the sixteenth century. When John Leland travelled the country in the early 1540s, compiling the notes that were to make his *Itinerary*, he was essentially making a map of the human experience of coming across one place after another; he describes the bridge into a town, jots down urban landmarks and mentions the distance between them. It is very much an experience on foot. By the time of William Camden's *Britannia* of 1586, plotting the urban landscape had become the work of specialist cartographers; describing buildings verbally was now evoking a different experience, one backed up by maps and plans that enabled the reader to grasp a concept of a totality of understanding, of seeing with the mind's eye whole groups of buildings and their relationship to one another.[1] If not always a bird's eye view, this was an experience of distance, appraisal and evaluation in several different senses. How did the visual representation of buildings play a role in these changes and shift the way that contemporaries looked at and used the structures of their everyday lives?

Discussion of changes in the representation of solid objects in the early modern world, be they people or buildings, inevitably confronts the issue of the role of one-point perspective in giving artists, whether painters, draughtsmen or cartographers, a seemingly new tool in order to simulate reality. Like the widening use of the classical language of architecture, the use of perspectival solutions for visual depiction can seem to have an inevitability about it and seems to make the key discoveries and achievements of Italian art of this period paramount and ultimately triumphant. With hindsight this may now seem the case, but for sixteenth-century artists and patrons it was not necessarily so. As several writers have variously suggested, England, like the rest of northern Europe, experienced Italy as a series of packages, of solutions to problems applied in the particular cir-

89 Wilton House, Wiltshire. Detail from the survey of lands for William Herbert, Earl of Pembroke, pen and ink on vellum, 1566. A drawing of two perspectives, showing the forecourt from above, in plan, and both gatehouse and the original entrance front to the house, in elevation. Collection of the Earl of Pembroke, Wilton House/The Bridgeman Art Library.

cumstances of each great commission, be it for a country house, a royal portrait, the making of a garden or a piece of furniture.[2] English patrons would raid treatises and pattern books for ideas without necessarily understanding the overall picture. What England did not see, that is to say, were the developmental stages of ideas presented to them through the conclusions of these books. Indeed, if someone from England were one of the minority who travelled, they equally did not see the origins, or understand the predecessors of the monuments of Italian art *in situ*. Thanks to the discipline of art history, these now come across in an organised chronological sequence. For contemporaries, the modern art they would have experienced in Florence in the second half of the sixteenth century, for example works for the first Medici Dukes of Tuscany, the paintings of Agnolo Bronzino, the sculpture of Benvenuto Cellini and Baccio Bandinelli, would have seemed in some ways bizarre and strange, even had their new religious sensibilities emerging from Protestantism not also been in the way.

One approach to ways of seeing and recording in northern Europe in the early modern period has sought not to propagate a kind of chaos that Italian art needed to organise, but a positive and all-encompassing approach that borrows the very term that plots the terrain discussed above. In her book *The Art of Describing*, Svetlana Alpers championed a means of rendering visual experience in northern Europe that is equated to 'mapping', taking and replicating the phenomena of that reality which privileges sight over the organising forces of a brain seeking selection and usually meaning in the things it experiences.[3] Objects large and small, things near and distant in the landscape, things colossal and minute, are given equal attention in form and detail. The intellectual processes here are those of curiosity and discovery rather than idealisation and simplification. This all-embracing approach to the visual world is not argued as at all non-selective when it comes to the physical means of conveying what is viewed; the oil painting, the miniature, the print, the drawing might all be severally useful in rendering the qualities and particularities of the object. Finding the technical means to do the job is very much part of the 'art of describing'; among these means new ideas coming from Italy might well have a role to play, but first the purpose of the exercise had to be determined and the audience both satisfied and pleased. At the point of pleasure the illusion of reality might be so astonishing as to simply give delight, but at the same time the very achievement of illusion might disturb the viewer. During Elizabeth's reign, for example, the German traveller Paul Hentzner recalled seeing the anamorphic portrait of Edward VI in Whitehall Palace in 1598, noting that it looked 'at first sight something quite deformed', but on taking the view through the small hole cut in the plate installed on its right, he found that 'you see it in its true proportions'.[4] Hans Holbein had earlier asked for a similar movement on the viewer's part in his painting known as *The Ambassadors* (now in the National Gallery, London), where the frontal view of two splendidly dressed young men gives way to a compressed image of a skull, a reminder of mortality, from the right-hand angle. This kind of leap of the imagination and the onlooker's sense of the bigger picture and possibilities of representation is present in all forms of the rendering of buildings, precisely because the purposes of illusion were to make the image suggest something that could actually be experienced.

It is clear that long before the sixteenth century the designers of buildings prepared flat, two-dimensional plans for discussion with their patrons; there are records of Henry VIII accepting these, passing what are often referred to as 'platts' between himself, the Office of the King's Works and certain courtiers and officials who might be involved at any one moment in the processes of royal building.[5] These might be highly diagrammatic: writing along a single line that expresses wall would have to explain doorways, projection and so on at a time when the symbolic vocabulary for such things was undeveloped. Sometimes, however, one façade of a building might be rendered to give the impression of what later came to be known as the elevation.[6] For a long time the orthogonal projection showing all sides of a building – or, with interiors, all walls of a room, as if the room could be folded up and assembled – proved invaluable in giving the patron a sense of what all the details of the project were to look like. Orthogonal projections therefore showed all the necessary information a viewer might want rather than attempting something that the eye, from a single given vantage point, actually sees. Given the frequent yoking together of classicism and perspectival illusion as new, as well as the development of persuasive methods of building and representation, it is worth noting that the older orthogonal methods in some senses support classical architecture: the proportionality of the latter and the clarity of the way one part of a façade, or wall of a room, relates to another, is better rendered through orthography's command of full knowledge.[7]

Orthogonal projections were immensely useful as documentation attached to any form of legal contract or dispute. The court house and market house at Barking in Essex were built in 1567–8 (fig. 90). It was a collaborative venture, the Crown paying for the cost of erection of the main buildings while the local people were to clear the site and build sixteen shops and some sheds in the market place. In 1595 an investigation took place when it was found that the inhabitants of the borough were failing to keep the market house in good repair because they believed it was to be granted out of their use. Carefully annotated drawings were prepared as part of the enquiry and these, in flat, orthogonal projection, show the constituent buildings, with the stocks, well and weighing station, and their relationship to each other in schematised fashion. Annotations give the various measurements. A different kind of use of this projection can be seen in the 1574 depiction of the largely fifteenth-century buildings of the Schools at Cambridge, where the ranges frame the information about their various

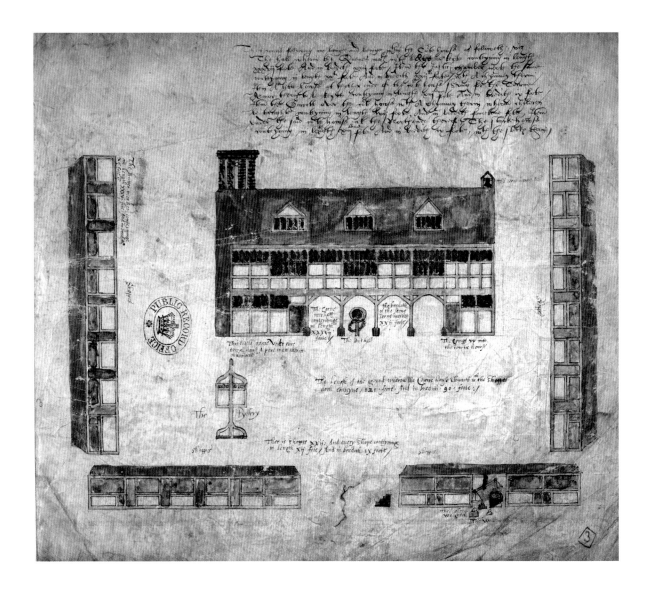

90 (*above*) Plan/drawing
of the 1567–8 court house
and market house, Barking,
Essex, 1595. National
Archives, E178/843.

91 (*facing page*) The Old
Schools and Library,
Cambridge. From a
presentation copy of
Matthew Parker's *De
antiquitate Britannicae*,
1574. By permission of
the Syndics of Cambridge
University Library.

lengths and breadths. The act of depiction may also have had a practical
end here, for in 1583–4 the buildings underwent their first major repair
since construction (fig. 91).[8]

The perspectival view was an alternative to this and was often used in
conjunction with the orthogonal, especially when the designer wished to
propose other solutions or, as is often the case, when a particular feature
such as an oriel window needs to stand out from the otherwise flat wall
surface. Sometimes perspective itself is taken from several different view-
points because the designer is choosing details from a variety of sources;
Inigo Jones does this often in his early drawings, a representative example
being his elevation for a new termination to the tower of St Paul's Cathe-

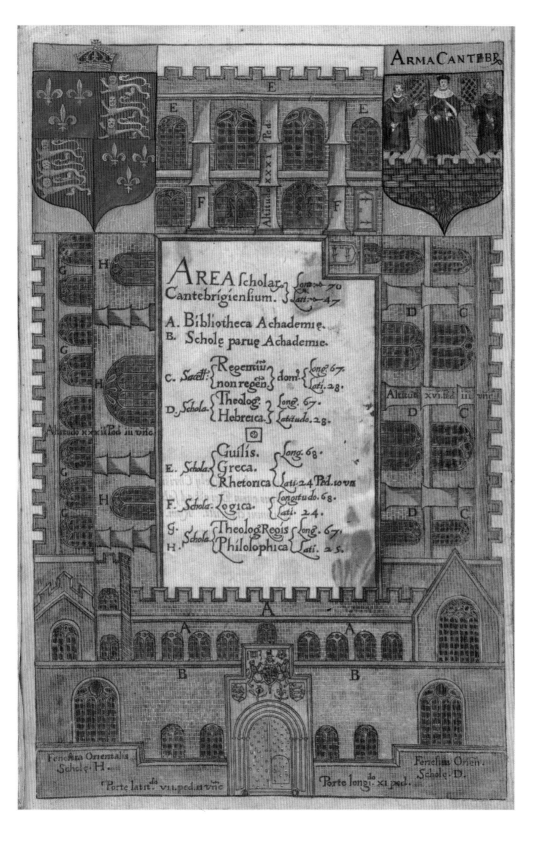

ARMA CANTEBR

AREA scholar. long. 70
Cantebrigiensium. lati. 47

A. Bibliotheca Achademiæ.
B. Scholæ paruæ Achademiæ.

C. Sacell: {Regemiū} dom: {long. 67.
         {non regen}   {lati. 28.

D. Schola {Theolog: } long. 67.
          {Hebreica } Latitudo. 28.

E. Schola {Guilis.   } long. 68.
          {Greca.   }
          {Rhetorica } lati. 24 Ped. 10 vn

F. Schola Logica. {longitudo. 68.
                  {lati. 24.

G. Schola {TheologRegis} long. 67.
H.   {Philosophica} lati. 25.

Fenestra Orientalis
Scholæ H.

Porte latit. VII. ped. II vnc

Fenestra Orien.
Scholæ D.

Porte longi. XI. ped.

dral of 1608 (fig. 92). Here are a multiplicity of souces, from Serlio and Palladio for the openings of the gallery to a print of Antonio da Sangallo's design for St Peter's in Rome for the spires.[9] What the perspectival view can do, however, is to render an impression of the experience of space and the physical sense of the wholeness of the design in bringing together the constituent parts. In John Smythson's view of a marble closet at Bolsover Castle, which may be one of the very first perspectival drawings of an interior, the floor, three walls and the vaulted ceiling are shown above the plan to give that full impression (fig. 93). The status of this drawing therefore must have been presentational, so that the patron could 'view' what the room would look like. It is but a step from here to the creation of the full model of the building, or of a single interior, a method that developed by leaps and bounds in the course of the seventeenth century.[10]

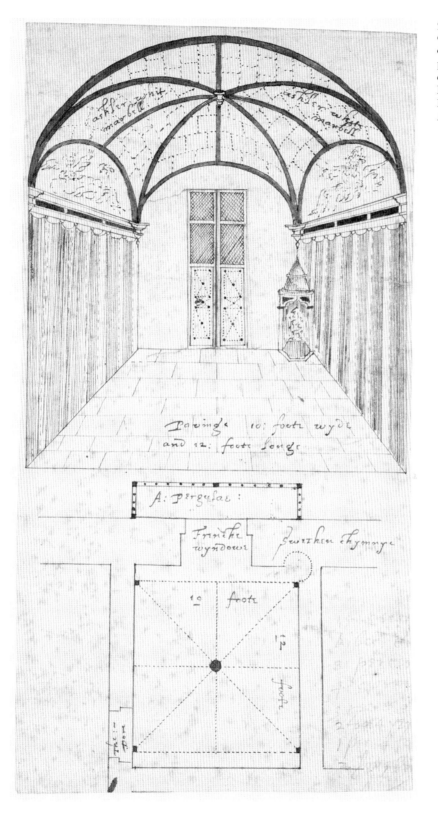

ashler whit marbell

ashler whit marbell

Pavinge 10: foote wyde and 12: foote longe

A: pergulae:

Frinche wyndowr

Swethin chymnye

10 foote

12 foote

93 John Smythson, drawing of a marble closet at Bolsover Castle, pen and ink, early 17th century. Smythson Drawings III/I (2), RIBA Library, Drawings and Archives Collections.

94 Anonymous, *Wisbech Castle, Cambridgeshire*, oil on panel, *c.* 1658–9. Wisbech and Fenland Museum, Wisbech. Copyright National Trust Picture Library/Christopher Hurst.

Orthogonal and perspective both feed into the history of the country-house view as it developed in painting and print through the seventeenth century.[11] The anonymous painting of Wisbech Castle, Cambridgeshire, of around 1658–9, could almost have been prepared as an architectural drawing of one sort by the way it practically fills the surface area and is cut exactly at those points where all the necessary details are rendered (fig. 94). Jan Siberechts's view of Wollaton Hall, of 1697, is a high-view-point perspective painting of a house then more than a century old. It was clearly commissioned because the current owner, Sir Thomas Willoughby, was proud of his new estate planning and gardens, but there is much else happening here (fig. 95). From the point of view of the prospect of the house, the rendition is all-encompassing: it depends on understanding that it is essentially a symmetrical structure, with a raised hall at its centre and four corner towers. The detailing of the building is in the florid style of the 1580s derived from Flemish decorative prints but it is consistently applied and the window openings are evenly spaced and consistent on each floor. Now one can 'see' the concealed further side of the building in the mind's eye because this is a building which depends on that symmetry and order. Planting a great house in a landscape like this could be familiar as a visual experience to late seventeenth-century viewers of this painting because, whatever surprises were within the house (and there were many, including a high great chamber above a hall with a hammer-beam roof), the building was comprehensible and integral as far as the eye could see, all at once. This was quite a different experience from the approach to a conventional early Tudor courtyard house, where each range was perceived separately and, as far as the unfamiliar visitor was concerned, to be approached axially. Individual features such as doorways and great windows would have been distinguished one from another; heraldry and inscription would give direction as to where to proceed next. When Wollaton was built in the 1580s, it was an extraordinarily singular design for its time. Siberechts's rendering of 1697 shows experience of buildings both increasingly classically designed and integrated into a single block as opposed to the rambling courtyards of the past. What has happened is that the viewer has been encouraged not to think in Leland's terms of separated parts but of the building as a whole. Seeing the world around the self as a map has played a vital role in this. It must have pleased Sir Thomas Willoughby greatly because of the extent of its vision. One is reminded of a text that dates from 1624, between the original building and the painting of it, Sir Henry Wotton's *Elements of Architecture*. In his opening section, 'The End is to Build Well', Wotton discusses 'The Seate and the Worke', considering various situations for the house and flattering the eye's insatiable curiosity:

95   Jan Siberechts, *Wollaton Hall, a Bird's Eye View from above the Bowling Green*, oil on canvas, 1697. Copyright Yale Center for British Art, Paul Mellon Collection, USA/The Bridgeman Art Library.

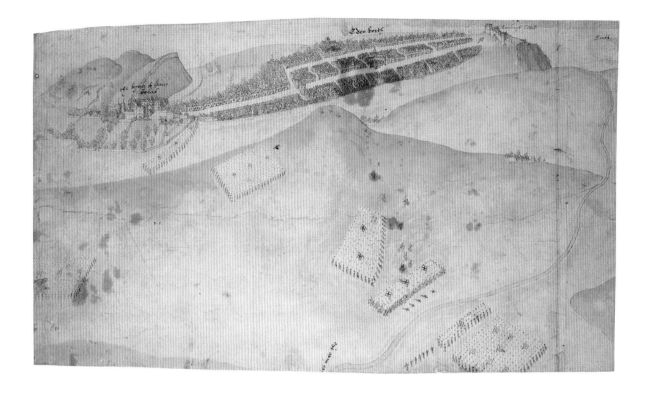

96 Anonymous, *View of Edinburgh*, 1544. A topographical map drawn for the invading English army. British Library, London, Cotton MS, Augustus I. ii. 56.

Some again may bee said to be Optical? Such I meane as concerne the *Properties* of a well chosen *Prospect*: which I will call the *Royaltie* of *Sight*. For there is a *Lordship* (as it were) of the *Feete*, wherein the Master doth much ioy when he walketh about the *Line* of his owne *Possessions*: So there is a *Lordship* likewise of the Eye which being a raunging, and Imperious, and (I might say) an *usurping Sence*, can indure no narrow *circumscription*, but must be fedde, both with extent and varietie.[12]

Much study has come to be devoted to the evolution of cartography in sixteenth-century England. At those levels of society where the ownership of property was a significant concern, there was demand for ever greater accuracy in delineating the landscape, both in maps and in panoramas. In royal circles, the demand for views of towns and great buildings within the royal dominions was an enthusiasm of Henry VIII and a necessity in the 1540s during the wars with France and Scotland. A map of Edinburgh, drawn in 1544 before the Earl of Hertford's attack on the city, shows the massing of English troops in preparation (fig. 96).[13] But as time went by maps also served a wider decorative purpose. The monarch's keenness for keeping maps led to their display in the royal palaces; the royal inventory taken in 1547 lists innumerable maps, including both countrywide maps such as 'a Mappe of all Europe of paper sette in a frame of woode' and others that appear to be something between a map or plan and a view of a particular

174

97   Anthonis van den Wyngaerde, from the *Panorama of London*, pen and ink, probably of 1543–4. Ashmolean Museum, University of Oxford/The Bridgeman Art Library.

building, for example 'the Discription of the Castell of Millayne painted vppon clothe'.[14] Royal patronage probably began the convention in England: by the late sixteenth century maps are common in houses of the aristocracy, often cited alongside paintings and other objects hanging on walls. From here it was a step to using maps in the decorative arts more generally and to place them either in panelling or on movable items such as screens.[15] From the last years of Henry VIII, probably of 1543–4, comes Anthonis van den Wyngaerde's panorama of London; the circumstances of its commission are unknown (fig. 97). Later, probably between 1558 and 1561, Wyngaerde was to draw the royal palaces around London, part of his extensive work for Philip II of Spain, both during and after the time of his marriage to Mary I.[16] While Elizabeth was frequently portrayed symbolically with maps and globes and while the principal atlases of her reign were dedicated to her, the leading expert on later Tudor map culture believes that the queen showed little interest in the practicalities and advantages of mapping and surveying, neglecting the need to initiate a full record of the royal estates.[17] This practice of recording and surveying came to promote among her leading subjects, headed by William Cecil her chief minister, a knowledge and expertise of their estate holdings – hence the wealth of estate maps of private property from this period, a true and vivid record of the outcomes of the post-dissolution settlement.[18]

Estate maps have proved a vital source for the reconstruction of country houses because they often give the best sense of the extent of the house at a given moment; sometimes these great buildings are shown with at least one orthogonally drawn façade, which can give clues about lost ranges of buildings if houses survive in an altered form. The great county maps of the Elizabethan age, however significant they are conceptually for giving the viewer a sense of the increasingly important county identity, its shape and geographical location, are not equally helpful when it comes to individual buildings. Christopher Saxton's celebrated maps, for example, completed by the time of the publication of his Atlas of 1579, tend to use formulaic notation for a range of places, so that towns of a known equal size are depicted in the same way as are great houses; it is often significant, however, that Saxton chooses certain individual sites as worthy of depiction in the first place and helps to establish the sense of hierarchy between these great seats, and therefore their owners, for a public audience.

Town maps offer a great deal of information. Even if schematically, they give a sense of that topographical relationship between buildings, the responsibility for their existence and maintenance between town governments and private individuals that is a key thread of this book. Also, the convention of putting vignettes of particular buildings along the edges of the map results in further details of their contemporary appearance. The list of significant buildings in John Speed's *c.* 1610 map of Salisbury, for example, takes the viewer around the city and in the bottom left-hand corner shows 'The forme of the counsel House'.

Buildings also feature in pictorial representations of significant contemporary events. From the series of wall paintings at Cowdray House, West Sussex, destroyed in the great fire there of 1793 but recorded shortly before that in a watercolour by S. H. Grimm, comes the well-known image of the coronation procession of Edward VI (fig. 5). It is not clear whether the wall painting was carried out at this date and thus within the ownership of Sir Anthony Browne, Master of the Horse in Henry VIII's last years, but it is likely to date from the ownership of his son, Viscount Montague. This image, especially through the wealth of textiles shown thrown from windows along the goldsmiths' houses of Cheapside, reflects how the city and its buildings were constantly changing. The travellers' accounts on which historians depend are likely to have been taken at moments of celebration, focusing on external decoration that temporarily but splendidly altered the city's appearance.

A different purpose of recording and possibly to make up for the impossibility of separate visits to the buildings was *Queen Elizabeth's Book of Oxford*, presented to the monarch on her visit in 1566 (fig. 98). Composed by Thomas Neale, Regius Professor of Hebrew, and illustrated by Thomas Bereblock, Fellow of Exeter College, it was devised as a Latin verse dialogue between the queen and the Earl of Leicester, Chancellor of the Uni-

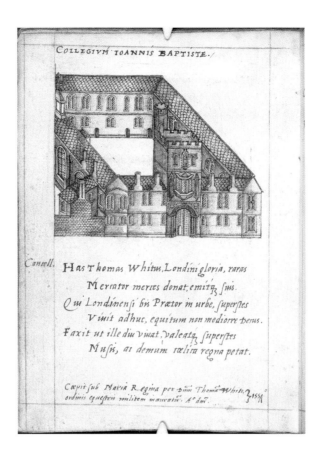

versity. In her edition of this extraordinary manuscript, published in 2006, Louise Durning suggests that this progression around the colleges was an imagined one. On her visit to Cambridge in 1564, the queen had been unable to visit all the colleges in turn. This second journey is therefore one of mental and intellectual exertion. As the translation of the opening of folio 4r puts it:

> Behold, (most distinguished Princess Elizabeth) you hold a topographical delineation of the Colleges and public Schools of your University of Oxford, partly represented by the draughtsman's pen, partly in poetic verse [. . . .] so that you might have the University's entire likeness to hand, as if laid out before your eyes.[19]

In the various depictions, Durning points out how Bereblock modifies the buildings to show them to their best advantage, sometimes altering the orientation between base and tower to incorporate important windows that would otherwise be obscured from view. The format is not quite standard but he uses a small range of possibilities and uses each of them to 'manage' the depiction of the entire quadrangle as fully as possible.

Almost everything discussed above has been intended either to record the specific nature of building and its surroundings as found by various artists, or to trace the prospecting for work by designers or architects. Usually what is depicted are new buildings in which some pride is shown. In the century after the Reformation, however, there is another growing purpose to rendering the built environment in pictorial form. Buildings also become part of national history and their depiction reflects this. Other than the practical depictions of old buildings for recording purposes, England did not especially develop a tradition of depicting the past, except for very particular political purposes – at least that has been how scholars since the mid-twentieth century have seen things. Just as certain images of the 'great deeds' of Henry VIII, still in the Royal Collection, were painted – some twenty years or more after the events portrayed, in order to propagandise the king's exploits from the days of his youth in the face of current war with France – so images of religious propaganda were produced in Elizabeth's reign to celebrate and rather mythologise the Protestant, affirmative events of the reign of her brother, Edward VI, in the face of renewed

Catholic aggression.[20] It is appropriate therefore that Frans Hogenberg's image of Nonsuch Palace, based on drawings by Joris Hoefnagel (one of which is dated 1568), was included in Braun and Hogenberg's *Civitates Orbis Terrarum* of 1598 (fig. 99).[21] This was just six years after Elizabeth had bought back the palace that she had used frequently in recent years but had been in the hands of the Earl of Arundel (subsequently his heir Lord Lumley) since 1557. The most famous of her father's palaces, arguably the only one he built from scratch, appears rather mirage-like above an enclosing wall; while it is often used as such it is probably far from being a literal depiction. Hogenberg discards the stream in the original Hoefnagel drawings and shows the queen herself approaching the palace from the wrong side because this is the more famous view, showing the stuccoes and great towers of the second court. It is indeed, as suggested by one of its most perceptive commentators, more the image of the building than its reality, more dependent on the history of buildings as depicted in manuscript illumination than an exact rendition.[22] Buildings can therefore take on the burden of their reputation and fame through such visual images.

This international context for the image of Nonsuch serves as a reminder that traditions of landscape painting are not yet embedded in English practice of this period. All the known depictions of buildings in context are generally ascribed to foreign artists, usually Flemish, as is the view of Richmond Palace from the Surrey bank of the Thames. It is often reproduced as it appears to be a straightforward, if strangely unlikely, image of a troupe of mummers performing for an aristocratic couple by the Thames (fig. 100).

100　Flemish School, *The Thames at Richmond, with Richmond Palace*, oil on canvas, 17th century. Reproduction by permission of the Syndics of the Fitzwilliam Museum, Cambridge.

In a quiet way it seems to prefigure the paintings of David Teniers, whose juxtaposition of different classes of people in landscape were produced for the Flemish market in considerable numbers. By the time this was painted, about 1620, the Palace of Richmond was almost a century and a quarter old but was seeing something of a revival; work had been undertaken there for Prince Henry about 1610 and Charles I was to present it to Henrietta Maria. More significantly, the palace had been the site of the death of Queen Elizabeth and both James I and Charles I were to express some displeasure that it was the dead queen's accession day that commanded more ceremony and charitable gifts than their own. Tucked into the left-hand corner of the painting, the palace already has an historicised quality, yet it is shown as the culmination of the sweep down from top right to middle left with other buildings, water gates and retaining fences against the river's encroachment. Is the palace the subject of the picture? It seems rather that the riverscape is the subject and the great building is simply the most significant eye-catcher on the horizon. Seeing the building in context is what this image is about, and a contemporary viewer's comprehension of it would be both topographical and historical. The people of England had come, by the time of the Civil War, to see the built environment in a similarly complex way, battered by time, renewed through adaptation and yet often incorporating the startlingly innovative in style, function and building materials.

Notes

Abbreviations

BAR British Archaeological Record
BL British Library, London
CBA Council for British Archaeology
CPR Calendar of Patent Rolls
HBMC Historic Buildings and Monuments Commission (English Heritage)
HMSO His/Her Majesty's Stationery Office
HPC *History of Parliament: House of Commons, 1509–58* (see Bindoff, ed., 1982) and *1558–1603* (Hasler, ed., 1981)
L&P *Letters and Papers [. . .] of Henry VIII* (see Bibliography)
MOLAS Museum of London Archaeology Service
ODNB *Oxford Dictionary of National Biography*
RCHM *Royal Commission on the Historical Monuments of England* (individual volumes cited in the notes)
RIBA Royal Institute of British Architects
SP State Papers
VCH *The Victoria History of the Counties of England* (individual volumes cited in the notes)

Introduction

1 Margaret Aston, 'English Ruins and English History: The Dissolution and the Sense of the Past', *Journal of the Warburg and Courtauld Institutes*, vol. 36, 1973, pp. 231–55. On the impact of monastic ruins on literature see Philip Schwyzer, *Archaeologies of English Renaissance Litereature*, Oxford, 2007, chap. 3 'Dissolving Images: Monastic Ruins in Elizabethan Poetry', pp. 72–107.

2 W. G. Hoskins, 'The Rebuilding of Rural England, 1570–1640', *Past and Present*, no. 4, 1953, pp. 44–59; R. Machin, 'The Great Rebuilding: A Reassessment', *Past and Present*, no. 77, 1977, pp. 33–56; Colin Platt, *The Great Rebuildings of Tudor and Stuart England*, London, 1994.

3 John Summerson, *Architecture in Britain 1530–1830*, Harmondsworth, 1953; many later editions.

4 H. M. Colvin et al., *The History of the King's Works*, vol. IV, *1485–1660* (part 2), London, 1982, pp. 1–364, covers the documented building activity at the royal palaces.

5 Eric Mercer, 'The Decoration of the Royal Palaces, 1553–1625', *Archaeological Journal*, vol. 110, 1954, pp. 150–63.

6 The classic study of the change of ritual and its manifestation in a particular town is Charles Phythian-Adams, 'Ceremony and the Citizen: The Communal Year at Coventry 1450–1550', in P. Clark, ed., *The Early Modern Town: A Reader*, London, 1976, pp. 106–28.

7 H. M. Colvin et al., *The History of the King's Works*, vol. III, *1485–1660* (part 1), London, 1975, pp. 225–333, discusses the royal castles.

8 R. Allen Brown, *English Castles*, 4th edn, London, 1976; Charles Coulson, 'Structural Symbolism in Medieval Castle Architecture', *British Archaeological Association Journal*, vol. 132, 1979, pp. 73–90.

9 John Leland, *The Itinerary of John Leland in or about the Years 1535–1543*, ed. L. Toulmin Smith, London, 1964, vol. I, pp. 73, 98.

10 Ibid., p. 73.

11 More fully on early Tudor changes to castles, see Maurice Howard, *The Early Tudor Country House: Architecture and Politics, 1490–1550*, London, 1987, chap. 3, pp. 43–58.

12 John R. Kenyon, *Raglan Castle*, Cardiff, 1988; Matthew Johnson, *Behind the Castle Gate: From Medieval to Renaissance*, London and New York, 2002.

13 Mark Girouard, *Robert Smythson and the Elizabethan Country House*, New Haven and London, 1983, chap. 6; Lucy Worsley, 'The Architectural Patronage of William Cavendish, first Duke of Newcastle, 1593–1676', unpubd Ph.D. thesis, University of Sussex, 2001.

Chapter 1

1 The dissolution is recorded at *L&P*, XIV (I), 100, 110; for Sharington's purchase, ibid., XV, 942 (110); and for discussion of the continuity of staff, see *VCH Wiltshire*, vol. III, 1956, pp. 314–15.

2 The seminal work on the dissolution remains Joyce Youings, *The Dissolution of the Monasteries*, London, 1971. The issue of tyranny is eloquently discussed by G. W. Bernard, 'The Tyranny of Henry VIII', in G. W. Bernard and S. J. Gunn, eds., *Authority and Consent in Tudor England: Essays presented to C. S. L. Davies*, Aldershot, 2002, pp. 113–30.

3 On Scotland and doctrinal matters, see Diarmaid MacCullough, *Reformation: Europe's House Divided 1490–1700*, Cambridge, 2003, pp. 202–4, 291–5. On the impact on the urban fabric of Scotland, see the relevant passages in Peter Clark, ed., *The Cambridge Urban History of Britain*, vol. II, *1540–1840*, Cambridge, 2000.

4 Christopher Haigh, *English Reformations: Religion, Politics and Society under the Tudors*, Oxford, 1993.

5 On the enactment and the particular circumstances of political decision-making, see R. W. Hoyle, 'The Origins of the Dissolution of the Monasteries', *Historical Journal*, vol. 38, no. 2, 1995, pp. 275–305.

6 On the earlier dissolutions, see David Knowles, *The Religious Orders in England*, vol. III, *The Tudor Age*, rev. edn, Cambridge, 1979, pp. 157–64; and on Wolsey's suppressions in order to found educational establishments, John Newman, 'Cardinal Wolsey's Collegiate Foundations', in S. J. Gunn and P. G. Lindley, eds., *Cardinal Wolsey: Church, State and Art*, Cambridge, 1991,

pp. 103–15. See also Deidre O'Sullivan, 'The "Little Dissolution" of the 1520s', *Post-Medieval Archaeology*, vol. 40, no. 2, 2006, pp. 227–58.

7 Felicity Heal, *Of Prelates and Princes: A Study of the Economic and Social Position of the Tudor Episcopate*, Cambridge, 1980; and on buildings in particular, Phyllis Hembry, 'Episcopal Palaces 1535–1660'; in E. W. Ives, J. J. Scarisbrick and R. J. Knecht, eds., *Wealth and Power in Tudor England: Essays presented to S. T. Bindoff*, London, 1978, pp. 146–66.

8 A. Krieder, *English Chantries: The Road to Dissolution*, Cambridge, Mass., 1979.

9 On the renewed iconoclasm at this point and the propagandistic images that resulted, see Margaret Aston, *The King's Bedpost: Reformation and Iconography in a Tudor Group Portrait*, Cambridge, 1993.

10 See, for example, J. C. Dickinson, 'The Buildings of the English Austin Canons after the Dissolution of the Monasteries', *Journal of the British Archaeological Association*, vol. 31, 1968, pp. 60–75; Nicholas Doggett, *Patterns of Re-Use: The Transformation of Former Monastic Buildings in Post-Dissolution Hertfordshire, 1540–1600*, BAR British Series, no. 331, Oxford, 2002.

11 On these links and continuities between courtyard and cloister, see Maurice Howard, *The Early Tudor Country House: Architecture and Politics, 1490–1550*, London, 1987, chap. 4, 'The Courtyard and the Household', pp. 59–107, and chap. 7, 'The Conversion of the Monasteries', pp. 136–62.

12 H. J. Habbakuk, 'The Market for Monastic Property, 1539–1603', *Economic History Review*, 2nd ser., vol. 10, 1958, pp. 362–80. There are many localised studies, many of them county based, such as T. H. Swales, 'The Redistribution of the Monastic Lands in Norfolk at the Dissolution', *Norfolk Archaeology*, vol. 34, part 1, 1966, pp. 14–43.

13 On the significance of credit, see Craig Muldrew, *The Economy of Obligation: The Culture of Credit and Social Relations in Early Modern England*, Basingstoke, 1998; on Sharington and his offences, C. E. Challis, *The Tudor Coinage*, Manchester, 1978, pp. 100–03.

14 Hoyle, 1995, pp. 290–91.

15 T. Wright, ed., *Three Chapters of Letters relating to the Suppression of the Monasteries*, London, 1843, p. 247.

16 Knowles, 1979, p. 308.

17 G. R. Elton, *The Tudor Constitution: Documents and Commentary*, Cambridge, 1960, p. 378.

18 Muriel St Clare Byrne, ed., *The Lisle Letters: An Abridgement*, London and Chicago, 1983, p. 223.

19 A letter from Sir William Petre on Lacock is at *L&P*, XIV (I), 100; on Titchfield, see *L&P*, XII (2), 1274, 1311 (40).

20 Byrne, ed., 1983, pp. 216–19, 221–3, 293–4, 335–7.

21 J. N. Hare, 'The Buildings of Battle Abbey', *Proceedings of the Battle Conference on Anglo-Norman Studies 1980*, Bury, 1981, pp. 78–95; Hare, *Battle Abbey: The Eastern Range and the Excavations of 1978–80*, HBMC Archaeological Reports, no. 2, 1985; on Battle Church, see Nikolaus Pevsner, with Ian Nairn, *The Buildings of England, Sussex*, Harmondsworth, 1965, pp. 407–8.

22 S. J. Gunn and P. G. Lindley, 'Charles Brandon's Westhorpe: An Early Tudor Courtyard House in Suffolk', *Archaeological Journal*, vol. 145, 1988, pp. 272–89.

23 Paul Everson and David Stocker, 'The Archaeology of Vice-Regality: Charles Brandon's Brief Rule in Lincolnshire', in David Gaimster and Roberta Gilchrist, eds., *The Archaeology of Reformation, 1480–1580*, Leeds, 2003, pp. 145–58.

24 H. M. Colvin et al., *The History of the King's Works*, vol. IV, *1485–1660* (part 2), London, 1982, pp. 355–7.

25 Habbakuk, 1958, p. 380.

26 National Archives, SP, 1/127, 109–10; the otherwise excellent article by W. H. St John Hope, 'The Making of Place House at Titchfield, near Southampton, in 1538', *Archaeological Journal*, vol. 63, 1906b, pp. 231–43, omits this part of the correspondence on Titchfield.

27 Colvin et al., 1982, pp. 59–63.

28 Ibid., pp. 234–7.

29 Ibid., pp. 68–74.

30 BL, Egerton MS, 2815.

31 For speculation on the footprint of the abbey church, see Jonathan Foyle, 'Syon Park: Rediscovering Medieval England's Only Bridgettine Monastery', *Current Archaeology*, no. 192, June 2004, pp. 550–55. On Somerset House, see John Stow, *A Survey of London* (1598), ed. with introduction and notes by C. L. Kingsford as *A Survey of London by John Stow, reprinted from the Text of 1603*, 3 vols, Oxford, 1908, vol. I, pp. 87–8; N. Pevsner, 'Old Somerset House', *Architectural Review*, vol. 116, 1954, pp. 163–7; Caroline Knight, 'Old Somerset House', *British Art Journal*, vol. 2, no. 2, 2000–2001, pp. 6–13.

32 S. Haynes, 'Interrogatories to be mynistred unto Sir W S towchynge the Coynage within the Mynte at Bristow', *A Collection of State Papers*, London, 1740, pp. 65–7.

33 Hope, 1906b, pp. 231–43.

34 Eamon Duffy, *The Stripping of the Altars: Traditional Religion in England 1400–1580*, New Haven and London, 1992, pp. 383–5.

35 Shirley Corke and Rob Poulton, 'The Historical Evidence *c.* 1275 to 1818', in Rob Poulton and Humphrey Woods, *Excavations on the Site of the Dominican Friary at Guildford in 1974 and 1976*, Surrey Archaeological Society Research, vol. 9, 1984, pp. 5–16.

36 On the Lincolnshire rising and its impact on the remaining large monasteries, see Knowles, 1979, pp. 322–35. On the establishment of royal supporters on monastic sites, Andrew White, *Sempringham Priory*, Lincolnshire Museums Information Series, no. 17, Lincoln, 1979; Everson and Stocker, 2003, pp. 145–58. On the city itself in the rising and its aftermath, J. W. F. Hill, *Tudor and Stuart Lincoln*, Cambridge, 1956, chap. 3, 'Religion and Social Change', pp. 40–68.

37 The full correspondence between Cromwell and Portinari is reproduced in W. H. St John Hope, 'The Cluniac Priory of St Pancras at Lewes', *Sussex Archaeological Collections*, vol. 49, 1906a, pp. 66–88.

38 Jamieson B. Hurry, *Reading Abbey*, London, 1901, chap. 9; Arthur E. Preston, 'The Demolition of Reading Abbey', *Berkshire Archaeological Journal*, vol. 39, no. 2, 1935, pp. 107–44; D. Sherlock, 'The Account of George Nycholl for St Augustine's, 1552–1553', *Archaeologia Cantiana*, vol. 99, 1983, pp. 25–44; Harold Brakspear, 'Stanley Abbey', *Archaeologia*, vol. 60, 1907, pp. 493–516; Brakspear, 'Excavations of Wiltshire Monasteries', *Archaeologia*, vol. 73, 1923, pp. 225–52.

39 Richard K. Morris, 'Monastic Architecture: Destruction and Reconstruction', in Gaimster and Gilchrist, eds., 2003, pp. 235–51; Warwick Rodwell, *Wells Cathedral: Excavations and Structural Studies 1978–93*, English Heritage Archaeological Report, no. 21, London, 2001, pp. 241–4.

40 Morris, 2003, p. 240.

41 Donald Woodward, ' "Swords into Ploughshares": Recycling in Pre-Industrial England', *Economic History Review*, 2nd ser., vol. 38, no. 2, 1985, pp. 175–91; David Stocker, with Paul Everson, 'Rubbish Recycled: A Study of the Re-Use of Stone in Lincolnshire', in David Parsons, ed., *Stone Quarrying and Building in England AD 43–1525*, Chichester, 1990, pp. 83–101.

42 Hare, 1985; *VCH Cheshire*, vol. III, 1980, pp. 161–5; R. McNeil and R. C. Turner, 'An Archi-

tectural and Topographical Survey of Vale Royal Abbey', *Journal of the Chester Archaeological and Historical Society*, vol. 70 (1987–8), 1990, pp. 51–79.

43 Preston, 1935, pp. 139–40. See also Brian Kemp, *Reading Abbey: An Introduction to the History of the Abbey*, Reading, 1968; Jeanette Martin, 'Leadership and Priorities in Reading during the Reformation', in Patrick Collinson and John Craig, eds., *The Reformation in English Towns 1500–1640*, Basingstoke and New York, 1998, pp. 113–29; and the biography of Thomas Vachell I, overseer of Reading's former lands, in *HPC 1509–58*, vol. III, 1982.

44 Colvin et al., 1982, pp. 472–6, 569–87.

45 Woodward, 1985, p. 181.

46 Colvin et al., 1982, p. 137.

47 Howard, 1987, p. 142.

48 P. G. Lindley, 'Structure, Sequence and Status: The Architectural History of Gainsborough Old Hall to c. 1600', in Phillip Lindley, ed., *Gainsborough Old Hall*, Occasional Papers in Lincolnshire History and Archaeology, no. 8, Lincoln, 1991, pp. 21–6.

49 R. Mitchell, ed., *Hinchingbrooke Documents 1530–1840*, Huntingdon, 1972; P. G. M. Dickinson, *Hinchingbrooke House*, Huntingdon, 1972.

50 Stow, ed. Kingsford, 1908, vol. I, pp. 176–7.

51 For Nedeham's work at Dartford, see Colvin et al., 1982, pp. 68–74.

52 Colvin et al., 1982, pp. 1–39; on bishops' palaces, see Hembry, 1978, pp. 146–66.

53 Colvin et al., 1982, pp. 47–8; *VCH Hertfordshire*, vol. II, 1908, p. 209.

54 Foyle, 2004.

55 Colvin et al., 1982, p. 73.

56 Ibid., p. 62.

57 Ibid., pp. 236–7.

58 Ibid., p. 48.

59 Ibid., p. 63.

60 Ibid., p. 74.

61 Ibid., p. 240.

62 Ibid., pp. 355–64; Christopher Norton, 'The Buildings of St Mary's Abbey, York and their Destruction', *Antiquaries Journal*, vol. 74, 1994, pp. 256–88.

63 Colvin et al., 1982, p. 74.

64 Hurry, 1901; Martin, 1998.

65 Robert S. Gottfried, *Bury St Edmunds and the Urban Crisis 1290–1539*, Princeton, 1982, pp. 236–53.

66 Barney Sloane, 'Tenements in London's Monasteries c. 1450–1540', in Gaimster and Gilchrist,

eds., 2003, pp. 290–98; John Schofield, 'Some Aspects of the Reformation of Religious Space in London, 1540–1660', ibid., pp. 310–24.

67 Morris, 2003, p. 238.

68 D. A. Stocker, 'The Archaeology of the Reformation in Lincoln: A Case Study in the Redistribution of Building Materials in the Mid Sixteenth Century', *Lincolnshire History and Archaeology*, vol. 25, 1990, pp. 18–32.

69 On the case of Dorchester-on-Thames, see Nicholas Doggett, 'The Dissolution and After: Dorchester Abbey, 1536–c. 1800', in Kate Tiller, ed., *Dorchester Abbey: Church and People 635–2005*, Witney, 2005, pp. 39–48.

70 Simon P. Ward, 'Dissolution or Reformation?: A Case Study from Chester's Urban Landscape', in Gaimster and Gilchrist, eds., 2003, pp. 267–79.

71 Eileen Roberts, *The Hill of the Martyr: An Architectural History of St Alban's Abbey*, Dunstable, 1993, summarises the public use of the monastic remains after the dissolution.

72 Woodward, 1985, p. 182.

73 The correspondence between Dr London and Cromwell is published in Wright, ed., 1843, pp. 221–9; on Reading after the Reformation, see Martin, 1998, and Maurice Howard, 'Recycling the Monastic Fabric: Beyond the Act of Dissolution', in Gaimster and Gilchrist, eds., 2003, pp. 221–34.

74 Woodward, 1985, p. 182.

75 Leland, ed. Toulmin-Smith, vol. 1, p. 132.

76 Stow, ed. Kingsford, 1908, vol. I, p. 171.

77 R. B. Harbottle and R. Fraser, 'Black Friars, Newcastle-upon-Tyne, after the Dissolution of the Monasteries', *Archaeologia Aeliana*, 5th ser., vol. 15, 1987, pp. 23–150.

78 John Schofield, *The Building of London from the Conquest to the Great Fire*, 2nd edn, London, 1993, pp. 145–9; John Schofield and Richard Lea, *Holy Trinity Priory, Aldgate, City of London: An Archaeological Reconstruction and History*, MOLAS, no. 24, London 2005, pp. 18–26.

79 Simon Ward, 'The Friaries in Chester: Their Impact and Legacy', in Alan Thacker, ed., *Medieval Archaeology: Art and Architecture at Chester*, Transactions of the British Archaeological Association Conference, vol. 22, London, 2000, pp. 121–31; *VCH Cheshire*, vol. V, part 2, 2005, pp. 244–5.

80 Schofield, 2003, pp. 310–24.

81 Roberts, 1993.

82 Paul Meyvaert, 'The Medieval Monastic Claustrum', *Gesta*, vol. 12, 1973, pp. 53–9; on the fundamental problems of adaptation, Howard, 1987, chap. 7.

83 For a plan of Titchfield, see Howard, 1987, p. 153. On galleries around gardens, see Howard, 1987, pp. 116–18; Rosalys Coope, 'The "Long Gallery": Its Origins, Development, Use and Decoration', *Architectural History*, vol. 29, 1986, pp. 43–72; Paula Henderson, *The Tudor House and Garden: Architecture and Landscape in the Sixteenth and Early Seventeenth Centuries*, New Haven and London, 2005, pp. 153–5.

84 On the construction of Hengrave, see Malcolm Airs, 'The Designing of Five East Anglian Country Houses, 1505–1637', *Architectural History*, vol. 21, 1978, pp. 58–67; Howard, 1987, pp. 90–92.

85 The most significant of the early commentaries on the conversion of Lacock are C. H. Talbot, 'Lacock Abbey: Notes on the Architectural History of the Building', *Journal of the British Archaeological Association*, new ser., vol. 11, 1905, pp. 175–210, and W. G. Clark-Maxwell, 'Sir William Sharington's Work at Lacock, Sudeley and Dudley', *Archaeological Journal*, vol. 70, 1913, pp. 175–82. On the cloister conversion in context, see Howard, 1987, pp. 152–62, with a plan of the transformation on p. 160.

86 For brief reports on Sopwell while archaeology was under way, see *Medieval Archaeology*, vol. 8, 1964, p. 242; vol. 9, 1965, p. 179; vol. 10, 1966, pp. 177–80; vol. 11, 1967, p. 274; see also Colin Platt, *Medieval England*, London, 1978, pp. 216–17. For a full account, see Doggett, 2002, pp. 187–98.

87 *RCHM Dorset*, vol. I, *West Dorset*, 1952, pp. 240–46.

88 An article on post-Reformation Newstead by Rosalys Coope is to be published in the *Thoroton Society Transactions*, forthcoming.

89 On Vale Royal, see n. 42 above.

90 The most useful discussion of the extended façade, incorporating all these houses, is that in Nicholas Cooper, *Houses of the Gentry, 1480–1680*, New Haven and London, 1999, pp. 74–93. On Parham, see Jayne Kirk, *Parham: An Elizabethan House and its Restoration*, forthcoming.

91 Paula Henderson, 'The Loggia in Tudor and Early Stuart England: The Adaptation and Function of Classical Form', in Lucy Gent, ed., *Albion's Classicism: The Visual Arts in Britain, 1550–1660*, New Haven and London, 1995, pp. 109–46.

92 Coope, forthcoming, on Newstead; on Vale Royal, see n. 42 above; J. Patrick Greene, 'The Impact of the Dissolution on Monasteries in Cheshire: The Case of Norton', in Thacker, ed., 2000, pp. 152–69, with Samuel and Nathaniel Buck's 1727 view of the 16th-century arrangement of steps up to the porch at pl. XXXII B.

93 On Chicksands, see *VCH Bedfordshire*, vol. II, 1908, pp. 271–5; S. Houfe, 'The Builders of Chicksands Priory', *Bedfordshire Magazine*, vol. 16, 1978, no. 125, pp. 185–9, no. 126, 228–31.

94 Dianne Duggan, 'Woburn Abbey: The First Episode of a Great Country House', *Architectural History*, vol. 46, 2003, pp. 57–80.

95 Maurice Howard and Edward Wilson, *The Vyne: A Tudor House Revealed*, London, 2003, pp. 97–8, 129–30.

96 On Battle, see note 21 above.

97 These are the conclusions found in Doggett, 2002, pp. 65–71.

98 G. W. Copeland, 'Some Problems of Buckland Abbey', *Transactions of the Devonshire Association*, vol. 85, 1953, pp. 41–52; Joyce Youings, 'Drake, Grenville and Buckland Abbey', *Transactions of the Devonshire Association*, vol. 112, 1980, pp. 95–9; *Buckland Abbey*, National Trust, 1991. On Netley, see John Hare, 'Netley Abbey: Monastery, Mansion and Ruin', *Proceedings of the Hampshire Field Club Archaeological Society*, vol. 49, 1993, pp. 207–27. On Worksop, Mark Girouard, *Robert Smythson and the Elizabethan Country House*, New Haven and London, 1983, pp. 131–4.

99 On Forde, see n. 87 above.

100 The survey of the Pembroke lands is published in Charles R. Straton, ed., *Survey of the Lands of William, 1st Earl of Pembroke*, 2 vols, Oxford, 1909; the sketch of Shaftesbury Abbey is in vol. II, p. 487. See also *RCHM Dorset*, vol. IV, *North Dorset*, pp. 57–61; F. C. Hopton, 'The Buildings of Shaftesbury Abbey in the Mid-Sixteenth Century', *Proceedings of the Dorset Natural History and Archaeological Society*, vol. 115, 1993, pp. 1–13.

101 Henderson, 2005, pp. 5–7.

102 An early example of this is the pre-1605 depiction of Audley End, formerly the Abbey of Walden. See P. J. Drury, 'No other palace in the kingdom will compare with it: The Evolution of Audley End, 1605–1745', *Architectural History*, vol. 23, 1980, pp. 1–39, pl. 1.

103 Stephen Porter, *Destruction in the English Civil Wars*, Stroud, 1994.

Chapter 2

1 W. G. Hoskins, 'The Rebuilding of Rural England, 1570–1640', *Past and Present*, no. 4, 1953, pp. 44–59.

2 R. Machin, 'The Great Rebuilding: A Reassessment', *Past and Present*, no. 77, 1977, pp. 33–56; Colin Platt, *The Great Rebuildings of Tudor and Stuart England*, London, 1994.

3 In the huge literature on this issue, see in particular G. R. Elton, *Policy and Police: The Enforcement of the Reformation in the Age of Thomas Cromwell*, Cambridge, 1972; and Steve Hindle, *The State and Social Change in Early Modern England, 1550–1640*, Basingstoke and New York, 2000. These books span the overall period and also introduce the idea of government as enforcer.

4 Paul Slack, *Poverty and Policy in Tudor and Stuart England*, London and New York, 1988, pp. 122–37, charts both the ideological background for new attitudes to the poor and the narrative of poor law legislation.

5 On the comparison of English cities with European counterparts, see Christopher R. Friedrichs, *The Early Modern City 1450–1750*, London and New York 1995; and Peter Clark, ed., *The Cambridge Urban History of Britain*, vol. II, 1540–1840, Cambridge, 2000. With useful European comparisons, Paul Courtney, 'Armies, Militias and the Urban Landscape: England, France and the Low Countries 1500–1900', in Adrian Green and Roger Leech, eds., *Cities in the World 1500–2000*, Leeds, 2006, pp. 167–93. See also D. M. Palliser, 'Town Defences in Medieval England and Wales', in A. Ayton and J. C. Price, eds., *The Medieval Military Revolution*, New York, 1995, pp. 105–20.

6 Sheila Collier, with Sarah Pearson, *Whitehaven 1660–1800. A New Town of the Late Seventeenth Century: A Study of its Buildings and Urban Development*, HMSO, London, 1991, pp. 2–3.

7 Dianne Duggan, '"London The Ring, Covent Garden The Jewel of That Ring": New Light on Covent Garden', *Architectural History*, vol. 43, 2000, pp. 140–61.

8 J. H. Bettey, 'The Dissolution and After at Cerne Abbas', in Katherine Barker, ed., *The Cerne Abbey Millennium Lectures*, Cerne Abbas, 1988, pp. 43–52.

9 Penelope Corfield, 'Urban Development in England and Wales in the Sixteenth and Seventeenth Centuries', in Jonathan Barry, ed., *The Tudor and Stuart Town: A Reader in English Urban History*, London and New York, 1990, pp. 35–62, with the editor's introduction to that volume, pp. 1–34; Alan D. Dyer, *Decline and Growth in English Towns 1400–1640*, London, 1991, 3rd edn, Cambridge, 1995. On the material evidence of decline, see Grenville Astill, 'Archae-

ology and the Late-Medieval Urban Decline', in T. R. Slater, ed., *Towns in Decline, AD 100–1600*, Aldershot, 2000, pp. 214–29. On a further useful study of a particular place, with reference to buildings, S. H. Rigby, '"Sore Decay" and "Fair Dwellings": Boston and Urban Decline in the Later Middle Ages', *Midland History*, vol. 10, 1985, pp. 47–61.

10 Richard Hooker, *Of the Laws of Ecclesiastical Polity*, with an introduction by Christopher Morris, London, 1907. On Hooker, see J. G. Davies, *The Secular Use of Church Buildings*, London, 1968, pp. 101–2. The standard edition of Hooker's works is W. Speed Hill, general editor, 6 vols, Cambridge, Mass., London and New York, 1977–93.

11 Robert Tittler, 'The Incorporation of Boroughs, 1540–1558', *History*, vol. 62, 1977, pp. 24–42; Joyce Youings, 'Tudor Barnstaple: New Life for an Ancient Borough', *Transactions of the Devonshire Association*, vol. 121, 1989, pp. 1–14.

12 Gideon Sjoberg, 'The Nature of the Pre-Industrial City', in Peter Clark, ed., *The Early Modern Town: A Reader*, London, 1976, pp. 43–52; for a counter to this, see Alexander Cowan, *Urban Europe, 1500–1700*, London, 1998, p. 130.

13 Robert Tittler, '"For the Re-edification of Townes": The Rebuilding Statutes of Henry VIII', *Albion*, vol. 22, no. 4, 1990, pp. 591–605.

14 Lena Cowen Orlin, 'Boundary Disputes in Early Modern London', in Orlin, ed., *Material London, ca. 1600*, Philadelphia, 2000, pp. 344–76; John Schofield, 'Some Aspects of the Reformation of Religious Space in London, 1540–1660', in David Gaimster and Roberta Gilchrist, eds., *The Archaeology of Reformation, 1480–1580*, Leeds, 2003, pp. 310–24.

15 Patricia Seed emphasises the differences in establishing possession of land between England and rival colonial powers in *Ceremonies of Possession in Europe's Conquest of the New World, 1492–1640*, Cambridge, 1996, chap. 1, 'Houses, Gardens and Fences', pp. 16–40.

16 For a particularly useful discussion of community, see Alexandra Shepard and Phil Withington, eds., *Communities in Early Modern England*, Manchester and New York, 2000, introduction, pp. 1–15.

17 Tittler, 1990.

18 N. B. Harte, 'State Control of Dress and Social Change in Pre-Industrial England', in D. C. Coleman and A. H. John, eds., *Trade, Government and Economy in Pre-Industrial England: Essays presented to F. J. Fisher*, London, 1976, pp.

132–65; A. Hunt, *Governance of the Consuming Passions: A History of Sumptuary Law*, London, 1996, p. 142.

19 Frances R. James, 'Copy of a Deed by Richard Phelips, dated 1535', *Transactions of the Woolhope Naturalists' Field Club for 1934–36*, 1938, pp. 100–04.

20 John Onians, *Bearers of Meaning: The Classical Orders in Antiquity, the Middle Ages, and the Renaissance*, Princeton, 1988, chap. 7, 'The Orders in the Christian Middle Ages', pp. 91–111.

21 Carlson, Leland H., ed., *Elizabethan Nonconformist Texts*, vol. III, *The Writings of Henry Barrow, 1587–90*, London, 1962, pp. 259–672.

22 *The Journal of George Fox edited from the MSS by Norman Penney*, with an introduction by T. Edmund Harvey, Cambridge, 1911.

23 On the English Catholics, see John Bossy, *The English Catholic Community, 1570–1850*, London, 1975; and A. Morey, *The Catholic Subjects of Elizabeth I*, London, 1978.

24 Morey, 1978, pp. 148–9.

25 Lisa McClain, 'Without Church, Cathedral or Shrine: The Search for Religious Space among Catholics in England, 1559–1625', *Sixteenth-Century Journal*, vol. 33, no. 2, 2002, pp. 381–99.

26 Parmiter, Geoffrey de C., 'The Imprisonment of Papists in Private Castles', *Recusant History*, vol. 19, no. 1, 1988, pp. 16–38.

27 *Second Book of Homilies*, as quoted in Davies, 1968, p. 100.

28 Davies, 1968, chap. 6, 'Secular Activities in Post-Reformation Churches', pp. 155–204.

29 Stanford E. Lehmberg, *The Reformation of Cathedrals: Cathedrals in English Society, 1485–1603*, Princeton, 1988; Gerald Cobb, *English Cathedrals. The Forgotten Centuries: Restoration and Change from 1530 to the Present Day*, London, 1980.

30 Gordon Higgott, 'The Fabric to 1670', in Derek Keene, Arthur Burns and Andrew Saint, eds., *St Paul's: The Cathedral Church of London 604–2004*, New Haven and London, 2004, pp. 171–90. Inigo Jones's work on the fabric has also been discussed and contextualised by Christy Anderson, *Inigo Jones and the Classical Tradition*, Cambridge and New York, 2007, pp. 183–96.

31 John Phillips, *The Reformation of Images: Destruction of Art in England, 1535–1660*, Berkeley, Los Angeles and London, 1973, chap. 4, 'Images Attacked', pp. 82–100.

32 This point is raised in Clark, ed., 2000, p. 274; on the late medieval neglect of public buildings, see Kate Giles, 'Public Space in Town and Village 1100–1500', in Giles and Christopher Dyer, eds., *Town and Country in the Middle Ages: Contrasts, Contacts and Interconnections, 1100–1500*, Society for Medieval Archaeology, Leeds, 2005, pp. 293–311. On town halls after the Reformation, Robert Tittler, *Architecture and Power: The Town Hall and the English Urban Community, c. 1500–1640*, Oxford, 1991.

33 Davies, 1968, chap. 6, 'Secular Activities in Post-Reformation Churches', pp. 155–204.

34 On the small sums given for church building, see W. K. Jordan, *Philanthropy in England, 1480–1660: A Study of the Changing Pattern of Social Aspirations*, London, 1959, pp. 314–21.

35 Steven Hobbs, 'Piety and Church Fabric in Sixteenth-Century Wiltshire: Evidence from Wills', *Wiltshire Studies: The Wiltshire Archaeological and Natural History Magazine*, vol. 98, 2005, pp. 81–9.

36 John Sayer, 'Charing Church', *Archaeologia Cantiana*, vol. 16, 1888, pp. 263–4.

37 Nigel Llewellyn, *Funeral Monuments in Post-Reformation England*, Cambridge, 2000, chap. 3, 'Building Monuments', pp. 146–216.

38 Hobbs, 2005, pp. 87, 88.

39 J. Charles Cox, *Churchwardens' Accounts from the Fourteenth Century to the Close of the Seventeenth Century*, London, 1913, p. 84.

40 G. W. O. Addleshaw and Frederick Etchells, *The Architectural Setting of Anglican Worship*, London, 1948, pp. 26–7.

41 Ibid., p. 31.

42 *VCH Berkshire*, vol. III, 1923, pp. 88–9.

43 Malcolm Airs, 'Lawrence Shipway, Freemason', *Architectural History*, vol. 27, 1984, pp. 368–75.

44 *VCH Rutland*, vol. II, 1935, pp. 37–40; Jack Simmons, 'Brooke Church, Rutland, with Notes on Elizabethan Church-Building', *Transactions of the Leicestershire Archaeological and Historical Society*, vol. 25, 1959, pp. 36–55.

45 *VCH Bedfordshire*, vol. III, repr. 1972, pp. 386–9.

46 Lawrence Butler, 'Leicester's Church, Denbigh: An Experiment in Puritan Worship', *Journal of the British Archaeological Association*, vol. 37, 1974, pp. 40–62.

47 Bruce Watson, 'Excavations and Observations on the Site of the Dutch Church, Austin Friars, in the City of London', *Transactions of the London and Middlesex Archaeological Society*, vol. 45, 1994, pp. 13–22.

48 H. F. Chettle, 'The Trinitarian Friars and Easton Royal', *Wiltshire Archaeological Magazine*, vol. 51, 1946, pp. 365–77; H. Bashford, 'Present and Past Churches at Easton Royal', *Wiltshire Archaeological Magazine*, vol. 56, 1955, pp. 66–7.

49 Nicholas Cooper, *Houses of the Gentry, 1480–1680*, New Haven and London, 1999, p. 88.

50 On John Jewel see the *ODNB*; see also Thomas Cocke and Peter Kidson, *Salisbury Cathedral: Perspectives on the Architectural History*, London, 1993, p. 17. Jewel was also responsible for instigating repairs around the close to the canons' houses and the walls; see *RCHM Salisbury: The Houses of the Close*, London, 1993, pp. 24, 40.

51 The presence of the woman leading the child into the church is discussed in John N. King, 'The Godly Woman in Elizabethan Iconography', *Renaissance Quarterly*, vol. 38, 1985, p. 47.

52 Howard Colvin, *Architecture and the After-Life*, New Haven and London, 1991, pp. 253–70.

53 On the broad issue of Gothic survival and revival of Gothic, see E. S. de Beer, 'Gothic: Origin and Diffusion of the Term: The Idea of Style in Architecture', *Journal of the Warburg and Courtauld Institutes*, vol. 11, 1948, pp. 143–62, and Peter Frankl, *The Gothic: Literary Sources and Interpretations through Eight Centuries*, Princeton, 1960. On England in the century after the Reformation, see Mark Girouard, 'Elizabethan Architecture and the Gothic Tradition', *Architectural History*, vol. 6, 1963, pp. 23–38; Thomas Cocke, 'The Wheel of Fortune: The Appreciation of Gothic since the Middle Ages', in Jonathan Alexander and Paul Binski, eds., *The Age of Chivalry: Art in Plantagenet England, 1200–1400*, London, 1987, pp. 183–91; Chris Brooks, *The Gothic Revival*, London, 1999; Howard Colvin, 'Gothic Survival and Gothick Revival', *Essays in English Architectural History*, New Haven and London, 1999, pp. 217–44; Maurice Howard, 'The Historiography of "Elizabethan Gothic"', in Michael Hall, ed., *Gothic Architecture and its Meanings, 1550–1830*, Reading, 2002, pp. 53–72.

54 I am especially indebted to the paper given by Thomas Cocke at a conference held at the Centre for Continuing Education, University of Oxford, May 2006.

55 On the view of Republicanism and Gothic, particularly its discussion in the Civil War, see Brooks, 1999, pp. 38–46.

56 S. E. Rigold, 'Two Types of Court Hall', *Archaeologia Cantiana*, vol. 83, 1968, pp. 1–22; Tittler, 1991, pp. 25–33. Also useful in this context is Giles, 2005, pp. 293–311.

57 Tittler, 1991, pp. 11, 160–68.

58 Nikolaus Pevsner, *The Buildings of England: Herefordshire*, Harmondsworth, 1963, p. 180; Norman Drinkwater, 'Hereford: Old Market Hall', *Transactions of the Woolhope Naturalists' Field Club*, vol. 33, 1949–51, pp. 1–13. On John Abel, its master carpenter, see D. L. Gregory, *John Abel of Sarnesfield*, London, 1980, and the *ODNB*; I am also indebted to the research of Gwyneth Guy, especially that presented at a conference held at the Centre for Continuing Education, University of Oxford, May 2006.

59 *VCH Leicestershire*, vol. V, 1964, pp. 137, 148.

60 On Tresham's buildings and their financing, see J. Alfred Gotch, *A Complete Account, Illustrated by Measured Drawings of the Buildings erected in Northamptonshire, by Sir Thomas Tresham, between the Years 1575 and 1605*, Northampton and London, 1883; M. E. Finch, *The Wealth of Five Northamptonshire Families, 1540–1640*, Northamptonshire Record Society, vol. 19, Oxford, 1956, pp. 66–99, 179–89; Felicity Heal and Clive Holmes, *The Gentry in England and Wales, 1500–1700*, Basingstoke, 1994, pp. 136–42; Malcolm Airs, *The Tudor and Jacobean Country House: A Building History*, Stroud, 1995, *passim*.

61 Robert Tittler, *Townspeople and Nation: English Urban Experiences, 1540–1640*, Stanford, 2001, pp. 60–80.

62 I am grateful to Sylvia Pinches for information on Ledbury. On the metaphorical aspects of the inscription at Leominster, see John Onians, 'Architecture, Metaphor and Mind', *Architectural History*, vol. 35, 1992, pp. 204–5; Maurice Howard, 'Classicism and Civic Architecture in Renaissance England', in Lucy Gent, ed., *Albion's Classicism: The Visual Arts in Britain, 1550–1660*, New Haven and London, 1995, pp. 29–49.

63 S. R. Blaylock, 'Exeter Guildhall', *Devon Archaeological Society Proceedings*, vol. 48, 1992, pp. 123–78. For a broad picture of Exeter's history at this period, see Wallace T. McCaffrey, *Exeter 1540–1640: The Growth of an English County Town*, Cambridge, Mass., 1958.

64 John Leland, *The Itinerary of John Leland in or about the Years 1535–1543*, ed. L. Toulmin Smith, with a foreword by Thomas Kendrick, 5 vols, London, 1964, vol. 1, p. 259.

65 Pen and wash drawings by Grose in the Salisbury and South Wiltshire Museum are reproduced in *VCH Wiltshire*, vol. VI, 1962, opposite p. 86, and Howard, 1995, p. 37.

66 Elizabeth Holland, 'The Earliest Bath Guildhall', *Bath History*, vol. 2, 1988, pp. 163–79; Jean Monco 'Bath and the "Great Rebuilding"' *Bath*

History IV 1992, see especially pp. 42–3; Michael Bishop, 'Bath's Second Guildhall, c. 1630–1776', *Bath History*, vol. 10, 2005, pp. 48–71.

67 Victor Morgan, 'The Elizabethan Shire House at Norwich', in Carole Rawcliffe, Roger Virgoe and Richard Wilson, eds., *Essays on East Anglian History presented to Hassell Smith*, Norwich, 1996, pp. 149–60.

68 J. Townsend, *A History of Abingdon*, London, 1910; R. Gilyard-Beer, *The County Hall, Abingdon*, HMSO, London, 1956; Nikolaus Pevsner, *The Buildings of England: Berkshire*, Harmondsworth, 1966, p. 56 where it is referred to as the 'town hall'. On the development of co-ordinated planning of later seventeenth-century public buildings that gave towns a sense of identity as places of cultural resort, see Peter Borsay, *The English Urban Renaissance: Culture and Society in the Provincial Town, 1660–1760*, Oxford, 1989.

69 On schools, see Joan Simon, *Education and Society in Tudor England*, Cambridge, 1967; on those of the Tudor period, Nicholas Orme, *English Schools in the Middle Ages*, London, 1973, pp. 252–89; on the buildings, Malcolm Seaborne, *The English School: Its Architecture and Organisation, 1370–1870*, London, 1971.

70 Orme, 1973, p. 254.

71 Simon, 1967, p. 303; Orme, 1973, pp. 286–7.

72 Orme, 1973, p. 259.

73 Ibid., pp. 272–83.

74 Lehmberg, 1988, pp. 297–301.

75 *VCH Surrey*, vol. II, 1905, pp. 155–62.

76 On problems of finance and malpractice over trusteeship of new Elizabethan foundations, see Jay P. Anglin, 'Frustrated Ideals: The Case of Elizabethan Grammar School Foundations', *History of Education*, vol. 11, no. 4, 1982, pp. 267–79.

77 *VCH Huntingdon*, vol. II, 1932, pp. 111–13.

78 Catherine F. Patterson, 'Leicester and Lord Huntingdon: Urban Patronage in Early Modern England', *Midland History*, vol. 16, 1991, pp. 45–62.

79 Simon, 1967, pp. 312–13.

80 On Shrewsbury School, see *VCH Shropshire*, vol. II, 1973, pp. 154–8; see also J. B. Oldham, 'A Sixteenth Century Shrewsbury School Inventory', *Transactions of the Shropshire Archaeology and Natural History Society*, vol. 47, 1933–4, pp. 121–37. On Ashbourne, *VCH Derbyshire*, vol. II, 1907, pp. 254–60; on Uppingham and Oakham, *VCH Rutland*, vol. I, 1908, pp. 261–8.

81 Erasmus, cited in N. Carlisle, *A Concise Description of the Endowed Grammar Schools of England and Wales*, 2 vols, London, 1818, vol. II, p. 82. For the plan of Guildford School, see Seaborne, 1971, p. 19.

82 Nicholas Orme, conference paper, 2003, 'English Schools 1400–1550', given at the conference *Biographies and Space: Placing the Subject in Art and Architecture*, Paul Mellon Centre, London, March 2003.

83 *VCH Hertfordshire*, vol. II, 1908, pp. 71–9. For the plan of Berkhamstead, see Seaborne, 1971, p. 15.

84 Richard Mulcaster, *Positions...*, London, 1581, p. 229.

85 Key works for this section on almshouses and hospitals are W. H. Godfrey, *The English Almshouse*, London, 1955; Rotha Mary Clay, *The Medieval Hospitals of England*, London, 1966; Elizabeth Prescott, *The English Medieval Hospital, 1050–1640*, Seaby, 1992; Nicholas Orme and Margaret Webster, *The English Hospital, 1070–1570*, New Haven and London, 1995.

86 Jordan, 1959; W. K. Jordan, *The Charities of Rural England*, London, 1961.

87 Slack, 1988, chap. 6, 'The Making of the Poor Law 1485–1610', pp. 113–37.

88 *VCH Berkshire*, vol. III, 1923, p. 93.

89 Slack, 1988, p. 38.

90 On witchcraft, see Keith Thomas, *Religion and the Decline of Magic: Studies in Popular Beliefs in Sixteenth- and Seventeenth-Century England*, London, 1971; on local accusation, James Sharpe, *Instruments of Darkness: Witchcraft in England, 1550–1750*, Harmondsworth, 1997, chap. 6, 'Accusations, Counter-Measures and the Local Community', pp. 148–68.

91 Prescott, 1992, p. 165.

92 Ibid., p. 170.

93 Heal and Holmes, 1994, p. 372.

94 On the Act of 1598, see Slack, 1988, p. 127.

95 Godfrey, 1955, pp. 28–9, 50–51. On Norwich, see F. W. Bennett-Symonds, 'The Hospital of St Giles, Norwich', *Journal of the British Archaeological Association*, new ser., vol. 5, 1925, pp. 55–67. On the hospital at Warwick, S. A. Pears, 'Leycester's Hospital', *Transactions of the Ancient Monuments Society*, new ser., vol. 13, 1966, pp. 35–41, and *VCH Warwickshire*, vol. VIII, 1969, pp. 423–6.

96 Godfrey, 1955, pp. 45–7.

97 Ibid., pp. 59–60, 54–7, 61–2, 47. Further on Abbot's Hospital, see J. W. Penycate, *A Guide to the Hospital of the Blessed Trinity (Abbot's Hospital), Guildford*, Guildford, 1976. On Whitgift's,

VCH Surrey, vol. IV, 1912, repr. 1967, pp. 213–15. On Ford's Hospital, J. Cleary and M. Orton, *So Long as the World Shall Endure: The Five Hundred Year History of Ford's and Bond's Hospitals*, Coventry, 1991.

98 Pauline Fenley, 'Charity and Status: The Activities of Sir John Kederminster at Langley Marish, Buckinghamshire (now Langley, Slough)', *Records of Buckinghamshire*, vol. 42, 2002, pp. 119–32.

99 Godfrey, 1955, p. 61; *VCH Berkshire*, vol. III, 1912, pp. 93, 111.

100 Prescott, 1992, pp. 88–9.

101 Ibid., p. 91.

102 Slack, 1988, p. 164.

103 Prescott, 1992, pp. 75–6.

Chapter 3

1 Juliet Fleming, *Graffiti and the Writing Arts of Early Modern England*, London, 2001.

2 This equation of language with shapes and the delight it was meant to inspire is discussed in Mark Girouard, *Robert Smythson and the Elizabethan Country House*, New Haven and London, 1983, pp. 21–8.

3 Nicholas Hilliard, *The Arte of Limninge* (*c*. 1600), ed. R. K. R. Thornton and T. G. S. Cain, Manchester, 1992.

4 Barbara Mowat, '"Knowing I loved my books": Reading *The Tempest* Intertextually', in Peter Hulme and William A. Sherman, eds., *The Tempest and its Travels*, London, 2000, pp. 27–36.

5 On basic changes in portraiture raised here, see Maurice Howard, *The Tudor Image*, London, 1995. On the specific point about the gateways of Smythson and Jones, Christy Anderson, *Inigo Jones and the Classical Tradition*, Cambridge and New York, 2007, pp. 125–7.

6 The standard accounts of fortification are those by J. R. Hale and John Summerson in Howard Colvin et al., *The History of the King's Works*, vol. IV, *1485–1660* (part 2), 'The Defence of the Realm 1485–1558' and 'The Defence of the Realm under Elizabeth I', London, 1982, pp. 367–401, 402–14. Lynn White, 'Jacopo Aconcio as an Engineer', *American Historical Review*, vol. 72, 1966–7, pp. 425–44; Marcus Merriman, 'Italian Military Engineers in Britain in the 1540s', in Sarah Tyacke, ed., *English Map-Making 1500–1650: Historical Essays*, London, 1983, pp. 57–67. See also Barbara Donagan, 'Halcyon Days and the Literature of War: England's Military Education before

1642', *Past and Present*, no. 147, 1995, pp. 65–100.

7 For an expert summary of architectural literature and its national adaptation, Vaughan Hart, ' "Paper Palaces" from Alberti to Scamozzi' in Vaughan Hart and Peter Hicks, eds., *Paper Palaces: The Rise of the Renaissance Architectural Treatise*, New Haven and London, 1998, pp. 1–29. Vasari's comment on the mis-use of Michelangelo runs thus: 'The licence he allowed himself has served as a great encouragement to others to follow his example; subsequently we have seen the creation of new kinds of fantastic ornament containing more of the grotesque than of rule or reason.' Translated from Giorgio Vasari, *Le vite de' più* (1550, rev. 1568), ed. Gaetano Milanesi, 9 vols, Florence, 1878–85, 2nd edn, 1906, vol. VII, p. 195.

8 Maurice Howard, 'The Ideal House and Healthy Life: The Origins of Architectural Theory in England', in Jean Guillaume, ed., *Les Traités d'architecture de la Renaissance*, Paris, 1988, pp. 425–33.

9 John Shute, *The First and Chiefe Groundes of Architecture*, London, 1563, sig. A.III.iv.

10 Ibid., sig. A.III.i.

11 Vaughan Hart, 'From Virgin to Courtesan in Early English Vitruvian Books', in Hart and Peter Hicks, eds., *Paper Palaces: The Rise of the Renaissance Architectural Treatise*, New Haven and London, 1998, pp. 297–318; Maurice Howard, 'Self-Fashioning and the Classical Moment in Mid-Sixteenth-Century English Architecture', in Lucy Gent and Nigel Llewellyn, eds., *Renaissance Bodies: The Human Figure in English Culture, c. 1540–1660*, London, 1990, pp. 198–217. See also the entry on John Shute in Eileen Harris, assisted by Nicholas Savage, *British Architectural Books and Writers 1556–1785*, Cambridge, 1990, pp. 418–22.

12 John Stow, *A Survey of London* (1598), ed. with introduction and notes by C. L. Kingsford as *A Survey of London by John Stow reprinted from the Text of 1603*, 3 vols, Oxford, 1908, vol. I, pp. 83, 193–4.

13 Robert Tittler, ' "For the Re-edification of Townes": The Rebuilding Statutes of Henry VIII', *Albion*, vol. 22, no. 4, 1990, pp. 591–605.

14 *The Statutes of the Realm [...] from Original Records and Authentic Manuscripts*, vol. III, 1817, pp. 959–60.

15 Stow, ed. Kingsford, 1908, vol. I, p. 259.

16 Paul L. Hughes and James F. Larkin, eds., *Tudor Royal Proclamations*, vol. III, *1588–1603*, New

Haven and London, 1969, pp. 245–48. On proclamation, see Felicity Heal, 'The Crown, the Gentry and London: The Enforcement of Proclamation, 1596–1640', in C. Cross, D. Loades, J. J. Scarisbrick, eds., *Law and Government under the Tudors*, Cambridge, 1988, pp. 211–26.

17 J. F. Larkin and P. L. Hughes, eds., *Stuart Royal Proclamations*, vol. I, *Royal Proclamations of King James I 1603–1625*, Oxford 1973, pp. 111–12.

18 Ibid., pp. 485–8.

19 Roger H. Leech, 'The Prospect from Rugman's Row: The Row House in Late Sixteenth- and Early Seventeenth-Century London', *Archaeological Journal*, vol. 153, 1996, pp. 201–42.

20 J. F. Larkin and P. L. Hughes, eds., *Stuart Royal Proclamations*, vol. II, *Charles I 1625–1646*, Oxford, 1983, pp. 20–26.

21 Thomas G. Barnes, 'The Prerogative and Environmental Control of London Building in the Early Seventeenth Century: The Lost Opportunity', *California Law Review*, vol. 58, 1970, pp. 1332–62.

22 Mrs Baldwyn-Childe, 'The Building of the Manor-House of Kyre Park, Worcestershire (1588–1618)', *The Antiquary*, vol. 21, 1890, pp. 202–5, 261–4; vol. 22, 1891, pp. 24–6, 50–53.

23 Maurice Howard, 'Inventories, Surveys and the History of Great Houses, 1480–1660', *Architectural History*, vol. 41, 1998, pp. 22–8. J. B. Oldham, 'A Sixteenth Century Shrewsbury School Inventory', *Transactions of the Shropshire Archaeological and Natural History Society*, vol. 47, 1933–4, pp. 121–37.

24 On paper and parchment, see L. F. Salzman, *Building in England down to 1540: A Documentary History*, Oxford, 1952, repr. 1967, p. 413; for the sixteenth-century documents, ibid., pp. 556–84.

25 Letter from Wren to the Bishop of Oxford, 25 June 1681, *Designs of Sir Christopher Wren for Oxford, Cambridge, London, Windsor, Eton*, Wren Society, vol. V, Oxford, 1928, pp. 19–20.

26 Malcolm Airs, *The Tudor and Jacobean Country House: A Building History*, Stroud, 1995, chap. 4, 'Methods of Undertaking', pp. 57–63.

27 On Exeter, see S. R. Blaylock, 'Exeter Guildhall', *Devon Archaeological Society Proceedings*, vol. 48, 1992, pp. 123–78; on Hull, Donald Woodward, *Men at Work: Labourers and Building Craftsmen in the Towns of Northern England, 1450–1750*, Cambridge, 1995, pp. 35–40.

28 Michelle O'Malley, *The Business of Art: Contracts and the Commissioning Process in Renaissance Italy*, New Haven and London, 2005, pp. 1–11, 251–4.

29 Salzman, 1952, repr. 1967, Appendix B, doc. 95.

30 Ibid., docs. 87, 88, 96.

31 Walter H. Godfrey, 'An Elizabethan Builder's Contract', *Sussex Archaeological Collections*, vol. 65, 1924, pp. 211–23 (p. 220).

32 James B. McVicar, 'Social Change and the Growth of Antiquarian Studies in Tudor and Stuart England', *Archaeological Review from Cambridge*, vol. 3, no. 1, 1984, pp. 48–67 (p. 62).

33 Thomas Platter, *Thomas Platter's Travels in England, 1599*, ed. Clare Williams, London, 1937.

34 Caroline Barron, Christopher Coleman and Claire Gobbi, eds., 'The London Journal of Alessandro Magno 1562', *London Journal*, vol. 9, no. 2, 1983, pp. 136–52 (p. 142).

35 *The Itinerary of John Leland in or about the Years 1535–1543*, ed. L. Toulmin Smith, with a foreword by Thomas Kendrick, 5 vols, London, 1964. For commentary on Leland, see T. D. Kendrick, *British Antiquity*, London, 1950, pp. 45–64; J. W. Binns, *Intellectual Culture in Elizabethan and Jacobean England: The Latin Writings of the Age*, Leeds, 1990; John Scattergood, 'John Leland's *Itinerary* and the Identity of England', in A. J. Piesse, ed., *Sixteenth-Century Identities*, Manchester, 2000, pp. 58–74. See also *ODNB*.

36 Leland, ed. Toulmin Smith, 1964, vol. II, p. 8; vol. I, p. 104.

37 Ibid., vol. V, pp. 103, 106.

38 Ibid., vol. V, p. 72.

39 Ibid., vol. V, p. 32.

40 Ibid., vol. IV, p. 7.

41 Ibid., vol. I, pp. 95, 164.

42 Ibid., vol. I, p. 181.

43 The standard modern edition of William Harrison's *Description of England* is that by Georges Edelen, subtitled *The Classic Contemporary Account of Tudor Social Life*, Ithaca, NY, 1968. See also Sheila Ahern, 'William Harrison, Author of the *Description of England* and the *Chronology*', *Essex Journal*, vol. 27, no. 3, 1992, pp. 61–70.

44 G. J. R. Parry, *A Protestant Vision: William Harrison and the Reformation of Elizabethan England*, Cambridge, 1987.

45 Harrison, ed. Edelen, 1968, p. 276.

46 Jack Simmons, ed., *English County Historians*, Wakefield, 1978, chap. 1, 'The Writing of English County History', pp. 1–21; Robert Tittler, *Townspeople and Nation: English Urban Experiences, 1540–1640*, Stanford, 2001, chap. 5, 'Henry Manship: Constructing the Civic Memory in Great Yarmouth', pp. 121–39.

47 On the broad issues of chronicling the city, see Peter Clark, 'Visions of the Urban Community: Antiquarians and the English City before 1800', in D. Fraser and A. Sutcliffe, eds., *The Pursuit of Urban History*, London, 1983, pp. 106–24. On Stow, M. J. Power, 'John Stow and his London', *Journal of Historical Geography*, vol. 11, no. 1, 1985, pp. 1–20; Lawrence Manley, 'From Matron to Monster: Tudor-Stuart London and the Languages of Urban Description', in Heather Dubrow and Richard Strier, eds., *The Historical Renaissance: New Essays on Tudor and Stuart Culture*, Chicago, 1988, pp. 347–74. See also the essays in Julia F. Merritt, ed., *Imagining Early Modern London: Perceptions and Portrayals of the City from Stow to Strype, 1598–1720*, Cambridge, 2001.

48 Sir Thomas Elyot, *The Boke named the Gouernour* (1531), ed. H. H. S. Croft, 1887, repr. New York, 1967, pp. 77–8.

49 Stow, ed. Kingsford, 1908, vol. II, p. 78.

50 Ian W. Archer, 'The Nostalgia of John Stow', in David L. Smith, Richard Strier and David Bevington, eds., *The Theatrical City: Culture, Theatre and Politics in London, 1576–1649*, Cambridge, 1995, pp. 17–34.

51 Ibid., p. 33.

52 Manley, 1988, p. 364.

53 Andrew McRae, '"On the Famous Voyage": Ben Jonson and Civic Space', in Andrew Gordon and Bernhard Klein, eds., *Literature, Mapping and the Politics of Space in Early Modern Britain*, Cambridge, 2001, pp. 181–203.

54 Ibid., p. 348 and p. 368, no. 8.

55 Kendrick, 1950, chap. 8, 'Britannia', pp. 134–67; Stuart Piggott, 'William Camden and the *Britannia*', *Proceedings of the British Academy*, vol. 37, 1951, pp. 199–217.

56 Wyman H. Herendeen, 'Wanton Discourse and the Engines of Time: William Camden – Historian among Poets-Historical', in Maryanne Cline Horowitz, Anne J. Cruz and Wendy A. Furman, eds., *Renaissance Rereadings, Intertext and Context*, Urbana and Chicago, 1988, pp. 142–56.

57 The literature on the country-house poem is vast, but of major importance here are the standard wide-ranging books on the subject by William A. McClung, *The Country House in English Renaissance Poetry*, Berkeley, 1977, and Alistair Fowler, *The Country House Poem*, Edinburgh, 1994.

58 Felicity Heal, *Hospitality in Early Modern England*, Oxford, 1990.

59 The quotations are from the standard edition of Jonson's works, *Ben Jonson, edited by C. H. Herford and Percy and Evelyn Simpson*, vol. VIII, *The Poems and Prose Works*, Oxford, 1947, pp. 93–6.

60 My first thoughts on the language of Jonson's poem and its relevance to the architectural historian were raised by Christy Anderson, '"Pallaces of the Poets": The Idea of the Tudor and Jacobean Country House', in Malcolm Airs, ed., *The Tudor and Jacobean Great House*, Oxford, 1994, pp. 19–27.

61 A. D. Cousins, 'Marvell's "Upon Appleton House, to my Lord Fairfax" and the Regaining of Paradise', in Conal Condren and Cousins, eds., *The Political Identity of Andrew Marvell*, Aldershot, 1990, pp. 53–84.

62 On the house, see McClung, 1977, pp. 157–65.

63 The quotations are from *Andrew Marvell: Complete Poetry*, ed. George de F. Lord, London and Melbourne, 1968, repr. 1984, pp. 61–88.

64 William H. Sherman, 'Bringing the World to England: The Politics of Translation in the Age of Hakluyt', *Transactions of the Royal Historical Society*, vol. 14, 2004, pp. 199–207.

65 Harris, assisted by Savage, 1990, pp. 120–22, 297–9, 414–17.

66 Lucy Gent, *Picture and Poetry, 1560–1620: Relations between Literature and the Visual Arts in the English Renaissance*, Leamington Spa, 1981, with a checklist of early editions of treatises known to be in collections of this period.

67 Thomas Coryat, *Coryat's Crudities hastily gobled up in Five Moneths Travells* (1611), ed. in 2 vols, Glasgow, 1905, vol. I, p. 352.

68 William Thomas, *The Historye of Italie* (1549), ed. George B. Parks, Ithaca, NY, 1963, p. 37.

69 Coryat, ed. 1905, vol. II, p. 50.

70 Harris, assisted by Savage, 1990, pp. 499–503.

71 Hart, 1998, pp. 314–16.

72 Anderson, 2007; John Newman, 'Inigo Jones's Architectural Education before 1614', *Architectural History*, vol. 35, 1992, pp. 18–50.

Chapter 4

1 C. H. Cook, *Medieval Churches and Chantry Chapels*, London, 1947; Howard Colvin, 'The Origin of Chantries', *Journal of Medieval History*, vol. 26, no. 2, 2000, pp. 163–73.

2 National Archives, Prerogative Court of Canterbury, 6 Spert.

3 For much of this information on Sandys and his houses, see Maurice Howard and Edward Wilson, *The Vyne: A Tudor House Revealed*, London,

2003, chap. 3, 'William Sandys, Courtier and Builder', pp. 40–56.

4   Ibid., pp. 114–15.

5   On the Holy Ghost Chapel, see *VCH Hampshire*, vol. IV, 1911, pp. 214–15, and Francis James Baigent and James Elwin Millard, *A History of the Ancient Town and Manor of Basingstoke in the County of Southampton, with a Brief Account of the Siege of Basing House, A.D. 1643–1645*, Basingstoke, 1889, pp. 110–71. On the tomb contract, see F. A. Greenhill, 'The Sandys Contract', *Transactions of the Monumental Brass Society*, vol. 9, 1952–4, pp. 354–61.

6   Sir Francis Bryan, appointed Chief Gentleman of Henry VIII's Privy Chamber in 1536, lived at Faulkbourne Hall, Essex, which he gained by marriage; he lived mainly out of his keepership, however, notably at Ampthill, where lodgings were built for him in 1536, and possibly at Woburn Abbey, which was leased to him in 1539 and he subsequently sublet in 1545. See Colvin et al., *The History of the King's Works*, vol. IV, *1485–1660* (part 2), London, 1982, p. 41; Dianne Duggan, 'Woburn Abbey: The First Episode of a Great Country House', *Architectural History*, vol. 46, 2003, p. 57.

7   For Sandys's activities at Calais, see Howard and Wilson, 2003, pp. 40–50. The discussion of the 'platt' is at *L&P*, III, 825.

8   John Stow, *A Survey of London* (1598), ed. with introduction and notes by C. L. Kingsford as *A Survey of London by John Stow, reprinted from the Text of 1603*, 3 vols, Oxford, 1908, vol. I, p. 112.

9   John Weever, *Ancient Funeral Monuments*, London, 1631, p. 598.

10 On Monoux at Walthamstow, see *VCH Essex*, vol. VI, 1973, pp. 288–9; Nikolaus Pevsner, rev. Bridget Cherry and Charles O'Brien as *The Buildings of England. London 5: East*, New Haven and London, 2005, p. 746.

11 For a full discussion of luxury and building, see David Thomson, *Renaissance Architecture: Critics, Patrons, Luxury*, Manchester, 1993.

12 Marillac's letter is at *L&P*, XVI, 321. On Weston, Marney, Brandon and their buildings, see Maurice Howard, *The Early Tudor Country House: Architecture and Politics, 1490–1550*, London, 1987, chap. 4, See also S. J. Gunn, *Charles Brandon, Duke of Suffolk, 1484–1545*, Oxford, 1988.

13 The main sources used here for the life of Rich are HPC, *1509–1558*, pp. 192–5, and the *ODNB*. For discussion of his role in the Reformation in Essex, see J. E. Oxley, *The Reformation in Essex*

14 *to the Death of Mary*, Manchester, 1965, *passim*.

14 The purchase of St Bartholomew's is at *L&P*, XIX (I), 610 (55).

15 E. A. Webb, 'St Bartholomew the Great: The Smithfield Gateway and the Cloister', *Transactions of the London and Middlesex Archaeological Society*, new ser., vol. 2, 1913, pp. 211–24; Webb, *The Records of St Bartholomew's Priory and of the Church and Parish of St Bartholomew the Great, West Smithfield*, 2 vols, Oxford, 1921, vol. I, pp. 253–76, 289–97; Nikolaus Pevsner, rev. Simon Bradley, *The Buildings of England, London I: The City of London*, New Haven and London, 1997, pp. 196–203.

16 Christopher Phillpotts, 'The Houses of Henry VIII's Courtiers in London', in David Gaimster and Roberta Gilchrist, eds., *The Archaeology of Reformation, 1480–1580*, Leeds, 2003, pp. 299–309.

17 Oxley, 1965, p. 252.

18 P. Benton, *The History of Rochford Hundred*, 2 vols, Rochford, 1867–83, vol. II; F. Chancellor, 'Rochford Hall', *Transactions of the Essex Archaeological Society*, new ser., vol. 9, 1906, pp. 298–300; *RCHM S.E. Essex*, 1923, pp. 127–9; L. R. Cryer, *A History of Rochford*, 1978; N. Barnes and L. Newman, 'Rochford Hall', *Rochford Hundred Historical Society*, vols 15–17, 1973.

19 The wills of Richard and Robert Rich are in F. G. Emmison, *Elizabethan Life: Wills of Essex Gentry and Merchants from the Prerogative Court of Canterbury*, Chelmsford, 1978, pp. 9–13.

20 *L&P*, X, 1015 (33).

21 R. C. Fowler, 'Inventories of Essex Monasteries in 1536', *Essex Archaeological Society Transactions*, vol. 9, 1904, pp. 391–5.

22 *L&P*, XII (I), 1330 (54), XIII (I), 646 (42); Oxley, 1965, p. 252.

23 A. W. Clapham, 'The Augustinian Priory of Little Leez and the Mansion of Leez Priory', *Transactions of the Essex Archaeological Society*, new ser., vol. 13, 1921, pp. 200–221, with a full bibliography; *RCHM Essex*, vol. II, 1921, pp. 158–61. Buck's view of the courtyard is reproduced in Howard, 1987, pp. 150–51.

24 Colvin et al., 1982, pp. 172–5.

25 K. A. Esdaile, 'The Monument of the First Lord Rich at Felsted', *Transactions of the Essex Archaeological Society*, new ser., vol. 22, 1936, pp. 59–67; Nigel Llewellyn, *Funeral Monuments in Post-Reformation England*, Cambridge, 2000, pp. 72, 333.

26 The licence to Rich is at CPR, *Philip and Mary*, II, 42. See also Andrew Clark, ed., *The Founda-*

tion Deeds of Felsted School and Charities, Oxford, 1916, pp. 1–11.

27 *VCH Essex*, vol. II, 1907, pp. 531–5; Clark, ed., 1916; Malcolm Seaborne, *The English School: Its Architecture and Organisation, 1370–1870*, London, 1971, p. 21; John Sergeaunt, *Felsted School*, Chelmsford and London, 1989. I am much indebted to J. J. Labno, 'English Schools and Almshouses/Hospitals: Pre- and Post-Reformation Foundations. The Evolution of Architectural Form', unpubd MA dissertation, University of Sussex, 1997.

28 Sergeaunt, 1989, p. 6.

29 For biographical details of Williams, HPC *1509–58*, pp. 620–23; *ODNB*.

30 Stow, ed. Kingsford, 1908, vol. I, pp. 294–5.

31 Christopher Hussey, 'Rycote Park, Oxfordshire', *Country Life*, vol. 63, 1928, pp. 16–24; Nikolaus Pevsner and Jennifer Sherwood, *The Buildings of England, Oxfordshire*, London, 1974, pp. 748–9.

32 *L&P*, IX, 422.

33 Prints by Winstanley, *Audley End*, London, 1688, and Kip, *Britannia Illustrata*, London, 1707.

34 W. K. Jordan, ed., *The Chronicle and Political Papers of King Edward VI*, London, 1966, p. 128.

35 *VCH Oxon*, vol. VII, 1962, pp. 160–219; for the school statutes, ibid., vol. I, 1939, p. 475.

36 Frederick George Lee, *The History and Antiquities of the Prebendal Church of the Blessed Virgin Mary of Thame*, London, 1883, cols. 427–32.

37 Ibid., cols. 457–92.

38 Felicity Heal, *Of Prelates and Princes: A Study of the Economic and Social Position of the Tudor Episcopate*, Cambridge, 1980. Her coverage of social responsibilities and resources is especially relevant to my discussion here; ibid., chap. 10, 'The Social Responsibilities of the Elizabethan Bishops', pp. 237–64, and chap. 11, 'The Resources of the Elizabethan Bishops', pp. 265–311.

39 Phyllis Hembry, 'Episcopal Palaces, 1535–1660', in E. W. Ives, J. J. Scarisbrick and R. J. Knecht, eds., *Wealth and Power in Tudor England: Essays presented to S.T. Bindoff*, London, 1978, pp. 146–66.

40 Colvin et al., 1982, pp. 217–19.

41 Hembry, 1978, p. 159.

42 Ibid., p. 163; Nikolaus Pevsner, rev. Enid Radcliffe, *The Buildings of England: Essex*, Harmondsworth, 1965, p. 435.

43 John Newman, 'Cardinal Wolsey's Collegiate Foundations', in S. J. Gunn and P. G. Lindley, eds., *Cardinal Wolsey: Church, State and Art*, Cambridge, 1991, pp. 103–15.

44 Heal, 1980, p. 247.

45 On the life of Whitgift, see John Strype, *The Life and Acts of John Whitgift, D.D., the Third and Last Lord Archbishop of Canterbury in the Reign of Queen Elizabeth*, Oxford, 1822; Powel Mills Dawley, *John Whitgift and the Reformation*, London, 1955; *ODNB*.

46 George Paule, *Life of John Whitgift*, 1612, cited in *ODNB*.

47 Nikolaus Pevsner, rev. Bridget Cherry, *The Buildings of England, London 2: South*, London, 1983, pp. 212–14.

48 Heal, 1980, p. 260.

49 *VCH Kent*, vol. II, 1926, p. 215.

50 *VCH Surrey*, vol. II, 1905, pp. 189–90.

51 *ODNB*; *VCH Surrey*, vol. IV, 1912, pp. 213–14; Pevsner, rev. Cherry, 1983, pp. 215–16; F. H. G. Percy, *Whitgift School: A History*, Croydon, 1991, with quotation from Paule at p. 41.

52 Llewellyn, 2000, p. 294, from his own translation of Henry Holland, *Herwologia Anglica hoc est clarissimorum et doctissmorum aliquot Angkorum qui floruerunt [...] Anno [...] MD [...] adMDCXX*, 1620, p. 227.

53 Howard, 1987, p. 37.

54 Malcolm Airs, *The Tudor and Jacobean Country House: A Building History*, Stroud, 1995, p. 99.

55 On the issue of the aristocracy's cost of living and the role of London in this, see Lawrence Stone, *The Crisis of the Aristocracy, 1558–1641*, Oxford, 1965.

56 Lawrence Stone, *Family and Fortune: Studies in Aristocratic Finance in the Sixteenth and Seventeenth Centuries*, Oxford, 1973, *passim*.

57 Ibid., pp. 30–31.

58 Lee, 1883, col. 431.

59 Caroline Knight, 'The Cecils at Wimbledon', in Pauline Croft, ed., *Patronage, Culture and Power: The Early Cecils, 1558–1612*, New Haven and London, 2002, pp. 47–66; J. F. Merritt, 'The Cecils and Westminster 1558–1612: The Development of an Urban Power Base', in ibid., pp. 231–46.

60 Jill Husselby and Paula Henderson, 'Location, Location, Location! Cecil House in the Strand', *Architectural History*, vol. 45, 2002, pp. 159–93.

61 Knight, 2002.

62 John Summerson, 'The Building of Theobalds, 1564–1585', *Archaeologia*, vol. 97, 1959, pp. 107–26; Malcolm Airs, '"Pomp or Glory": The Influence of Theobalds', in Croft, ed., 2002, pp. 3–19.

63 Mark Girouard, 'Burghley House, Lincolnshire', *Country Life*, vol. 186, 1992, no. 17, pp. 56–9,

no. 18, pp. 58–61; J. Husselby, 'Architecture at Burghley House: The Patronage of William Cecil', unpubd Ph.D. thesis, Warwick University, 1996; Eric L. Till, 'Fact and Conjecture: The Building of Burghley House 1555–1587', *Northamptonshire Past and Present*, vol. 9, no. 4, 1997–8, pp. 323–32; Jill Husselby, 'The Politics of Pleasure: William Cecil and Burghley House', in Croft, ed., 2002, pp. 21–45.

64 Peter Barber, 'England II: Monarchs, Ministers and Maps, 1550–1625', in David Buisseret, ed., *Monarchs, Ministers and Maps: The Emergence of Cartography as a Tool of Government in Early Modern Europe*, Chicago, 1992, pp. 57–98.

65 On Cecil's grasp of economic matters, see Felicity Heal and Clive Holmes, 'The Economic Patronage of William Cecil', in Croft, ed., 2002, pp. 199–229.

66 Joan Thirsk, 'Stamford in the Sixteenth and Seventeenth Centuries', in Alan Rogers, ed., *The Making of Stamford*, Leicester, 1965, pp. 58–76.

67 *RCHM The Town of Stamford*, London, 1977, pp. 42–3.

68 'Ordinances made by Sir William Cecill, Knight of the Order of the Garter, Baron of Burghley, for the order and gouernment of xiij poore men whereof one to be Warden of the Hospital at Stamford Baron in the Countie of Northampton', *Proclamations Elizabeth 1591–1602*, no. 115 of a bound collection of Proclamations in the Society of Antiquaries Library, London.

69 *ODNB*; further to this, the same author, Simon Adams, *Leicester and the Court: Essays on Elizabethan Politics*, Manchester, 2002.

70 Adams, 2002, p. 225; Lawrence Butler, 'Leicester's Church, Denbigh: An Experiment in Puritan Worship', *Journal of the British Archaeological Association*, vol. 37, 1974, pp. 40–62 (60).

71 Adams, 2002, p. 327; inventories of Leicester House, Wanstead and Kenilworth are in *Archaeologia*, vol. 73, 1923, pp. 28–54.

72 M. W. Thompson, *Kenilworth Castle, Warwickshire*, HMSO, London, 1977; Derek Renn, *Kenilworth Castle, Warwickshire*, HMSO, London, 1991; J. Nichols, *The Progresses and Public Processions of Queen Elizabeth*, 3 vols, London, 1823; Jean Wilson, *Entertainments for Elizabeth I*, London, 1980.

73 Butler, 1974; Edward Hubbard, *The Buildings of Wales: Clwyd*, Harmondsworth, 1986, pp. 145–6; Adams, 2002, p. 225.

74 Thomas Kemp, ed., *The Black Book of Warwick*, Warwick, 1898; all subsequent quotations are from the record of Dudley's visit, pp. 26–51.

75 *VCH Warwickshire*, vol. VIII, 1969, pp. 423–6, 548–9.

76 E. G. Tibbits, 'The Hospital of Robert, Earl of Leicester, in Warwick', *Transactions of the Birmingham Archaeological Society* (1936), vol. 60, 1940, pp. 112–44 (122).

77 *VCH Warwickshire*, vol. VIII, 1969, p. 549.

78 Tibbits, 1940, p. 127.

79 *VCH Warwickshire*, vol. VIII, 1969, p. 549; Adams, 2002, pp. 225–6.

80 Philip B. Chatwin, 'The Hospital of Lord Leycester, formerly the Hall and other Buildings of the Medieval Guilds in Warwick', *Transactions of the Birmingham Archaeological Society*, vol. 70, 1952, pp. 37–48; this article reconstructs the medieval rather than the late sixteenth-century arrangements.

81 Adams, 2002, p. 310.

82 Linda Levy Peck, *Northampton: Patronage and Policy at the Court of James I*, London, 1982; *ODNB*.

83 Colvin et al., 1982, pp. 122–3.

84 Peck, 1982, pp. 73–4 (without identifying Simon Basil as the King's Surveyor).

85 Evelyn P. Shirley, 'An Inventory of the Effects of Henry Howard, K.G., Earl of Northampton, taken on his death in 1614, together with a transcript of his Will', *Archaeologia*, vol. 42, 1869, pp. 347–78; the inventory of Northumberland House is at pp. 369–74.

86 G. Gater and W. H. Godfrey, eds., *Survey of London*, vol. XVIII, *The Strand (The Parish of St. Martin-in-the-Fields, Part II)*, London, 1937, pp. 10–12.

87 For the Smythson drawing, see Mark Girouard, 'The Smythson Collection of the Royal Institute of British Architects', *Architectural History*, vol. 5, 1962, p. 32, no. I/12. On the Thorpe drawings, John Summerson, ed., *The Book of Architecture of John Thorpe in the Sir John Soane's Museum*, Walpole Society, vol. 40, 1966, pp. 108–9, nos. T 279–80, 275–6. See also Jeremy Wood, 'The Architectural Patronage of Algernon Percy, 10th Earl of Northumberland', in John Bold and Edward Chaney, eds., *English Architecture Public and Private: Essays for Kerry Downes*, London and Rio Grande, 1993, pp. 55–80. On Vertue's comments, Gater and Godfrey, eds., 1937, p. 16, and his drawing of the frontispiece, pl. 4.

88 H. L. Bradfer-Lawrence, *Castle Rising: A Short History of the Castle, Honor, Church and Borough of Castle Rising, Norfolk*, King's Lynn, 1932, pp. 60–81.

89 Shirley, 1869, pp. 375–7.

90 Peck, 1982, p. 75; Nikolaus Pevsner, rev. Bridget Cherry, *The Buildings of England, London 2: South*, Harmondsworth, 1983, p. 271; Nikolaus Pevsner, rev. Bill Wilson, *The Buildings of England, Norfolk 2: North-West and South*, New Haven and London, 2002, p. 254; Nikolaus Pevsner, rev. John Newman, *The Buildings of England, Shropshire*, New Haven and London, 2006, pp. 223–4; Bradfer-Lawrence, 1932, pp. 60–61. Castle Rising and Greenwich are discussed, with plans, in W. H. Godfrey, *The English Almshouse*, London, 1955, pp. 57–9.

91 On particular aspects of women, building and space, see Anne Laurence, *Women in England 1500–1760: A Social History*, London, 1996, pp. 152–7; Sara Mendelson and Patricia Crawford, *Women in Early Modern England, 1550–1720*, Oxford, 1998, pp. 205–12. On the Countess of Shrewsbury, the established biography is that of David N. Durant, *Bess of Hardwick: An Elizabethan Dynast*, London, 1977. On Hardwick Hall, Mark Girouard, *Robert Smythson and the Elizabethan Country House*, New Haven and London, 1983, pp. 143–64. See also Gillian White, ' "that whyche ys made nedefoulle and nesasary": The Nature and Purpose of the Original Furnishings and Decoration of Hardwick Hall, Derbyshire', unpubd Ph.D. thesis, University of Warwick, 2005. On Lady Anne Clifford, Alice Friedman, 'Constructing an Identity in Prose, Plaster and Paint: Lady Anne Clifford as Writer and Patron of the Arts', in Lucy Gent, ed., *Albion's Classicism: The Visual Arts in Britain, 1550–1660*, New Haven and London, 1995, pp. 359–76; Richard T. Spence, *Lady Anne Clifford, Countess of Pembroke, Dorset and Montgomery (1590–1676)*, Stroud, 1997.

92 Alice T. Friedman, *House and Household in Elizabethan England: Wollaton Hall and the Willoughby Family*, Chicago, 1989, chap. 3, 'A House Divided', pp. 53–70.

93 D. J. H. Clifford, ed., *The Diaries of Lady Anne Clifford*, Stroud, 1990.

94 Maurice Howard, ' "His Lordship was the chiefest architect": Patrons and Builders in 16th-Century England', in Giles Worsley, ed., *The Role of the Amateur Architect*, London, 1994, pp. 7–13. Conclusions there are based on the published building accounts: David N. Durant and Philip Riden, 'The Building of Hardwick Hall', part 1, 'The Old Hall, 1587–91', *Derbyshire Record Society*, vol. 4, 1980, pp. 1–152, and part 2, 'The New Hall, 1591–8', ibid., vol. 9, 1984, pp. 153–264.

95 White, 2005. See also Mark Girouard, 'The Ghost of Elizabethan Chatsworth', in *Town and Country*, New Haven and London, 1992, pp. 211–20.

96 Barbara J. Harris, *English Aristocratic Women 1450–1550: Marriage and Family, Property and Careers*, Oxford, 2002, chap. 7, 'Widows: Women of Property and Custodians of their Families' Futures', pp. 127–74.

97 *ODNB* on Frances Sidney.

98 G. M. Edwards, *Sidney Sussex College*, London, 1899, pp. 8–13; *RCHM The City of Cambridge*, 1959, part 2, pp. 203–9.

99 M. K. Jones and M. G. Underwood, *The King's Mother: Lady Margaret Beaufort, Countess of Richmond and Derby*, Cambridge, 1992; on the college buildings, *RCHM The City of Cambridge*, 1959, part 1, pp. 25–37, part 2, pp. 187–202.

100 Katherine Duncan-Jones, *Sir Philip Sidney: Courtier Poet*, New Haven and London, 1991.

101 G. K. Waller, *Mary Sidney, Countess of Pembroke: A Critical Study of her Writings and Literary Milieu*, London, 1979; M. P. Hannay, *Philip's Phoenix: Mary Sidney, Countess of Pembroke*, New York and Oxford, 1990; on her poems and Protestant internationalism, Louise Schleiner, *Tudor and Stuart Women Writers*, Bloomington and Indianapolis, 1994, chap. 3, 'Authorial Identity for a Second-Generation Protestant Aristocrat', pp. 52–81.

102 John Harris and Gordon Higgott, *Inigo Jones: Complete Architectural Drawings*, London, 1989, pp. 84–5; Paula Henderson, 'The Loggia in Tudor and Early Stuart England: The Adaptation and Function of Classical Form', in Gent, ed., 1995, pp. 109–46; Giles Worsley, *Inigo Jones and the European Classicist Tradition*, New Haven and London, 2007, p. 105.

103 David Howarth, 'The Patronage and Collecting of Aletheia, Countess of Arundel 1606–54', *Journal of the History of Collections*, vol. 10, no. 2, 1998, pp. 125–37. The quotation from the correspondence of Arundel is taken from M. F. S. Hervey, *The Life, Correspondence and Collections of Thomas Howard Earl of Arundel*, Cambridge, 1921, p. 142.

104 Elizabeth V. Chew, 'The Countess of Arundel and Tart Hall', in Edward Chaney, ed., *The Evolution of English Collecting: The Reception of Italian Art in the Tudor and Stuart Periods*, New Haven and London, 2003, pp. 285–314; Dianne Duggan, ' "A rather fascinating hybrid", Tart Hall: Lady Arundel's Casino at Whitehall', *British Art Journal*, vol. 4, 2003, pp. 54–64, with Hollar's *Spring* reproduced on pp. 54 and 56 (detail).

105 This discussion of Dorothy Hopton is much indebted to 'The Letters and Will of Lady Dorothy Bacon, 1597–1629', *Norfolk Record Society*, vol. 56, 1991, pp. 77–112. The ODNB entry (by A. Hassell Smith) has a different view of Dorothy Hopton's marriage.

106 Robert Wilson-North and Stephen Porter, 'Witham, Somerset: From Carthusian Monastery to Country House to Gothic Folly', *Architectural History*, vol. 40, 1997, pp. 81–98.

107 Francis Blomefield, continued by the Rev. Charles Parkin (vols VI–XI), *An Essay towards a Topographical History of the County of Norfolk*, 11 vols, London, 1805–10. This work mentions the Smiths' burial in the church but not where exactly they had lived (vol. VI, p. 101), which was certainly not at the early Tudor Great Cressingham Manor House, a residence that remained in the possession of the Jenney family who had built it. Blomefield also states that Lady Dorothy 'kept court' at her husband's manor of Eccles in 1622 (vol. I, p. 408).

108 Malcolm Airs, 'The Designing of Five East Anglian Country Houses, 1505–1637', *Architectural History*, vol. 21, 1978, pp. 58–67.

Chapter 5

1 T. D. Kendrick, *British Antiquity*, London, 1950, p. 149.

2 Lucy Gent, 'The Rash Gazer: Economies of Vision in Britain, 1550–1660', in Gent, ed., *Albion's Classicism: The Visual Arts in Britain, 1550–1660*, New Haven and London, 1995, pp. 377–93. On the selectivity and creativity of the use of foreign examples, see Alice Friedman, 'Did England Have a Renaissance? Classical and Anti-Classical Themes in Elizabethan Culture', in Susan J. Barnes, ed., *Cultural Differentiation and Cultural Identity in the Visual Arts*, Washington, 1989, pp. 95–111, and Christy Anderson, 'The Secrets of Vision in Renaissance England', in Lyle Massey, ed., *The Treatise on Perspective: Published and Unpublished*, New Haven and London, 2003, pp. 323–47.

3 Svetlana Alpers, *The Art of Describing: Dutch Art in the Seventeenth Century*, London and Chicago, 1983.

4 Paul Hentzner, trans. Horace, Earl of Orford, as *Paul Hentzner's Travels in England, during the Reign of Queen Elizabeth*, London, 1797, p. 23.

5 In May 1520, for example, the three commissioners charged with the temporary palace for the Field of Cloth of Gold wrote to Wolsey, noting the king's complaint that they have made more buildings than were mentioned in the 'platt': *L&P*, III, 825.

6 John H. Harvey, 'Four Fifteenth-Century London Plans', *London Topographical Society*, vol. 20, 1952, pp. 1–8.

7 On the sorting of the uses of orthogonal and perspective, I am much indebted to Laura Jacobus, 'On "Whether a man could see before him and behind him both at once": The Role of Drawing in the Design of Interior Space in England *c.* 1600–1800', *Architectural History*, vol. 31, 1988, pp. 148–66.

8 *RCHM The City of Cambridge*, repr. 1988, vol. 1, pp. 11–18.

9 See Christy Anderson, *Inigo Jones and the Classical Tradition*, Cambridge and New York, 2007, p. 30.

10 On the techniques and tools of representation in the designer's workshop, see Malcolm Airs, *The Tudor and Jacobean Country House: A Building History*, Stroud, 1995, chap. 7, 'The Realization of the Design', pp. 86–93.

11 John Harris, *The Artist and the Country House: A History of Country House and Garden View Painting in Britain, 1540–1870*, London, 1979.

12 Henry Wotton, *The Elements of Architecture collected by Henry Wotton Knight from the Best Authors and Examples*, London, 1624, p. 4.

13 Peter Barber, 'England I: Pageantry, Defense and Government: Maps at Court to 1550', in David Buisseret, ed., *Monarchs, Ministers and Maps: The Emergence of Cartography as a Tool of Government in Early Modern Europe*, Chicago, 1992, pp. 26–56.

14 David Starkey, ed., *The Inventory of King Henry VIII: Society of Antiquaries MS 129 and British Library MS Harley 1419*, London, 1998, nos. 10768 and 10779.

15 For an enigmatic example, see William Ravenhill and Margery Rowe, 'A Decorated Screen Map of Exeter based on John Hooker's Map of 1587', in Todd Gray, Margery M. Rowe and Audrey M. Erskine, eds., *Tudor and Stuart Devon. The Common Estate and Government: Essays presented to Joyce Youings*, Exeter, 1992, pp. 1–12; the dating of this may be as late as around 1700.

16 Howard Colvin and Susan Foister, eds., *The Panorama of London circa 1544 by Anthonis van den Wyngaerde*, London, 1996.

17 Peter Barber, 'England II: Monarchs, Ministers and Maps, 1550–1625', in Buisseret, ed., 1992, pp. 57–98; Barber, 'Was Elizabeth I interested in maps – and did it matter?', *Transactions of the*

Royal Historical Society, vol. 14, 2004, pp. 185–98.

18   J. B. Harley, 'Maps, Knowledge and Power', in Denis Cosgrove and Stephen Daniels, eds., *The Iconography of Landscape*, Cambridge, 1988, pp. 277–312; P. D. A. Harvey, 'Estate Surveyors and the Spread of the Scale-Map in England 1550–80', *Landscape History*, vol. 15, 1993, pp. 37–50; Paula Henderson, *The Tudor House and Garden: Architecture and Landscape in the Sixteenth and Early Seventeenth Centuries*, New Haven and London, 2005.

19   Louise Durning, ed., *Queen Elizabeth's Book of Oxford*, MS Bodley 13a, trans. Sarah Knight and Helen Spurling, Oxford, 2006.

20   The royal images are 'Henry VIII at the Field of Cloth of Gold', 'The Embarkation of Henry VIII at Dover', 'The Battle of the Spurs' and 'The Meeting of Henry VIII and Maximilien', all reproduced in Christopher Lloyd and Simon Thurley, *Henry VIII: Images of a Tudor King*, Oxford, 1990, at fig. 48, title page, figs. 40 and 38 respectively. On the issues around a renewed national Protestant awareness *c.* 1570, see Margaret Aston, *The King's Bedpost: Reformation and Iconography in a Tudor Group Portrait*, Cambridge, 1993.

21   On the engraving, see my entry in David Starkey (curator), *Elizabeth: The Exhibition at the National Maritime Museum*, ed. Susan Doran, London, 2003, p. 103, cat. no. 96.

22   Geoffrey Quilley, 'The Image of Nonsuch Palace: Mythology and Meaning', in Maurice Howard, ed., *The Image of the Building: Papers from the Annual Symposium of the Society of Architectural Historians of Great Britain*, Milton Keynes, 1996, pp. 17–36.

Bibliography

Abrams, Lesley, and Carley, James, P., eds., *The Archaeology and History of Glastonbury Abbey: Essays in Honour of the 90th Birthday of C. A. Ralegh Radford*, Woodbridge, 1991

Adams, Simon, ed., *Household Accounts and Disbursement Books of Robert Dudley, Earl of Leicester, 1558–1561, 1584–1586*, Camden 5th ser., Royal Historical Society, Cambridge, 1995

Adams, Simon, *Leicester and the Court: Essays on Elizabethan Politics*, Manchester, 2002

Addleshaw, G. W. O., and Etchells, Frederick, *The Architectural Setting of Anglican Worship*, London, 1948

Agnew, Jean-Christophe, *Worlds Apart: The Market and the Theater in Anglo-American Thought, 1550–1750*, Cambridge, 1986

Ahern, Sheila, 'William Harrison, Author of the *Description of England* and the *Chronology*', *Essex Journal*, vol. 27, no. 3, 1992, pp. 61–70

Airs, Malcolm, 'The Designing of Five East Anglian Country Houses, 1505–1637', *Architectural History*, vol. 21, 1978, pp. 58–67

Airs, Malcolm, *Tudor and Jacobean: A Guide and Gazetteer*, Buildings of Britain series, London, 1982

Airs, Malcolm, 'Lawrence Shipway, Freemason', *Architectural History*, vol. 27, 1984, pp 368–75

Airs, Malcolm, ed., *The Tudor and Jacobean Country House*, Oxford, 1994

Airs, Malcolm, *The Tudor and Jacobean Great House: A Building History*, Stroud, 1995

Airs, Malcolm, ' "Pomp or Glory": The Influence of Theobalds', in Croft, ed., 2002, pp. 3–19

Alexander, Jonathan, and Binski, Paul, eds., *The Age of Chivalry: Art in Plantagenet England, 1200–1400*, London, 1987

Alford, B. W., and Barker, T. C., eds., *A History of the Carpenters' Company*, London, 1968

Alpers, Svetlana, *The Art of Describing: Dutch Art in the Seventeenth Century*, London and Chicago, 1983

Anderson, Christy, ' "Pallaces of the Poets": The Idea of the Tudor and Jacobean Country House', in Airs, ed., 1994, pp. 19–28

Anderson, Christy, 'Learning to Read Architecture in the English Renaissance', in Gent, ed., 1995, pp. 239–86

Anderson, Christy, 'The Secrets of Vision in Renaissance England', in Massey, ed., 2003, pp. 323–47

Anderson, Christy, *Inigo Jones and the Classical Tradition*, Cambridge and New York, 2007

Anglin, J. P., 'Frustrated Ideals: The Case of Elizabethan Grammar School Foundations', *History of Education*, vol. 11, no. 4, 1982, pp. 267–79

Archer, Ian W., 'The Nostalgia of John Stow', in Smith, Strier and Bevington, eds., 1995, pp. 17–34

Archer, Ian W., 'The Arts and Acts of Memorialization in Early Modern London', in Merritt, ed., 2001, pp. 89–113

Arnold, A. A., 'Rochester Bridge in A.D. 1561', *Archaeologia Cantiana*, vol. 17, 1887, pp. 212–40

Ash, Eric H., *Power, Knowledge and Expertise in Elizabethan England*, Baltimore, 2004

Astill, Grenville, 'Archaeology and the Late-Medieval Urban Decline', in Slater, ed., 2000, pp. 214–29

Aston, Margaret, 'English Ruins and English History: The Dissolution and the Sense of the Past', *Journal of the Warburg and Courtauld Institutes*, vol. 36, 1973, pp. 231–55

Aston, Margaret, *England's Iconoclasts*, vol. I, Oxford, 1988

Aston, Margaret, *The King's Bedpost: Reformation and Iconography in a Tudor Group Portrait*, Cambridge, 1993

Ayton, A., and Price, J. C., eds., *The Medieval Military Revolution*, New York, 1995

Baigent, Francis James, and Millard, James Elwin, *A History of the Ancient Town and Manor of Basingstoke in the County of Southampton, with a Brief Account of the Siege of Basing House, A.D. 1643–1645*, Basingstoke, 1889

Baldwyn-Childe, Mrs, 'The Building of the Manor-House of Kyre Park, Worcestershire (1588–1618)', *The Antiquary*, vol. 21, 1890, pp. 202–5, 261–4; vol. 22, 1891, pp. 24–6, 50–53

Barber, Bruno, Chew, Steve, Dyson, Tony, and White, Bill, *The Cistercian Abbey of St Mary Stratford Langthorne, Essex: Archaeological Excavations for the London Underground Limited Jubilee Line Extension Project*, MOLAS, no. 18, 2004

Barber, Peter, 'England I: Pageantry, Defense and Government: Maps at Court to 1550' and 'England II: Monarchs, Ministers and Maps, 1550–1625', in Buisseret, ed., 1992, pp. 26–56, 57–98

Barber, Peter, 'Was Elizabeth I interested in maps – and did it matter?', *Transactions of the Royal Historical Society*, vol. 14, 2004, pp. 185–98

Barker, Katherine, ed., *The Cerne Abbas Millennium Lectures*, Cerne Abbas, 1988

Barnes, N., and Newman, L., 'Rochford Hall', *Rochford Hundred Historical Society*, vols 15–17, 1973

Barnes, Susan J., ed., *Cultural Differentiation and Cultural Identity in the Visual Arts*, Washington, 1989

Barnes, Thomas G., 'County Politics and a Puritan *Cause célèbre*: Somerset Church Ales in 1633', *Transactions of the Royal Historical Society*, 5th ser., vol. 9, 1959, pp. 103–22

Barnes, Thomas G., 'The Prerogative and Environmental Control of London Building in the Early Seventeenth Century: The Lost Opportunity', *California Law Review*, vol. 58, 1970, pp. 1332–1362

Barron, Caroline, Coleman, Christopher, and Gobbi, Claire, eds., 'The London Journal of Alessandro Magno 1562', *London Journal*, vol. 9, no. 2, 1983, pp. 136–52

Barrow, Henry, see Carlson, Leland H., ed., 1962

Barry, Jonathan, ed., *The Tudor and Stuart Town: A Reader in English Urban History*, London and New York, 1990

Barry, Jonathan, 'Provincial Town Culture, 1640–1780: Urbane or Civic?', in Pittock and Wear, eds., 1991, pp. 198–234

Barry, Jonathan, 'Civility and Civic Culture in Early Modern England: The Meanings of Urban Freedom', in Burke, Harrison and Slack, eds., 2000, pp. 181–96

Bashford, H., 'Present and Past Churches at Easton Royal', *Wiltshire Archaeological Magazine*, vol. 56, 1955, pp. 66–7

Batho, Gordon, 'Notes and Documents on Petworth House', *Sussex Archaeological Collections*, vol. 96, 1958, pp. 108–34

Baumann, G., ed., *The Written Word*, Oxford, 1986

Bearman, Robert, ed., *The History of an English Borough: Stratford-upon-Avon 1196–1996*, Stroud, 1997

Beavitt, Paul, 'Geophysical and Building Survey at Launde Abbey', *Transactions of the Leicestershire Archaeological and Historical Society*, vol. 69, 1995, pp. 22–31

Belsey, Catherine, *The Subject of Tragedy: Identity and Difference in Renaissance Drama*, London and New York, 1985

Bennett-Symonds, F. W., 'The Hospital of St Giles, Norwich', *Journal of the British Archaeological Association*, new ser., vol. 5, 1925, pp. 55–67

Benton, P., *The History of Rochford Hundred*, 2 vols, Rochford, 1867–83, vol. II

Berlin, Michael, 'Civic Ceremony in Early Modern London', *Urban History Yearbook*, 1986, pp. 15–27

Bernard, G. W., 'The Dating of Church Towers: Huntingdonshire Re-examined', *Archaeological Journal*, vol. 149, 1992, pp. 344–50

Bernard, G. W., and Gunn, S. J., eds., *Authority and Consent in Tudor England: Essays presented to C.S.L. Davies*, Aldershot, 2002

Bernard, G. W., 'The Tyranny of Henry VIII', in Bernard and Gunn, eds., 2002, pp. 113–29

Bernard G. W., *The King's Reformation: Henry VIII and the Remaking of the English Church*, New Haven and London, 2005

Bettey, J. H., 'The Dissolution and After at Cerne Abbas', in Barker, ed., 1988, pp. 43–52

Bindoff, S. T., ed., *History of Parliament: House of Commons: Appendices, Constituencies, Members, 1509–1558*, 3 vols, 1982

Bindoff, S. T., Hurstfield, J., and Williams, C. H., eds., *Elizabethan Government and Society*, London, 1961

Binns, J. W., *Intellectual Culture in Elizabethan and Jacobean England: The Latin Writings of the Age*, Leeds, 1990

Bishop, Michael, 'Bath's Second Guildhall, *c*. 1630–1776', *Bath History*, vol. 10, 2005, pp. 48–71

Blaylock, S. R., 'Exeter Guildhall', *Devon Archaeological Society Proceedings*, vol. 48, 1992, pp. 123–78

Blomefield, Francis, continued by the Rev. Charles Parkin (vols VI–XI), *An Essay towards a Topographical History of the County of Norfolk*, 11 vols, London, 1805–10

Bold, John, and Chaney, Edward, eds., *English Architecture Public and Private: Essays for Kerry Downes*, London and Rio Grande, 1993

Boorde, Andrew, *The boke for to Lerne a man to be wyse in building of his howse for the helth of his soule, and body*, London, *c*. 1540

Boorde, Andrew, *A Compendyous Regyment or A Dyetary of Helth made in Mountpyllier, compiled by Andrewe Boorde of Physycke Doctour*, London 1542; expanded with a life of Andrew Boorde and large extracts from his *Breuuyary*, ed. F. J. Furnivall, London, 1870

Borsay, Peter, 'Culture, Status and the English Urban Landscape', *History*, vol. 67, 1982, pp. 1–12

Borsay, Peter, *The English Urban Renaissance: Culture and Society in the Provincial Town, 1660–1760*, Oxford, 1989

Bossy, John, *The English Catholic Community, 1570–1850*, London, 1975

Bradfer-Lawrence, H. L., *Castle Rising: A Short History of the Castle, Honor, Church and Borough of Castle Rising, Norfolk*, King's Lynn, 1932

Brakspear, Harold, 'Stanley Abbey', *Archaeologia*, vol. 60, 1907, pp. 493–516

Brakspear, Harold, 'Excavations of Wiltshire Monasteries', *Archaeologia*, vol. 73, 1923, pp. 225–52

Brayshay, Mark, ed., *Topographical Writers in South-West England*, Exeter, 1996

Brenner, Robert, *Merchants and Revolution: Commercial Change, Political Conflict and London's Overseas Traders, 1550–1653*, Princeton, 1993

Brett-James, N. G., *The Growth of Stuart London*, London, 1935

Brigden, Susan, 'Religion and Social Obligation in Early Sixteenth-Century London', *Past and Present*, no. 103, 1984, pp. 67–112

Bright, Charles Curtis, 'Caressing the Great: Viscount Montague's Entertainment of Elizabeth at Cowdray, 1591', *Sussex Archaeological Collections*, vol. 127, 1989, pp. 147–66

Brinkworth, E. R. C., ed., *South Newington Church-wardens' Accounts 1553–1684*, Banbury Historical Society, vol. 6, 1964

Broad, J. 'Gentry Finance and the Civil War: The Case of the Buckinghamshire Verneys', *Economic History Review*, 2nd ser., vol. 32, 1979, pp. 183–200

Brooks, Chris, *The Gothic Revival*, London, 1999

Brown, Cedric C., and Marotti, Arthur F., eds., *Texts and Cultural Change in Early Modern England*, Basingstoke, 1997

Brown, R. Allen, *English Castles*, 4th edn, London, 1976

Buisseret, David, ed., *Monarchs, Ministers and Maps: The Emergence of Cartography as a Tool of Government in Early Modern Europe*, Chicago, 1992

Burke, Peter, *The Renaissance Sense of the Past*, London, 1969

Burke, Peter, Harrison, Brian, and Slack, Paul, eds., *Civil Histories: Essays presented to Sir Keith Thomas*, Oxford, 2000

Burke, Peter, 'A Civil Tongue: Language and Politeness in Early Modern Europe', in Burke, Harrison and Slack, eds., 2000, pp. 31–48

Burt, Richard, and Archer, John Michael, eds., *Enclosure Acts: Sexuality, Property and Culture in Early Modern England*, Ithaca, NY, 1994

Butler, Lawrence, 'Leicester's Church, Denbigh: An Experiment in Puritan Worship', *Journal of the British Archaeological Association*, vol. 37, 1974, pp. 40–62

Butler, Lawrence, 'Medieval Urban Religious Houses', in Schofield and Leech, eds., 1987, pp. 167–91

Buxton, Antony, 'Domestic Culture in Early Seventeenth-Century Thame', *Oxoniensia*, vol. 67, 2002, pp. 79–115

Byrne, Muriel St Clare, ed., *The Lisle Letters: An Abridgement*, London and Chicago, 1983

Camden, William, *Britannia, or a Chorographical Description of Great Britain and Ireland, together with the adjacent islands. Written in Latin by William camsden, and translated into English, with additions and improvements; by Edmund Gibson*, 2 vols, London, 1772

Cameron, Alan, 'Some Social Consequences of the Dissolution of the Monasteries in Nottinghamshire', *Transactions of the Thoroton Society*, vol. 79, 1975, pp. 50–59

Carlisle, N., *A Concise Description of the Endowed Grammar Schools of England and Wales*, 2 vols, London, 1818

Carlson, Eric Josef, ed., *Religion and the English People, 1500–1640: New Voices, New Perspectives*, Kirksville, Missouri, 1998

Carlson, Leland H., ed., *Elizabethan Nonconformist Texts*, vol. III, *The Writings of Henry Barrow, 1587–90*, London, 1962

Cast, David, 'Speaking of Architecture: The Evolution of a Vocabulary in Vasari, Jones and Sir John Vanbrugh', *Journal of the Society of Architectural Historians*, vol. 52, 1993, pp. 179–88

Chalkin, Christopher, *English Counties and Public Building 1650–1850*, London and Rio Grande, 1998

Challis, C. E., *The Tudor Coinage*, Manchester, 1978

Chancellor, F., 'Rochford Hall', *Transactions of the Essex Archaeological Society*, new ser., vol. 9, 1906, pp. 298–300

Chaney, Edward, ed., *The Evolution of English Collecting: The Reception of Italian Art in the Tudor and Stuart Periods*, New Haven and London, 2003

Chatwin, Philip B., 'The Hospital of Lord Leycester, formerly the Hall and other Buildings of the Medieval Guilds in Warwick', *Transactions of the Birmingham Archaeological Society*, vol. 70, 1952, pp. 37–48

Chettle, H. F., 'The Trinitarian Friars and Easton Royal', *Wiltshire Archaeological Magazine*, vol. 51, 1946, pp. 365–77

Chew, Elizabeth V., 'The Countess of Arundel and Tart Hall', in Chaney, ed., 2003, pp. 285–314.

Churchwardens' Accounts of Pittington and other Parishes in the County of Durham 1580–1700, Surtees Society, vol. 74, 1888

Clapham, A. W., 'The Augustinian Priory of Little Leez and the Mansion of Leez Priory', *Transactions of the Essex Archaeological Society*, new ser., vol. 13, 1921, pp. 200–221

Clark, Andrew, ed., *The Foundation Deeds of Felsted School and Charities*, Oxford, 1916

Clark, Peter, ed., *The Early Modern Town: A Reader*, London, 1976

Clark, Peter, ed., *County Towns in Pre-Industrial England*, Leicester, 1981

Clark, Peter, 'Visions of the Urban Community: Antiquarians and the English City before 1800', in Fraser and Sutcliffe, eds., 1983, pp. 106–24

Clark, Peter, 'The Civic Leaders of Gloucester 1580–1800', in Clark, ed., 1984, pp. 311–45

Clark, Peter, ed., *The Transformation of English Provincial Towns*, London, 1984

Clark, Peter, ed., *The Cambridge Urban History of Britain*, vol. II, *1540–1840*, Cambridge, 2000

Clark, Peter, 'Improvement, Policy and Tudor Towns', in Bernard and Gunn, eds., 2002, pp. 233–47

Clark-Maxwell, W. G., 'Sir William Sharington's Work at Lacock, Sudeley and Dudley', *Archaeological Journal*, vol. 70, 1913, pp. 175–82

Clay, Rotha Mary, *The Medieval Hospitals of England*, London, 1966

Cleary, J., and Orton, M., *So Long as the World Shall Endure: The Five Hundred Year History of Ford's and Bond's Hospitals*, Coventry, 1991

Clifford, D. J. H., ed., *The Diaries of Lady Anne Clifford*, Stroud, 1990

Cobb, Gerald, *English Cathedrals. The Forgotten Centuries: Restoration and Change from 1530 to the Present Day*, London, 1980

Cocke, Thomas, 'Le gothique anglais sous Charles Ier', *Révue de l'art*, vol. 30, 1975, pp. 21–30

Cocke, Thomas, 'The Wheel of Fortune: The Appreciation of Gothic since the Middle Ages', in Alexander and Binski, eds., 1987, pp. 183–91

Cocke, Thomas, and Kidson, Peter, *Salisbury Cathedral: Perspectives on the Architectural History*, London, 1993

Colchester, L. S., *Wells Cathedral Fabric Accounts 1390–1600*, Wells, 1983

Coleman, D. C., and John, A. H., eds., *Trade, Government and Economy in Pre-Industrial England: Essays presented to F. J. Fisher*, London, 1976

Collier, Sheila, with Pearson, Sarah, *Whitehaven 1660–1800. A New Town of the Late Seventeenth Century: A Study of its Buildings and Urban Development*, HMSO, London, 1991

Collinson, Patrick, 'John Stow and Nostalgic Antiquarianism', in Merritt, ed., 2001, pp. 27–51

Collinson, Patrick, *Elizabethans*, London, 2003

Collinson, Patrick, and Craig, John, eds., *The Reformation in English Towns 1500–1640*, Basingstoke and New York, 1998

Colvin, Howard, 'Castles and Government in Tudor England', *English Historical Review*, vol. 83, 1969, pp. 125–39

Colvin, H. M., 'Inigo Jones and the Church of St Michael le Querne', *London Journal*, vol. 12, no. 1, 1986, pp. 36–9

Colvin, Howard, *Architecture and the After-Life*, New Haven and London, 1991

Colvin, Howard, 'Gothic Survival and Gothick Revival', in his *Essays in English Architectural History*, New Haven and London, 1999, pp. 217–44

Colvin, Howard, 'The Origin of Chantries', *Journal of Medieval History*, vol. 26, no. 2, 2000, pp. 163–73

Colvin, Howard, and Foister, Susan, eds., *The Panorama of London circa 1544 by Anthonis van den Wyngaerde*, London, 1996

Colvin, H. M., Ransome, D. R., and Summerson, John, *The History of the King's Works*, vol. III, *1485–1660* (part 1), London, 1975

Colvin, H. M., Summerson, John, Biddle, Martin, Hale, J. R., and Merriman, Marcus, *The History of the King's Works*, vol. IV, *1485–1660* (part 2), London, 1982

Condren, Conal, and Cousins, A. D., eds., *The Political Identity of Andrew Marvell*, Aldershot, 1990

Cook, C. H., *Medieval Churches and Chantry Chapels*, London, 1947

Cook, G. H., ed., *Letters to Cromwell and others on the Suppression of the Monasteries*, London, 1965

Coope, Rosalys, 'The "Long Gallery": Its Origins, Development, Use and Decoration', *Architectural History*, vol. 29, 1986, pp. 43–72

Coope, Rosalys, article on post-Reformation Newstead, *Thoroton Society Transactions*, forthcoming

Cooper, Janet, 'Civic Ceremonial in Tudor and Stuart Colchester', *Essex Journal*, vol. 23, no. 3, 1988, pp. 65–7

Cooper, Nicholas, *Houses of the Gentry, 1480–1680*, New Haven and London, 1999

Copeland, G. W., 'Some Problems of Buckland Abbey', *Transactions of the Devonshire Association*, vol. 85, 1953, pp. 41–52

Copeland, G. W., 'Devonshire Church Houses', *Reports and Transactions of the Devonshire Association*, vol. 92, 1960, pp. 116–41; vol. 93, 1961, pp. 250–65; vol. 94, 1962, pp. 427–39

Coppack, Glyn, 'Some Descriptions of Rievaulx Abbey in 1538–9: The Disposition of a Major Cistercian Precinct in the Early Sixteenth Century', *Journal of the British Archaeological Association*, vol. 139, 1986, pp. 100–33

Corfield, Penelope, 'Urban Development in England and Wales in the Sixteenth and Seventeenth Centuries', in Barry, ed., 1990, pp. 35–62

Corke, Shirley, and Poulton, Rob, 'The Historical Evidence *c.* 1275 to 1818', in Poulton and Woods, 1984, pp. 5–16

Coryat, Thomas, *Coryat's Crudities hastily gobled up in Five Moneths Travells (1611)*, ed. in 2 vols, Glasgow, 1905

Cosgrove, Denis, and Daniels, Stephen, eds., *The Iconography of Landscape*, Cambridge, 1988

Coulson, Charles, 'Structural Symbolism in Medieval Castle Architecture', *British Archaeological Association Journal*, vol. 132, 1979, pp. 73–90

Courtney, Paul, 'Armies, Militias and the Urban Landscape: England, France and the Low Countries 1500–1900', in Green and Leech, eds., 2006, pp. 167–93

Cousins, A. D., 'Marvell's "Upon Appleton House, to my Lord Fairfax" and the Regaining of Paradise', in Conal Condren and Cousins, eds., *The Political Identity of Andrew Marvell*, Aldershot, 1990, pp. 53–84

Cowan, Alexander, *Urban Europe, 1500–1700*, London, 1998

Cowper, J. Meadows, 'Accounts of St Dunstan's Canterbury, part two, A.D. 1508–80', *Archaeologia Cantiana*, vol. 17, 1887, pp. 77–149

Cox, J. Charles, *Churchwardens' Accounts from the Fourteenth Century to the Close of the Seventeenth Century*, London, 1913

Craig, J. S., 'Co-operation and Initiatives: Elizabethan Churchwardens and the Parish Accounts of Mildenhall', *Social History*, vol. 18, 1993, pp. 357–80

Crane, Mary Thomas, *Framing Authority: Sayings, Self and Society in Sixteenth-Century England*, Princeton, 1993

Cressy, David, *Literacy and the Social Order: Reading and Writing in Tudor and Stuart England*, Cambridge, 1980

Croft, Pauline, ed., *Patronage, Culture and Power: The Early Cecils, 1558–1612*, New Haven and London, 2002

Cross, C., Loades, D, and Scarisbrick, J. J., eds., *Law and Government under the Tudors*, Cambridge, 1988

Cross, M. Claire, *The Free Grammar School of Leicester*, Department of English Local History, University of Leicester, Occasional Papers, no. 4, Leicester, 1953

Cryer, L. R., *A History of Rochford*, London, 1978

Curran, John E., 'The History Never Written: Bards, Druids, and the Problem of Antiquarianism in *Poly Olbion*', *Renaissance Quarterly*, vol. 51, no. 2, 1998, pp. 498–525

Currie, C. R. J., and Lewis, C. P., eds., *A Guide to English County Histories*, Stroud, 1997

Davies, Horton, *Worship and Theology in England from Cranmer to Hooker, 1534–1603*, Princeton and Oxford, 1970

Davies, J. G., *The Secular Use of Church Buildings*, London, 1968

Dawley, Powel Mills, *John Whitgift and the Reformation*, London, 1955

de Beer, E. S., 'Gothic: Origin and Diffusion of the Term: The Idea of Style in Architecture', *Journal of the Warburg and Courtauld Institutes*, vol. 11, 1948, pp. 143–62

de Vries, J., *European Urbanization 1500–1800*, Cambridge, Mass., 1984

Dickinson, J. C., 'The Buildings of the English Austin Canons after the Dissolution of the Monasteries', *Journal of the British Archaeological Association*, vol. 31, 1968, pp. 60–75

Dickinson, P. G. M., *Hinchingbrooke House*, Huntingdon, 1972

Doggett, Nicholas, *Patterns of Re-Use: The Transformation of Former Monastic Buildings in Post-Dissolution Hertfordshire, 1540–1600*, BAR British Series, no. 331, Oxford, 2002

Doggett, Nicholas, 'The Dissolution and After: Dorchester Abbey, 1536–c. 1800', in Tiller, ed., 2005, pp. 39–48

Donagan, Barbara, 'Halcyon Days and the Literature of War: England's Military Education before 1642', *Past and Present*, no. 147, 1995, pp. 65–100

Drew, Charles, ed., *Lambeth Churchwardens' Accounts 1504–1645 and Vestry Book of 1610*, Surrey Record Society, vol. 18, 1941

Drinkwater, Norman, 'Hereford: Old Market Hall', *Transactions of the Woolhope Naturalists' Field Club*, vol. 33, 1949–51, pp. 1–13

Drury, P. J., 'No other palace in the kingdom will compare with it: The Evolution of Audley End, 1605–1745', *Architectural History*, vol. 23, 1980, pp. 1–39

Dubrow, Heather, and Strier, Richard, eds., *The Historical Renaissance: New Essays on Tudor and Stuart Culture*, Chicago, 1988

Duffy, Eamon, *The Stripping of the Altars: Traditional Religion in England 1400–1580*, New Haven and London, 1992

Duggan, Dianne, '"London The Ring, Covent Garden The Jewel of That Ring": New Light on Covent Garden', *Architectural History*, vol. 43, 2000, pp. 140–61

Duggan, Dianne, '"A rather fascinating hybrid", Tart Hall: Lady Arundel's Casino at Whitehall', *British Art Journal*, vol. 4, 2003, pp. 54–64

Duggan, Dianne, 'Woburn Abbey: The First Episode of a Great Country House', *Architectural History*, vol. 46, 2003, pp. 57–80

Duncan-Jones, Katherine, *Sir Philip Sidney: Courtier Poet*, New Haven and London, 1991

Dunning, Robert W., 'The Tribunal, Glastonbury, Somerset', in Abrams and Carley, eds., 1991, pp. 88–92

Durant, David N., *Bess of Hardwick: An Elizabethan Dynast*, London, 1977

Durant, David, and Riden, Philip, 'The Building of Hardwick Hall', part 1, 'The Old Hall, 1587–91', *Derbyshire Record Society*, vol. 4, 1980, pp. 1–152, and part 2 'The New Hall, 1591–8', ibid., vol. 9, 1984, pp. 153–264

Durning, Louise, ed., *Queen Elizabeth's Book of Oxford*, MS Bodley 13a, trans. Sarah Knight and Helen Spurling, Oxford, 2006

Dyer, Alan D., *The City of Worcester in the Sixteenth Century*, Leicester, 1973

Dyer, Alan, 'Crisis and Resolution: Government and Society in Stratford, 1540–1640', in Bearman, ed., 1997, pp. 80–96

Dyer, Alan D., *Decline and Growth in English Towns 1400–1640*, London, 1991, 3rd edn, Cambridge, 1995

Edwards, G. M., *Sidney Sussex College*, London, 1899

Elton, G. R., *The Tudor Constitution: Documents and Commentary*, Cambridge, 1960

Elton, G. R., *Policy and Police: The Enforcement of the Reformation in the Age of Thomas Cromwell*, Cambridge, 1972

Elyot, Sir Thomas, *The Boke named the Gouernour* (1531), ed. H. H. S. Croft, 1887, repr. New York, 1967

Emmison, F. G., *Elizabethan Life: Wills of Essex Gentry and Merchants from the Prerogative Court of Canterbury*, Chelmsford, 1978

English, J. A., *The Old House, Rochford*, London, 1984

Esdaile, K. A., 'The Monument of the First Lord Rich at Felsted', *Transactions of the Essex Archaeological Society*, new ser., vol. 22, 1936, pp. 59–67

Evans, J., 'Extracts from the Account Book of Sir William More, of Loseley, in Surrey, in the Time of Queen Mary and of Queen Elizabeth', *Archaeologia*, vol. 36, 1855, pp. 284–310

Everitt, Alan, 'The Market Town', in Thirsk, ed., 1967, pp. 467–506; and as 'The Market Towns', in Clark, ed., 1976, pp. 168–204

Everitt, Alan, ed., *Perspectives in English Urban History*, London and Basingstoke, 1973

Everson, Paul, and Stocker, David, 'The Archaeology of Vice-Regality: Charles Brandon's Brief Rule in Lincolnshire', in Gaimster and Gilchrist, eds., 2003, pp. 145–58

Fenley, Pauline, 'Charity and Status: The Activities of Sir John Kederminster at Langley Marish, Buckinghamshire (now Langley, Slough)', *Records of Buckinghamshire*, vol. 42, 2002, pp. 119–32

Finch, M. E., *The Wealth of Five Northamptonshire Families, 1540–1640*, Northamptonshire Record Society, vol. 19, Oxford, 1956

Fleming, Juliet, *Graffiti and the Writing Arts of Early Modern England*, London, 2001

Fowler, Alistair, *The Country House Poem*, Edinburgh, 1994

Fowler, R. C., 'Inventories of Essex Monasteries in 1536', *Essex Archaeological Society Transactions*, vol. 9, 1904, pp. 391–5

Fox, George, *The Journal of George Fox edited from the MSS by Norman Penney*, with an introduction by T. Edmund Harvey, Cambridge, 1911

Foxe, John, *The Acts and Monuments*, London, 1563, 2nd edn, 3rd edn, 1563–76

Foyle, Jonathan, 'Syon Park: Rediscovering Medieval England's Only Bridgettine Monastery', *Current Archaeology*, no. 192, June 2004, pp. 550–55

Frankl, Peter, *The Gothic: Literary Sources and Interpretations through Eight Centuries*, Princeton, 1960

Fraser, D., and Sutcliffe, A., eds., *The Pursuit of Urban History*, London, 1983

Friedman, Alice, 'Did England Have a Renaissance? Classical and Anti-Classical Themes in Elizabethan Culture', in Barnes, ed., 1989, pp. 95–111

Friedman, Alice T., *House and Household in Elizabethan England: Wollaton Hall and the Willoughby Family*, Chicago, 1989

Friedman, Alice, 'Constructing an Identity in Prose, Plaster and Paint: Lady Anne Clifford as Writer and Patron of the Arts', in Gent, ed., 1995, pp. 359–76

Friedrichs, Christopher R., *The Early Modern City 1450–1750*, London and New York, 1995

Gadd, Derek, 'The London Inn of the Abbots of Waltham: A Revised Reconstruction of a Medieval Town House in Lovat Lane', *Transactions of the London and Middlesex Archaeological Society*, vol. 34, 1983, pp. 171–7

Gaimster, David, 'The Archaeology of Post-Medieval Society, c. 1450–1750: Material Culture Studies in Britain Since the War', in B. Vyner, ed., 1994, pp. 283–312

Gaimster, David, and Gilchrist, Roberta, eds., *The Archaeology of Reformation, 1480–1580*, Leeds, 2003

Gaimster, David, and Stamper, Paul, eds., *The Age of Transition: The Archaeology of English Culture, 1400–1600*, Oxford, 1997

Gater, G., and Godfrey, W. H., eds., *Survey of London*, vol. XVIII, *The Strand (The Parish of St. Martin-in-the-Fields, Part II)*, London, 1937

Gent, Lucy, *Picture and Poetry, 1560–1620: Relations between Literature and the Visual Arts in the English Renaissance*, Leamington Spa, 1981

Gent, Lucy, ed., *Albion's Classicism: The Visual Arts in Britain, 1550–1660*, New Haven and London, 1995

Gent, Lucy, and Llewellyn, Nigel, eds., *Renaissance Bodies: The Human Figure in English Culture, c. 1540–1660*, London, 1990

Gilchrist, Roberta, and Mytum, Harold, eds., *The Archaeology of Rural Monasteries*, BAR British Series, no. 203, 1989

Gilchrist, Roberta, and Mytum, Harold, eds., *Advances in Monastic Archaeology*, BAR British Series, no. 227, 1993

Giles, Kate, 'Public Space in Town and Village 1100–1500', in Giles and Dyer, eds., 2005, pp. 293–311

Giles, Kate, and Dyer, Christopher, eds., *Town and Country in the Middle Ages: Contrasts, Contacts and Interconnections, 1100–1500*, Society for Medieval Archaeology, Leeds, 2005

Gilyard-Beer, R., *The County Hall, Abingdon*, HMSO, London, 1956

Girouard, Mark, 'The Development of Longleat House between 1546 and 1572', *Archaeological Journal*, vol. 116, 1961, pp. 200–222

Girouard, Mark, 'The Smythson Collection of the Royal Institute of British Architects', *Architectural History*, vol. 5, 1962, pp. 21–184

Girouard, Mark, 'Elizabethan Architecture and the Gothic Tradition', *Architectural History*, vol. 6, 1963, pp. 23–38

Girouard, Mark, *Robert Smythson and the Elizabethan Country House*, New Haven and London, 1983

Girouard, Mark, *The English Town*, New Haven and London, 1992

Girouard, Mark, 'Burghley House, Lincolnshire', *Country Life*, vol. 186, 1992, no. 17, pp. 56–9, no. 18, pp. 58–61

Godfrey, Walter H., 'An Elizabethan Builder's Contract', *Sussex Archaeological Collections*, vol. 65, 1924, pp. 211–23

Godfrey, W. H., *The English Almshouse*, London, 1955

Goodall, John A. A., *God's House at Ewelme: Life, Devotion and Architecture in a Fifteenth-Century Almshouse*, Aldershot, 2001

Goose, N. R., 'Decay and Regeneration in Seventeenth Century Reading: A Study in a Changing Economy', *Southern History*, vol. 6, 1984, pp. 53–74

Gordon, Andrew, and Klein, Bernhard, eds., *Literature, Mapping and the Politics of Space in Early Modern Britain*, Cambridge, 2001

Gotch, J. Alfred, *A Complete Account, Illustrated by Measured Drawings of the Buildings erected in Northamptonshire, by Sir Thomas Tresham, between the Years 1575 and 1605*, Northampton and London, 1883

Gottfried, Robert S., *Bury St Edmunds and the Urban Crisis 1290–1539*, Princeton, 1982

Grady, Kevin, 'The Records of the Charity Commissioners: A Source for Urban History', *Urban History Yearbook*, no. 9, 1982

Graves, Pamela C., 'Social Space in the English Medieval Parish Church', *Economy and Society*, vol. 18, no. 3, 1989, pp. 297–322

Gray, I. E., and Potter, W. E., *Ipswich School 1400–1950*, Ipswich, 1950

Gray, Todd, Rowe, Margery M., and Erskine, Audrey M., eds., *Tudor and Stuart Devon. The Common Estate and Government: Essays presented to Joyce Youings*, Exeter, 1992

Green, Adrian, and Leech, Roger, eds., *Cities in the World 1500–2000*, Leeds, 2006

Greene, J. Patrick, *Medieval Monasteries*, Leicester, 1992

Greene, J. Patrick, 'The Impact of the Dissolution on Monasteries in Cheshire: The Case of Norton', in Thacker, ed., 2000, pp. 152–69

Greenhill, F. A., 'The Sandys Contract', *Transactions of the Monumental Brass Society*, vol. 9, 1952–4, pp. 354–61

Gregory, D. L., *John Abel of Sarnesfield*, London, 1980

Griffiths, Paul, and Jenner, Mark S. R., *Londonopolis: Essays in the Cultural and Social History of Early Modern London*, Manchester, 2000

Guillaume, Jean, ed., *Les Traités d'architecture de la Renaissance*, Paris, 1988

Gunn, S. J., *Charles Brandon, Duke of Suffolk, 1484–1545*, Oxford, 1988

Gunn, Steven, 'War, Dynasty and Public Opinion in Early Tudor England', in Bernard and Gunn, eds., 2002, pp. 131–49

Gunn, S. J., and Lindley, P. G., 'Charles Brandon's West-horpe: An Early Tudor Courtyard House in Suffolk', *Archaeological Journal*, vol. 145, 1988, pp. 272–89

Gunn, S. J., and Lindley, P. G., eds., *Cardinal Wolsey: Church, State and Art*, Cambridge, 1991

Habbakuk, H. J., 'The Market for Monastic Property, 1539–1603', *Economic History Review*, 2nd ser., vol. 10, 1958, pp. 362–80

Haigh, Christopher, *English Reformations: Religion, Politics and Society under the Tudors*, Oxford, 1993

Hall, J., *A History of the Town and Parish of Nantwich*, Didsbury, 1883, repr. 1972

Hall, Michael, ed., *Gothic Architecture and its Meanings, 1550–1830*, Reading, 2002

Hallam, Elizabeth M., 'Henry VIII's Monastic Refoundations of 1536–7 and the Course of the Dissolution', *Bulletin of the Institute of Historical Research*, vol. 51, 1978, pp. 124–31

Hanham, Alison, ed., *Churchwardens' Accounts of Ashburton 1479–1580*, Devon and Cornwall Record Society, new ser., no. 15, 1970

Hannay, M. P., *Philip's Phoenix: Mary Sidney, Countess of Pembroke*, New York and Oxford, 1990

Harbottle, R. B., and Fraser, R., 'Black Friars, Newcastle-upon-Tyne, after the Dissolution of the Monasteries', *Archaeologia Aeliana*, 5th ser., vol. 15, 1987, pp. 23–150

Hare, J. N. 'The Buildings of Battle Abbey', *Proceedings of the Battle Conference on Anglo-Norman Studies 1980*, Bury, 1981, pp. 78–95

Hare, J. N., *Battle Abbey: The Eastern Range and the Excavations of 1978–80*, HBMC Archaeological Reports, no. 2, 1985

Hare, John, 'Netley Abbey: Monastery, Mansion and Ruin', *Proceedings of the Hampshire Field Club Archaeological Society*, vol. 49, 1993, pp. 207–27

Hare, John, *The Dissolution of the Monasteries in Hampshire*, Hampshire Papers, no. 16, Winchester, 1999

Harley, J. B., 'Maps, Knowledge and Power', in Cosgrove and Daniels, eds., 1988, pp. 277–312

Harris, Barbara J., *English Aristocratic Women 1450–1550: Marriage and Family, Property and Careers*, Oxford, 2002

Harris, Eileen, assisted by Nicholas Savage, *British Architectural Books and Writers 1556–1785*, Cambridge, 1990

Harris, John, *The Artist and the Country House: A History of Country House and Garden View Painting in Britain, 1540–1870*, London, 1979

Harris, John, and Higgott, Gordon, *Inigo Jones: Complete Architectural Drawings*, London, 1989

Harris, Jonathan Gil, 'This Is Not a Pipe: Water Supply, Incontinent Sources, and the Leaky Body Politic', in Burt and Archer, eds., 1994, pp. 203–28

Harrison, William, *The Description of England: The Classic Contemporary Account of Tudor Social Life* (1570s), ed. Georges Edelen, Ithaca, NY, 1968

Hart, Vaughan, 'A peece of good *Heraldry*, than of *Architecture*: Heraldry and the Orders of Architecture as Joint Emblems of Chivalry', *Res*, vol. 23, 1993, pp. 52–66

Hart, Vaughan, 'From Virgin to Courtesan in Early English Vitruvian Books', in Hart and Hicks, eds., 1998, pp. 297–318

Hart, Vaughan, and Hicks, Peter, eds., *Paper Palaces: The Rise of the Renaissance Architectural Treatise*, New Haven and London, 1998

Harte, N. B., 'State Control of Dress and Social Change in Pre-Industrial England', in D. C. Coleman and A. H. John, eds., 1976, pp. 132–65

Hartwell, Clare, *The History and Architecture of Chetham's School and Library*, New Haven and London, 2004

Harvey, John H., 'Four Fifteenth-Century London Plans', *London Topographical Society*, vol. 20, 1952, pp. 1–8

Harvey, P. D. A., 'Estate Surveyors and the Spread of the Scale-Map in England 1550–80', *Landscape History*, vol. 15, 1993, pp. 37–50

Hassell-Smith, *County and Court: Government and Politics in Norfolk 1558–1603*, Oxford, 1974

Hay, Denys, 'The Dissolution of the Monasteries in the Diocese of Durham', *Archaeologia Aeliana*, 4th ser., vol. 15, 1938, pp. 69–114

Haynes, S., *A Collection of State Papers*, London, 1740

Heal, Felicity, *Of Prelates and Princes: A Study of the Economic and Social Position of the Tudor Episcopate*, Cambridge, 1980

Heal, Felicity, 'The Crown, the Gentry and London: The Enforcement of Proclamation, 1596–1640', in Cross, Loades and Scarisbrick, eds., 1988, pp. 211–26

Heal, Felicity, *Hospitality in Early Modern England*, Oxford, 1990

Heal, Felicity, and Holmes, Clive, *The Gentry in England and Wales, 1500–1700*, Basingstoke, 1994

Heal, Felicity, and Holmes, Clive, 'The Economic Patronage of William Cecil', in Croft, ed., 2002, pp. 199–229

Hembry, Phyllis, 'Episcopal Palaces 1535–1660', in Ives, Scarisbrick and Knecht, eds., 1978, pp. 146–66

Henderson, Paula, 'The Loggia in Tudor and Early Stuart England: The Adaptation and Function of Classical Form', in Gent, ed., 1995, pp. 109–46

Henderson, Paula, *The Tudor House and Garden: Architecture and Landscape in the Sixteenth and Early Seventeenth Centuries*, New Haven and London, 2005

Hentzner, Paul, trans. Horace, Earl of Orford, as *Paul Hentzner's Travels in England, during the Reign of Queen Elizabeth*, London, 1797

Herendeen, Wyman H., 'Wanton Discourse and the Engines of Time: William Camden – Historian among Poets-Historical', in Horowitz, Cruz and Furman, eds., 1988, pp. 142–56

Hervey, M. F. S., *The Life, Correspondence and Collections of Thomas Howard Earl of Arundel*, Cambridge, 1921

Heylyn, Peter, *Cosmographie in four bookes: containing the chorographie of the whole world, and all the principall kingdoms, provinces, seas and isles thereof*, London, 1652.

Higgott, Gordon, 'The Fabric [of St Paul's] to 1670', in Keene, Burns and Saint, eds., 2004, pp. 171–90

Hill, J. W. F., *Tudor and Stuart Lincoln*, Cambridge, 1956

Hilliard, Nicholas, *The Arte of Limninge* (*c*. 1600), ed. R. K. R. Thornton and T. G. S. Cain, Manchester, 1992

Hindle, Steve, *The State and Social Change in Early Modern England, 1550–1640*, Basingstoke and New York, 2000

Hoak, Dale, ed., *Tudor Political Culture*, Cambridge, 1995

Hobbs, Steven, 'Piety and Church Fabric in Sixteenth-Century Wiltshire: Evidence from Wills', *Wiltshire Studies: The Wiltshire Archaeological and Natural History Magazine*, vol. 98, 2005, pp. 81–9

Holland, Elizabeth, 'The Earliest Bath Guildhall', *Bath History*, vol. 2, 1988, pp. 163–79

Hollander, A. E. J., and Kellaway, W., eds., *Studies in London History presented to Philip Edmund Jones*, London, 1969

Hooker, Richard, *Of the Laws of Ecclesiastical Polity*, with an introduction by Christopher Morris, London, 1907

Hope, W. H. St John, 'The Cluniac Priory of St Pancras at Lewes', *Sussex Archaeological Collections*, vol. 49, 1906a, pp. 66–88

Hope, W. H. St John, 'The Making of Place House at Titchfield, near Southampton, in 1538', *Archaeological Journal*, vol. 63, 1906b, pp. 231–43

Hopkins, Lisa, 'We were the Trojans: British National Identities in 1633', *Renaissance Studies*, vol. 16, no. 1, 2002, pp. 36–51

Hopton, F. C., 'The Buildings of Shaftesbury Abbey in the Mid-Sixteenth Century', *Proceedings of the Dorset Natural History and Archaeological Society*, vol. 115, 1993, pp. 1–13

Horowitz, Maryanne Cline, Cruz, Anne J., and Furman, Wendy A., eds., *Renaissance Rereadings, Intertext and Context*, Urbana and Chicago, 1988

Hoskins, W. G., 'The Rebuilding of Rural England, 1570–1640', *Past and Present*, no. 4, 1953, pp. 44–59

Hoskins, W. G., 'The Elizabethan Merchants of Exeter', in Bindoff, Hurstfield and Williams, 1961, pp. 163–87; also in Clark, ed., 1976, pp. 148–67

Hoskins, W. G., 'English Provincial Towns in the Early Sixteenth Century', *Provincial England*, London, 1963, pp. 68–85; also in Clark, ed., 1976, pp. 91–105

Houfe, S., 'The Builders of Chicksands Priory', *Bedfordshire Magazine*, vol. 16, 1978, no. 125, pp. 185–9, no. 126, pp. 228–31

Houlbrooke, Ralph, 'Civility and Civil Observances in the Early Modern English Funeral', in Burke, Harrison and Slack, eds., 2000, pp. 67–85

Howard, Deborah, 'Scotland's Thrie Estates', in Gent, ed., 1995, pp. 51–78

Howard, Deborah, 'The Protestant Renaissance', *Architectural Heritage: The Journal of the Architectural Heritage Society of Scotland*, vol. 9, 1998, pp. 1–15

Howard, Maurice, *The Early Tudor Country House: Architecture and Politics, 1490–1550*, London, 1987

Howard, Maurice, 'The Ideal House and Healthy Life: The Origins of Architectural Theory in England', in Guillaume, ed., 1988, pp. 425–33

Howard, Maurice, 'Self-Fashioning and the Classical Moment in Mid-Sixteenth-Century English Architecture', in Gent and Llewellyn, eds., 1990, pp. 198–217

Howard, Maurice, ' "His Lordship was the chiefest architect": Patrons and Builders in 16th-Century England', in Worsley, ed., 1994, pp. 7–13

Howard, Maurice, 'Classicism and Civic Architecture in Renaissance England', in Gent, ed., 1995, pp. 29–48

Howard, Maurice, *The Tudor Image*, London, 1995

Howard, Maurice, ed., *The Image of the Building: Papers from the Annual Symposium of the Society of Architectural Historians of Great Britain*, Milton Keynes, 1996

Howard, Maurice, 'Inventories, Surveys and the History of Great Houses, 1480–1660', *Architectural History*, vol. 41, 1998, pp. 14–29

Howard, Maurice, 'The Historiography of "Elizabethan Gothic" ', in Hall, ed., 2002, pp. 53–70

Howard, Maurice, 'Recycling the Monastic Fabric: Beyond the Act of Dissolution', in Gaimster and Gilchrist, eds., 2003, pp. 221–34

Howard, Maurice, and Wilson, Edward, *The Vyne: A Tudor House Revealed*, London, 2003

Howarth, David, 'The Patronage and Collecting of Aletheia, Countess of Arundel 1606–54', *Journal of the History of Collections*, vol. 10, no. 2, 1998, pp. 125–37

Hoyle, R. W., 'The Origins of the Dissolution of the Monasteries', *Historical Journal*, vol. 38, no. 2, 1995, pp. 275–305

Hubbard, Edward, *The Buildings of Wales: Clwyd*, Harmondsworth, 1986

Hughes, Ann, 'Building a Godly Town: Religious and Cultural Divisions in Stratford-upon-Avon, 1560–1640', in Bearman, ed., 1997, pp. 97–109

Hughes, Paul L., and Larkin, James F., eds., *Tudor Royal Proclamations*, vol. II, *The Later Tudors 1553–1587*, vol. III, *1588–1603*, New Haven and London, 1969

Hulme, Peter, and Sherman, William A., eds., *The Tempest and its Travels*, London, 2000

Humphreys, John, 'The Elizabethan Estate Book of Grafton Manor, near Bromsgrove, with Particulars of the Re-Building of the Mansion in 1568–1569', *Transactions and Proceedings of the Birmingham Archaeological Society*, vol. 44, 1918, pp. 1–124

Hunt, A., *Governance of the Consuming Passions: A History of Sumptuary Law*, London, 1996

Hurry, Jamieson B., *Reading Abbey*, London, 1901

Husselby, J., 'Architecture at Burghley House: The Patronage of William Cecil', unpubd PhD thesis, Warwick University, 1996

Husselby, Jill, 'The Politics of Pleasure: William Cecil and Burghley House', in Croft, ed., 2002, pp. 21–45

Husselby, Jill, and Paula Henderson, 'Location, Location, Location! Cecil House in the Strand', *Architectural History*, vol. 45, 2002, pp. 159–93

Hussey, Christopher, 'Rycote Park, Oxfordshire', *Country Life*, vol. 63, 1928, pp. 16–24

Ives, E. W., Scarisbrick, J. J., and Knecht, R. J., eds., *Wealth and Power in Tudor England: Essays presented to S. T. Bindoff*, London, 1978

Jack, Sybil M., 'Dissolution Dates for Monasteries dissolved under the Act of 1536', *Bulletin of the Institute of Historical Research*, vol. 43, 1970, pp. 161–81

Jackson, Christine, 'Functionality, Commemoration and Civic Competition: A Study of Early Seventeenth-Century Workhouse Design and Building in Reading and Newbury', *Architectural History*, vol. 47, 2004, pp. 77–112

Jacobus, Laura, 'On "Whether a man could see before him and behind him both at once": The Role of Drawing in the Design of Interior Space in England *c*. 1600–1800', *Architectural History*, vol. 31, 1988, pp. 148–66

James, Frances R., 'Copy of a Deed by Richard Phelips, dated 1535', *Transactions of the Woolhope Naturalists' Field Club for 1934–36*, 1938, pp. 100–04

Jenner, Mark S., 'Civilization or Deodorization? Smell in Early Modern English Culture', in Burke, Harrison and Slack, eds., 2000, pp. 127–44

Johnson, Matthew H., 'Assumptions and Interpretations in the Study of the Great Rebuilding', *Archaeological Review from Cambridge*, vol. 5, no. 2, 1986, pp. 141–53

Johnson, Matthew, 'Reconstructing Castles and Refashioning Identities in Renaissance England', in Tarlow and West, eds., 1999, pp. 69–86

Johnson, Matthew, *Behind the Castle Gate: From Medieval to Renaissance*, London and New York, 2002

Jones, E. L., Porter, S., and Turner, M., *A Gazetteer of English Urban Fire Disasters, 1500–1900*, Historical Geography Research Series, no. 13, 1984

Jones, G. P., 'The Repairing of Crummock Bridge, Holm Cultram, 1554', *Transactions of the Cumberland and Westmorland Antiquarian and Archaeological Society*, vol. 52, 1952, pp. 85–100

Jones, M. K., and Underwood, M. G., *The King's Mother: Lady Margaret Beaufort, Countess of Richmond and Derby*, Cambridge, 1992

Ben Jonson, edited by C. H. Herford and Percy and Evelyn Simpson, vol. VIII, *The Poems and Prose Works*, Oxford, 1947

Jordan, W. K., *Philanthropy in England, 1480–1660: A Study of the Changing Pattern of Social Aspirations*, London, 1959

Jordan, W. K., *The Charities of Rural England*, London, 1961

Jordan, W. K., ed., *The Chronicle and Political Papers of King Edward VI*, London, 1966

Keene, Derek, Burns, Arthur, and Saint, Andrew, eds., *St Paul's: The Cathedral Church of London, 604–2004*, New Haven and London, 2004

Kemp, Brian, *Reading Abbey: An Introduction to the History of the Abbey*, Reading, 1968

Kemp, Thomas, ed., *The Black Book of Warwick*, Warwick, 1898

Kendrick, T. D., *British Antiquity*, London, 1950

Kennedy, Joseph, 'Laymen and Monasteries in Hampshire, 1530–1558', *Proceedings of the Hampshire Field Club*, vol. 27, 1970, pp. 65–85

Kent, Joan, *The English Village Constable, 1580–1642*, Oxford, 1986

Kenyon, John R., *Raglan Castle*, Cardiff, 1988

Key, Jane, ed., 'The Letters and Will of Lady Dorothy Bacon, 1597–1629', *Norfolk Record Society*, vol. 56, 1991, pp. 77–112

King, John N., 'The Godly Woman in Elizabethan Iconography', *Renaissance Quarterly*, vol. 38, 1985, pp. 41–84

Kitching, C. J., 'Fire Disasters and Fire-Relief in Sixteenth-Century England: The Nantwich Fire of 1583', *Bulletin of the Institute of Historical Research*, vol. 54, 1981, pp. 171–87

Kitching, Christopher, 'Re-Roofing Old St Paul's Cathedral, 1561–66', *London Journal*, vol. 12, no. 2, 1986, pp. 123–33

Knight, Caroline, 'Old Somerset House', *British Art Journal*, vol. 2, no. 2, 2000–2001, pp. 6–13

Knight, Caroline, 'The Cecils at Wimbledon', in Croft, ed., 2002, pp. 47–66

Knowles, David, *The Religious Orders in England*, vol. III, *The Tudor Age*, rev. edn, Cambridge, 1979

Knowles, M. D., and Hadcock, R. N., *Medieval Religious Houses*, London, 1954

Knowles, James, 'Cecil's Shopping Centre: The Rediscovery of a Ben Jonson Masque in Praise of Trade', *Times Literary Supplement*, 7 February 1997, pp. 14–15

Krieder, A., *English Chantries: The Road to Dissolution*, Cambridge, Mass., 1979

Kumin, Beat, *The Shaping of a Community: The Rise and Reformation of the English Parish, c.1400–1560*, Aldershot, 1996

Labno, J. J., 'English Schools and Almshouses/ Hospitals: Pre- and Post-Reformation Foundations. The Evolution of Architectural Form', unpubd MA dissertation, University of Sussex, 1997

Laithwaite, Michael, 'The Buildings of Burford: A Cotswold Town in the Fourteenth to Nineteenth Centuries', in Everitt, ed., 1973, pp. 60–90

Laithwaite, Michael, 'Totnes Houses 1500–1800', in Clark, ed., 1984, pp. 62–98

Larkin and Hughes, eds., *Stuart Royal Proclamations*, vol. II, *Charles I 1625–1646*, Oxford, 1983, pp. 20–6.

Laurence, Anne, *Women in England 1500–1760: A Social History*, London, 1996

Laurence, Anne, 'Women Using Building in Seventeenth-Century England: A Question of Sources?', *Transactions of the Royal Historical Society*, vol. 13, 2003a, pp. 293–303

Laurence, Anne, 'Space, Status and Gender in English Topographical Paintings c.1660–c.1740', *Architectural History*, vol. 46, 2003b, pp. 81–94

Lawson, Terence, and Killingray, David, *An Historical Atlas of Kent*, Chichester, 2004

Lee, Frederick George, *The History and Antiquities of the Prebendal Church of the Blessed Virgin Mary of Thame*, London, 1883

Leech, Roger H., 'The Prospect from Rugman's Row: The Row House in Late Sixteenth- and Early Seventeenth-Century London', *Archaeological Journal*, vol. 153, 1996, pp. 201–42

Lehmberg, Stanford E., *The Reformation of Cathedrals: Cathedrals in English Society, 1485–1603*, Princeton, 1988

Leland, John, *The Itinerary of John Leland in or about the Years 1535–1543*, ed. L. Toulmin Smith, with a foreword by Thomas Kendrick, 5 vols, London, 1964

Letters and Papers Foreign and Domestic of the Reign of Henry VIII 1509–47, eds. J. S. Brewer, J. Gairdner and R. H. Brodie, London, 1862–1910, 1920, 1929–32 (*L&P*)

Lindley, Phillip, ed., *Gainsborough Old Hall*, Occasional Papers in Lincolnshire History and Archaeology, no. 8, Lincoln, 1991

Lister, John, and Brown, William, 'Seventeenth Century Builders' Contracts', *Yorkshire Archaeological Journal*, vol. 16, 1902, pp. 108–13

Llewellyn, Nigel, *Funeral Monuments in Post-Reformation England*, Cambridge, 2000

Lloyd, Christopher, and Thurley, Simon, *Henry VIII: Images of a Tudor King*, Oxford, 1990

Lloyd, David, *The Making of English Towns*, London, 1984

Lomazzo, Giovanni Paolo, trans. Richard Haydocke as *A Tracte containing the Artes of Curious Paintinge,*

Carvinge and Buildinge (1598), repr. Farnborough, 1970

Longford, E. *Images of Chelsea*, Richmond, 1980

MacCaffrey, Wallace T., *Exeter 1540–1640: The Growth of an English County Town*, Cambridge, Mass., 1958

McClain, Lisa, 'Without Church, Cathedral or Shrine: The Search for Religious Space among Catholics in England, 1559–1625', *Sixteenth-Century Journal*, vol. 33, no. 2, 2002, pp. 381–99

McClung, William A., *The Country House in English Renaissance Poetry*, Berkeley, 1977

McClung, William A., 'The Matter of Metaphor: Literary Myths of Construction', *Journal of the Society of Architectural Historians*, vol. 40, no. 4, 1981, pp. 279–88

MacCullough, Diarmaid, *Reformation: Europe's House Divided 1490–1700*, Cambridge, 2003

MacCullough, Diarmaid, and Blatchly, John, 'A House Fit for a Queen: Wingfield House in Tacket Street, Ipswich and its Heraldic Room', *Proceedings of the Suffolk Institute*, vol. 38, 1996, pp. 13–34

McNeil, R., and Turner, R. C., 'An Architectural and Topographical Survey of Vale Royal Abbey', *Journal of the Chester Archaeological and Historical Society*, vol. 70 (1987–8), 1990, pp. 51–79

McRae, Andrew, '"On the Famous Voyage": Ben Jonson and Civic Space', in Gordon and Klein, eds., 2001, pp. 181–203

McVicar, James B., 'Social Change and the Growth of Antiquarian Studies in Tudor and Stuart England', *Archaeological Review from Cambridge*, vol. 3, no. 1, 1984, pp. 48–67

Machin, R. 'The Great Rebuilding: A Reassessment', *Past and Present*, no. 77, 1977, pp. 33–56

Magno, Alessandro, see Barron, Coleman and Gobbi, eds., 1983

Maltby, Judith D., *Prayer Book and People in Elizabethan and Early Stuart England*, Cambridge, 1998

Manco, Jean, 'Bath and "The Great Rebuilding"', *Bath History*, vol. IV, 1992, pp. 25–51

Manley, Lawrence, 'From Matron to Monster: Tudor-Stuart London and the Languages of Urban Description', in Dubrow and Strier, eds., 1988, pp. 347–74

Manley, Lawrence, *Literature and Culture in Early Modern London*, Cambridge, 1995

Manley, Lawrence, 'Of Sites and Rites', in Smith, Strier and Bevington, eds., 1995, pp. 35–53

Manning, Roger B., *Religion and Society in Elizabethan Sussex: A Study in the Enforcement of the Religious Settlement 1558–1603*, Leicester, 1969

Marchant, R. A., *The Puritans and the Church Courts in the Diocese of York 1560–1642*, London, 1960

Markus, Thomas A., *Buildings and Power: Freedom and*

Control in the Origin of Modern Building Types, London and New York, 1993

Marotti, Arthur F., 'Southwell's Remains: Catholicism and Anti-Catholicism in Early Modern England', in Brown and Marotti, eds., 1997, pp. 37–65

Martin, Jeanette, 'Leadership and Priorities in Reading during the Reformation', in Collinson and Craig, eds., 1998, pp. 113–29

Andrew Marvell: Complete Poetry, ed. George de F. Lord, London and Melbourne, 1968, repr. 1984

Massey, Lyle, ed., *The Treatise on Perspective: Published and Unpublished*, New Haven and London, 2003

Masters, Betty R., 'The Mayor's Household before 1600', in Hollander and Kellaway, eds., 1969, pp. 95–116

Mayhew, Graham, *Tudor Rye*, Falmer, 1987

Mendelson, Sara, and Crawford, Patricia, *Women in Early Modern England, 1550–1720*, Oxford, 1998

Mercer, Eric, 'The Decoration of the Royal Palaces, 1553–1625', *Archaeological Journal*, vol. 110, 1954, pp. 150–63

Mercer, Eric, *English Art 1553–1625*, Oxford, 1962

Merriman, Marcus, 'Italian Military Engineers in Britain in the 1540s', in Tyacke, ed., 1983, pp. 57–67

Merritt, Julia, 'The Social Context of the Parish Church in Early Modern Westminster', *Urban History Yearbook*, vol. 18, 1991, pp. 20–31

Merritt, J. F., 'Puritans, Laudians, and the Phenomenon of Church-Building in Jacobean London', *Historical Journal*, vol. 41, no. 4, 1998, pp. 935–60

Merritt, Julia F., ed., *Imagining Early Modern London: Perceptions and Portrayals of the City from Stow to Strype, 1598–1720*, Cambridge, 2001

Merritt, J. F., 'The Cecils and Westminster 1558–1612: The Development of an Urban Power Base', in Croft, ed., 2002, pp. 231–46

Meyvaert, Paul, 'The Medieval Monastic Claustrum', *Gesta*, vol. 12, 1973, pp. 53–9

Millican, Percy, 'The Rebuilding of Wroxham Bridge in 1576: A Transcript of the Account Book', *Norfolk Archaeology*, vol. 26, 1936–8, pp. 281–95

Mills, Joan, and Mills, Dennis, 'A Case Study at Canwick of the Enduring Influence of Monastic Houses', *Lincolnshire History and Archaeology*, vol. 33, 1998, pp. 47–54

Mitchell, R., ed., *Hinchingbrooke Documents 1530–1840*, Huntingdon, 1972

Morey, A., *The Catholic Subjects of Elizabeth I*, London, 1978

Morgan, Victor, 'The Elizabethan Shire House at Norwich', in Rawcliffe, Virgoe and Wilson, eds., 1996, pp. 149–60

Morris, Richard K., 'Monastic Architecture: Destruction and Reconstruction', in Gaimster and Gilchrist, eds., 2003, pp. 235–51

Mowat, Barbara, '"Knowing I loved my books": Reading *The Tempest* Intertextually', in Hulme and Sherman, eds., 2000, pp. 27–36

Mowl, Timothy, ' "The Wrong Things at the Wrong Time": 17th-Century Gothic Churches', in Hall, ed., 2002, pp. 73–96

Mulcaster, Richard, *Positions wherein those primitive circumstances be examined, which are ncessarie for the training up of children, either for skill in their booke, or health in the bodie* (1561), London, 1581.

Muldrew, Craig, *The Economy of Obligation: The Culture of Credit and Social Relations in Early Modern England*, Basingstoke, 1998

Murray, Hugh, 'The Great Chamber at Gilling Castle', *St Lawrence Papers*, vol. VIII, York, 1996, pp. 1–33

Myers, A. R., 'Tudor Chester', *Journal of the Chester Archaeological Society*, vol. 63, 1980, pp. 43–57

Neville-Singleton, Pamela, '"A very good trumpet": Richard Hakluyt and the Politics of Overseas Expansion', in Brown and Marotti, eds., 1997, pp. 66–79

Newman, John, 'Nicholas Stone's Goldsmiths' Hall: Design and Practice in the 1630s', *Architectural History*, vol. 14, 1971, pp. 30–39

Newman, John, 'Cardinal Wolsey's Collegiate Foundations', in Gunn and Lindley, eds., 1991, pp. 103–15

Newman, John, 'Inigo Jones's Architectural Education before 1614', *Architectural History*, vol. 35, 1992, pp. 18–50

Nichols, J., *The Progresses and Public Processions of Queen Elizabeth*, 3 vols, London, 1823

Ní Chuilleanán, Eiléan, ' "Strange Ceremonies": Sacred Space and Bodily Presence in the English Reformation', in Piesse, ed., 2000, pp. 133–54

Nield, Theodore, 'The Cross, Leominster', *Transactions of the Woolhope Naturalists' Field Club*, 1918–20, pp. 43–6

North, Thomas, ed., *The Accounts of the Churchwardens of Saint Martin's, Leicester, 1489–1844*, Leicester, 1884

Norton, Christopher, 'The Buildings of St Mary's Abbey, York and their Destruction', *Antiquaries Journal*, vol. 74, 1994, pp. 256–88

Oldham, J. B., 'A Sixteenth Century Shrewsbury School Inventory', *Transactions of the Shropshire Archaeological Society*, vol. 47, 1933–4, pp. 121–37

O'Malley, Michelle, *The Business of Art: Contracts and the Commissioning Process in Renaissance Italy*, New Haven and London, 2005

Onians, John, *Bearers of Meaning: The Classical Orders in Antiquity, the Middle Ages, and the Renaissance*, Princeton, 1988

Onians, John, 'Architecture, Metaphor and the Mind', *Architectural History*, vol. 35, 1992, pp. 192–207

Orlin, Lena Cowan, 'Boundary Disputes in Early

Modern London', in Orlin, ed., *Material London, ca. 1600*, Philadelphia, 2000, pp. 344–76

Orme, Nicholas, *English Schools in the Middle Ages*, London, 1973

Orme, Nicholas, and Webster, Margaret, *The English Hospital, 1070–1570*, New Haven and London, 1995

Orme, Nicholas, 'English Schools 1400–1550', Paper given at the conference *Biographies and Space: Placing the Subject in Art and Architecture*, Paul Mellon Centre, London, March 2003

O'Sullivan, Deidre, 'The "Little Dissolution" of the 1520s', *Post-Medieval Archaeology*, vol. 40, no. 2, 2006, pp. 227–58

Oxley, J. E., *The Reformation in Essex to the Death of Mary*, Manchester, 1965

Palliser, D. M., 'York under the Tudors: The Trading Life of a Northern Capital', in Everitt, ed., 1973, pp. 39–59

Palliser, D. M., *Tudor York*, Oxford, 1979

Palliser, D. M., 'Civic Mentality and the Environment in Tudor York', *Northern History*, vol. 18, 1982, pp. 78–115; also in Barry, ed., 1990, pp. 206–43

Palliser, D. M., 'Town Defences in Medieval England and Wales', in Ayton and Price, eds., 1995, pp. 105–20

Palmer, Anthony, ed., *Tudor Churchwardens' Accounts*, Hertfordshire Record Society Publications, vol. 1, 1985

Parfitt, George, *English Poetry of the Seventeenth Cenury*, 2nd edn, London, 1992

Parker, Vanessa, *The Making of King's Lynn: Secular Buildings from the 11th to the 17th Century*, London and Chichester, 1971

Parmiter, Geoffrey de C., 'The Imprisonment of Papists in Private Castles', *Recusant History*, vol. 19, no. 1, 1988, pp. 16–38

Parry, G. J. R., *A Protestant Vision: William Harrison and the Reformation of Elizabethan England*, Cambridge, 1987

Parsons, David, ed., *Stone Quarrying and Building in England AD 43–1525*, Chichester, 1990

Patterson, Catherine F., 'Leicester and Lord Huntingdon: Urban Patronage in Early Modern England', *Midland History*, vol. 16, 1991, pp. 45–62

Pears, S. A., 'Leycester's Hospital', *Transactions of the Ancient Monuments Society*, new ser., vol. 13, 1966, pp. 35–41

Peck, Linda Levy, *Northampton: Patronage and Policy at the Court of James I*, London, 1982

Peck, Linda Levy, *Consuming Splendor: Society and Culture in Seventeenth-Century England*, Cambridge, 2005

Penycate, J. W., *A Guide to the Hospital of the Blessed Trinity (Abbot's Hospital), Guildford*, Guildford, 1976

Percy, F. H. G., *Whitgift School: A History*, Croydon, 1991

Pevsner, Nikolaus and among others, *The Buildings of England*, 46 vols, Harmondsworth, 1951–74; later rev. edns by Simon Bradley, Bridget Cherry et al., New Haven and London, 2002–, individual volumes as cited in the notes above

Pevsner, Nikolaus, 'Old Somerset House', *Architectural Review*, vol. 116, 1954, pp. 163–7

Phillips, John, *The Reformation of Images: Destruction of Art in England, 1535–1660*, Berkeley, Los Angeles and London, 1973

Phillpotts, Christopher, 'The Houses of Henry VIII's Courtiers in London', in Gaimster and Gilchrist, eds., 2003, pp. 299–309

Phythian-Adams, Charles, 'Ceremony and the Citizen: The Communal Year at Coventry 1450–1550', in Clark, ed., 1976, pp. 106–28

Pierce, S. R., 'A Drawing for a New Spire for Old St. Paul's London', *Antiquaries Journal*, vol. 43, 1963, pp. 128–31

Piesse, A. J., ed., *Sixteenth-Century Identities*, Manchester, 2000

Piggott, Stuart, 'William Camden and the *Britannia*', *Proceedings of the British Academy*, vol. 37, 1951, pp. 199–217

Piggott, Stuart, *Ruins in a Landscape: Essays in Antiquarianism*, Edinburgh, 1976

Pittman, Susan, 'The Social Structure and Parish Community of St. Andrew's Church, Calstock, as Reconstituted from its Seating Plan, c.1587/8', *Southern History*, nos. 20–21, 1998–9, pp. 44–67

Pittock, J., and Wear, A., eds., *Interpretation and Cultural History*, New York, 1991

Platt, Colin, *Medieval England*, London, 1978

Platt, Colin, *The Great Rebuildings of Tudor and Stuart England*, London, 1994

Platter, Thomas, *Thomas Platter's Travels in England, 1599*, ed. Clare Williams, London, 1937

Porter, Stephen, *Destruction in the English Civil Wars*, Stroud, 1994

Poulton, Rob, and Woods, Humphrey, *Excavations on the Site of the Dominican Friary at Guildford in 1974 and 1976*, Surrey Archaeological Society, vol. 9, 1984

Pound, J. F., 'The Social Trade and Structure of Norwich 1525–1575', *Past and Present*, no. 34, 1966, pp. 49–69; also in Clark, ed., 1976, pp. 129–47

Pound, J. F., *Tudor and Stuart Norwich*, Norwich, 1988

Power, M. J., 'John Stow and his London', *Journal of Historical Geography*, vol. 11, no. 1, 1985, pp. 1–20

Prescott, Elizabeth, *The English Medieval Hospital, 1050–1640*, Seaby, 1992

Preston, Arthur E., 'The Demolition of Reading Abbey', *Berkshire Archaeological Journal*, vol. 39, no. 2, 1935, pp. 107–44

Preston, W. E., 'A Sixteenth-Century Account Roll of the Building of a House at Chevet', *Yorkshire Archaeological Journal*, vol. 32, 1934–6, pp. 326–30

Price, J., *Historical Account of Leominster and its Vicinity*, 1795

Quilley, Geoffrey, 'The Image of Nonsuch Palace: Mythology and Meaning', in Howard, ed., 1996, pp. 17–36

Quiney, Anthony, *Town Houses of Medieval Britain*, New Haven and London, 2003

Rappaport, Steve, *Worlds Within Worlds: Structures of Life in Sixteenth-Century London*, Cambridge, 1989

Ravenhill, William, and Rowe, Margery, 'A Decorated Screen Map of Exeter based on John Hooker's Map of 1587', in Gray, Rowe and Erskine, eds., 1992

Rawcliffe, Carole, Virgoe, Roger, and Wilson, Richard, eds., *Essays on East Anglian History presented to Hassell Smith*, Norwich, 1996

Rawcliffe, Carole, and Wilson, Richard, eds., with Christine Clark, *Norwich since 1550*, London and New York, 2004

Renn, Derek, *Kenilworth Castle, Warwickshire*, HMSO, London, 1991

Richeson, A. W., *English Land Measuring to 1800: Instruments and Practices*, Cambridge and London, 1966

Richmond, Colin, 'The English Reformation: Report from a Stationary Train', in Bernard and Gunn, eds., 2002, pp. 97–111

Rideout, Edna, 'The Account Book of the New Haven, Chester, 1567–8', *Transactions of the Historic Society of Lancashire and Cheshire*, vol. 80, 1929, pp. 86–128

Ridley, Jasper, *A History of the Carpenters' Company*, London, 1995

Rigby, S. H., '"Sore Decay" and "Fair Dwellings": Boston and Urban Decline in the Later Middle Ages', *Midland History*, vol. 10, 1985, pp. 47–61

Rigold, S. E., 'Two Types of Court Hall', *Archaeologia Cantiana*, vol. 83, 1968, pp. 1–22

Roberts, Eileen, *The Hill of the Martyr: An Architectural History of St Alban's Abbey*, Dunstable, 1993

Rockett, William, '*Britannia*, Ralph Brooke, and the Representation of Privilege in Elizabethan England', *Renaissance Quarterly*, vol. 53, 2000, pp. 474–99

Rodwell, Warwick, *Wells Cathedral: Excavations and Structural Studies 1978–93*, English Heritage Archaeological Report, no. 21, London, 2001

Rogers, Alan, ed., *The Making of Stamford*, Leicester, 1965

Rosser, Gervase, 'Myth, Image and Social Process in the English Medieval Town', *Urban History*, vol. 23, part 1, 1966, pp. 5–25

Rosser, Gervase, and Thurley, Simon, 'Whitehall Palace and King Street, Westminster: The Urban Cost of Princely Magnificence', *London Topographical Record*, vol. 26, 1990, pp. 57–77

Royal Commission on the Historical Monuments of England, 1910– (*RCHM*)

Rutton, W. L. 'St Martin's Church, New Romney: Records relating to its Removal in A.D. 1550', *Archaeologia Cantiana*, vol. 20, 1893, pp. 155–60

Sacks, David Harris, *The Widening Gate: Bristol and the Atlantic Economy 1450–1700*, Berkeley and London, 1991

Sadler, Ernest A., 'The Earliest Records of Ashbourne Grammar School', *Journal of the Derbyshire Archaeological and Natural History Society*, new ser., vol. 5, 1931

Salzman, L. F., *Building in England down to 1540: A Documentary History*, Oxford, 1952, repr. 1967

Sandeen, Ernest R., 'The Building of Redgrave Hall, 1545–1554', *Proceedings of the Suffolk Institute of Archaeology*, vol. 29, 1961–3, pp. 1–33

Saunders, Ann, *The Royal Exchange*, London Topographical Society, no. 152, 1997

Sayer, John, 'Charing Church', *Archaeologia Cantiana*, vol. 16, 1888, pp. 263–4

Scattergood, John, 'John Leland's *Itinerary* and the Identity of England', in Piesse, ed., 2000, pp. 58–74

Schleiner, Louise, *Tudor and Stuart Women Writers*, Bloomington and Indianapolis, 1994

Schofield, John, *The Building of London from the Conquest to the Great Fire*, 2nd edn, London, 1993

Schofield, John, *Medieval London Houses*, New Haven and London, 1994

Schofield, John, 'Urban Housing in England 1400–1600', in Gaimster and Stamper, eds., 1997, pp. 127–44

Schofield, John, 'Some Aspects of the Reformation of Religious Space in London, 1540–1660', in Gaimster and Gilchrist, eds., 2003, pp. 310–24

Schofield, John, and Lea, Richard, *Holy Trinity Priory, Aldgate, City of London: An Archaeological Reconstruction and History*, MOLAS, no. 24, 2005

Schofield, John, and Leech, Roger, eds., *Urban Archaeology in Britain*, CBA report, no. 61, 1987

Schwyzer, Philip, *Archaeologies of English Renaissance Literature*, Oxford, 2007.

Seaborne, Malcolm, *The English School: Its Architecture and Organisation, 1370–1870*, London, 1971

Seed, Patricia, *Ceremonies of Possession in Europe's Conquest of the New World, 1492–1640*, Cambridge, 1996

Sergeaunt, John, *Felsted School*, Chelmsford and London, 1989

Serlio, Sebastiano, *L'architettura* (1537–51), trans. as *The First Booke of Architecture*, London, 1611, later as *The Five Books of Architecture*

Sharpe, James, *Instruments of Darkness: Witchcraft in England, 1550–1750*, Harmondsworth, 1997

Sharpe, Sir Montagu, and Westlake, the late Minor-Canon, 'The Mending of the Brynt Bridge', *London and Middlesex Archaeological Society Transactions*, new ser., vol. 5, 1929, pp. 449–66

Shepard, Alexandra, and Withington, Phil, eds., *Communities in Early Modern England*, Manchester and New York, 2000

Sherlock, D., 'The Account of George Nycholl for St Augustine's, 1552–1553', *Archaeologia Cantiana*, vol. 99, 1983, pp. 25–44

Sherman, William H., *John Dee: The Politics of Reading and Writing in the English Renaissance*, Amherst, 1995

Sherman, William H., 'Bringing the World to England: The Politics of Translation in the Age of Hakluyt', *Transactions of the Royal Historical Society*, vol. 14, 2004, pp. 99–207

Shirley, Evelyn P., 'An Inventory of the Effects of Henry Howard, K.G., Earl of Northampton, taken on his death in 1614, together with a transcript of his Will', *Archaeologia*, vol. 42, 1869, pp. 347–78

Shute, John, *The First and Chiefe Groundes of Architecture*, London, 1563

Simmons, Jack, 'Brooke Church, Rutland, with Notes on Elizabethan Church-Building', *Transactions of the Leicestershire Archaeological and Historical Society*, vol. 25, 1959, pp. 36–55

Simmons, Jack, ed., *English County Historians*, Wakefield, 1978

Simon, Joan, *Education and Society in Tudor England*, Cambridge, 1967

Sjoberg, Gideon, 'The Nature of the Pre-Industrial City', in Clark, ed., 1976, pp. 43–52

Slack, Paul, *Poverty and Policy in Tudor and Stuart England*, London and New York, 1988

Slack, Paul, *From Reformation to Improvement: Public Welfare in Early Modern England. The Ford Lectures delivered in the University of Oxford 1994–1995*, Oxford, 1998

Slack, Paul, 'Perceptions of the Metropolis in Seventeenth-Century England', in Burke, Harrison and Slack, eds., 2000, pp. 161–80

Slater, T. R., ed., *Towns in Decline, AD 100–1600*, Aldershot, 2000

Sloane, Barney, 'Tenements in London's Monasteries c. 1450–1540', in Gaimster and Gilchrist, eds., 2003, pp. 290–98

Sloane, Barney, and Malcolm, Gordon, *Excavations at the Priory of the Order of the Hospital of St John of Jerusalem, Clerkenwell, London*, MOLAS, no. 20, 2004

Smith, Frederick Francis, *A History of Rochester*, London, 1928

Smith, David L., Strier, Richard, and Bevington, David, eds., *The Theatrical City: Culture, Theatre and Politics in London, 1576–1649*, Cambridge, 1995

Speed, John, *The Theatre of the Empire of Great Britaine*, London, 1611–12

Spence, Richard T., *Lady Anne Clifford, Countess of Pembroke, Dorset and Montgomery (1590–1676)*, Stroud, 1997

Spurr, John, 'The English "Post-Reformation?"', *Journal of Modern History*, vol. 74, 2002, pp. 101–19

Starkey, David, ed., *The Inventory of King Henry VIII: Society of Antiquaries MS 129 and British Library MS Harley 1419*, London, 1998

Starkey, David (curator), *Elizabeth: The Exhibition at the National Maritime Museum*, ed. Susan Doran, London, 2003

The Statutes of the Realm [. . .] from Original Records and Authentic Manuscripts, vol. III, 1817, pp. 959–60.

Stevenson, Christine, *Medicine and Magnificence: British Hospital and Asylum Architecture 1660–1815*, New Haven and London, 2000

Stevenson, Christine, 'Occasional Architecture in Seventeenth-Century London', *Architectural History*, vol. 49, 2006, pp. 35–74

Stocker, D. A., 'The Archaeology of the Reformation in Lincoln: A Case Study in the Redistribution of Building Materials in the Mid Sixteenth Century', *Lincolnshire History and Archaeology*, vol. 25, 1990, pp. 18–32

Stocker, David, with Everson, Paul, 'Rubbish Recycled: A Study of the Re-Use of Stone in Lincolnshire', in Parsons, ed., 1990, pp. 83–101

Stone, Lawrence, 'The Building of Hatfield House', *Archaeological Journal*, vol. 112, 1965, pp. 100–128

Stone, Lawrence, *The Crisis of the Aristocracy 1558–1641*, Oxford, 1965

Stone, Lawrence, *Family and Fortune: Studies in Aristocratic Finance in the Sixteenth and Seventeenth Centuries*, Oxford, 1973

Stone, Lawrence, and Stone, Jeanne Fawtier, *An Open Elite? England 1540–1880*, abridged edn, Oxford, 1986

Stow, John, *A Survey of London* (1598), ed. with introduction and notes by C. L. Kingsford as *A Survey of London by John Stow, reprinted from the Text of 1603*, 3 vols, Oxford, 1908

Straton, Charles R., ed., *Survey of the Lands of William, 1st Earl of Pembroke*, 2 vols, Oxford, 1909

Strype, John, *The Life and Acts of John Whitgift, D.D., the Third and Last Lord Archbishop of Canterbury in the Reign of Queen Elizabeth*, Oxford, 1822

Summerson, John, *Architecture in Britain 1530–1830*, Harmondsworth, 1953; many later edns

Summerson, John, 'Three Elizabethan Architects', *Bulletin of the John Rylands Library*, vol. 40, 1957, pp. 202–28

Summerson, John, 'The Building of Theobalds, 1564–1585', *Archaeologia*, vol. 97, 1959, pp. 107–26

Summerson, John, ed., *The Book of Architecture of John Thorpe in the Sir John Soane's Museum*, Walpole Society, vol. 40, 1966

Swales, T. H., 'The Redistribution of the Monastic Lands in Norfolk at the Dissolution', *Norfolk Archaeology*, vol. 34, part 1, 1966, pp. 14–43

Talbot, C. H., 'Lacock Abbey: Notes on the Architectural History of the Building', *Journal of the British Archaeological Association*, new ser., vol. 11, 1905, pp. 175–210

Tarlow, Sarah, and West, Susie, eds., *The Familiar Past? Archaeologies of Later Historical Britain*, London and New York, 1999

Taylor, E. G. R., *The Mathematical Practitioners of Tudor & Stuart England*, Cambridge, 1954

Thacker, Alan, ed., *Medieval Archaeology: Art and Architecture at Chester*, Transactions of the British Archaeological Association Conference, vol. 22, London, 2000

Thirsk, Joan, 'Stamford in the Sixteenth and Seventeenth Centuries', in Rogers, ed., 1965, pp. 58–76

Thirsk, J., ed., *The Agrarian History of England and Wales*, vol. IV, Cambridge, 1967

Thirsk, Joan, *The Rural Economy of England*, London, 1984

Thomas, Keith, *Religion and the Decline of Magic: Studies in Popular Beliefs in Sixteenth- and Seventeenth-Century England*, London, 1971

Thomas, Keith, 'The Meaning of Literacy in Early Modern England', in Baumann, ed., 1986, pp. 97–131

Thomas, William, *The Historye of Italie* (1549), ed. George B. Parks, Ithaca, NY, 1963

Thompson, Benjamin, 'Monasteries and their Patrons at Foundation and Dissolution', *Transactions of the Royal Historical Society*, 6th ser., vol. 4, 1994, pp. 103–23

Thompson, M. W., *Kenilworth Castle, Warwickshire*, HMSO, London, 1977

Thomson, David, *Renaissance Architecture: Critics, Patrons, Luxury*, Manchester, 1993

Thurley, Simon, *The Royal Palaces of Tudor England: Architecture and Court Life 1460–1547*, New Haven and London, 1993

Tibbits, E. G., 'The Hospital of Robert, Earl of Leicester, in Warwick', *Transactions of the Birmingham Archaeological Society* (1936), vol. 60, 1940, pp. 112–44

Till, Eric L., 'Fact and Conjecture: The Building of Burghley House 1555–1587', *Northamptonshire Past and Present*, vol. 9, no. 4, 1997–8, pp. 323–32

Tiller, Kate, ed., *Dorchester Abbey: Church and People 635–2005*, Witney, 2005

Tittler, Robert, 'The Incorporation of Boroughs, 1540–1558', *History*, vol. 62, 1977, pp. 24–42

Tittler, Robert, 'The Vitality of an Elizabethan Port: The Economy of Poole, c. 1550–1600', *Southern History*, vol. 7, 1985, pp. 95–113

Tittler, Robert, 'The End of the Middle Ages in the English Country Town', *Sixteenth-Century Journal*, vol. 18, 1987, pp. 471–87

Tittler, Robert, '"For the Re-edification of Townes": The Rebuilding Statutes of Henry VIII', *Albion*, vol. 22, no. 4, 1990, pp. 591–605

Tittler, Robert, *Architecture and Power: The Town Hall and the English Urban Community, c. 1500–1640*, Oxford, 1991

Tittler, Robert, 'Seats of Honor, Seats of Power: The Symbolism of Public Seating in the English Urban Community, c.1560–1620', *Albion*, vol. 24, no. 2, 1992, pp. 205–23

Tittler, Robert, 'Political Culture and the Built Environment of the English Country Town, c.1540–1620', in Hoak, ed., 1995, pp. 133–56

Tittler, Robert, 'Reformation, Civic Culture and Collective Memory in English Provincial Towns', *Urban History*, vol. 24, no. 3, 1997, pp. 283–300

Tittler, Robert, *The Reformation and the Towns in England*, Oxford, 1998

Tittler, Robert, *Townspeople and Nation: English Urban Experiences, 1540–1640*, Stanford, 2001

Townsend, J., *A History of Abingdon*, London, 1910

Trevor-Roper, H. R., *Archbishop Laud*, 2nd edn, London, 1962

Tyacke, Sarah, ed., *English Map-Making 1500–1650: Historical Essays*, London, 1983

The Victoria History of the Counties of England, 1900– (*VCH*); individual volumes as cited in the notes above

Vasari, Giorgio, *Le vite de' più eccellenti pittori, scultori, e architettori*, ed. Gaetanno Milanesi, 9 vols, Florence, 1878–85, 2nd edn, 1906

Vyner, B., ed., *Building on the Past: Papers Celebrating 150 Years of the Royal Archaeological Institute*, London, 1994

Wadmore, J. F., 'Sir Thomas Smythe, Knt. (A.D. 1558–1625)', *Archaeologia Cantiana*, vol. 20, 1893, pp. 82–103

Walker, Greg, *Writing Under Tyranny: English Literature and the Henrician Reformation*, Oxford, 2005

Waller, G. K., *Mary Sidney, Countess of Pembroke: A Critical Study of her Writings and Literary Milieu*, London, 1979

Ward, Jennifer, and Marshall, Kenneth, *Old Thorndon Hall*, Essex Record Office Publications, no. 61, Chelmsford, 1972

Ward, Simon, 'The Friaries in Chester: Their Impact and Legacy', in Thacker, ed., 2000, pp. 121–31

Ward, Simon P., 'Dissolution or Reformation?: A Case Study from Chester's Urban Landscape', in Gaimster and Gilchrist, eds., 2003, pp. 267–79

Watson, Bruce, 'Excavations and Observations on the Site of the Dutch Church, Austin Friars, in the City of London', *Transactions of the London and Middlesex Archaeological Society*, vol. 45, 1994, pp. 13–22

Webb, E. A., 'St Bartholomew the Great: The Smithfield Gateway and the Cloister', *Transactions of the London and Middlesex Archaeological Society*, new ser., vol. 2, 1913, pp. 211–24

Webb, E. A., *The Records of St Bartholomew's Priory and of the Church and Parish of St Bartholomew the Great, West Smithfield*, 2 vols, Oxford, 1921

Webb, John, 'Peter Moore of Ipswich (d. 1601): A Tudor Tailor, Poet and Gospeller and his Circle', *Proceedings of the Suffolk Institute*, vol. 38, 1996, pp. 35–55

Webb, Sidney, and Webb, Beatrice, *English Local Government: The Story of the King's Highway*, London, 1920

Weever, John, *Ancient Funeral Monuments*, London, 1631

Welch, Edwin, ed., *Plymouth Building Accounts of the Sixteenth and Seventeenth Centuries*, Devon and Cornwall Record Society, Torquay, 1967

Wells-Cole, Anthony, *Art and Decoration in Elizabethan and Jacobean England: The Influence of Continental Prints, 1558–1625*, New Haven and London, 1997

White, Andrew, *Sempringham Priory*, Lincolnshire Museums Information Series, no. 17, Lincoln, 1979

White, Gillian, ' "that whyche ys made nedefoulle and nesasary": The Nature and Purpose of the Original Furnishings and Decoration of Hardwick Hall, Derbyshire', unpubd PhD thesis, University of Warwick, 2005

White, Lynn, 'Jacopo Aconcio as an Engineer', *American Historical Review*, vol. 72, 1966–7, pp. 425–44

Willan, T. S., *Elizabethan Manchester*, Manchester, 1980

Wilson, Jean, *Entertainments for Elizabeth I*, London, 1980

Wilson-North, Robert, and Porter, Stephen, 'Witham, Somerset: From Carthusian Monastery to Country House to Gothic Folly', *Architectural History*, vol. 40, 1997, pp. 81–98

Wood, Jeremy, 'The Architectural Patronage of Algernon Percy, 10th Earl of Northumberland', in Bold and Chaney, eds., 1993, pp. 55–80

Woodger, Andrew, 'Post-Reformation Mixed Gothic in Huntingdonshire Church Towers and its Campanological Associations', *Archaeological Journal*, vol. 141, 1984, pp. 269–308

Woodger, Andrew, 'St Cuthbert's Wells, Reconsidered', *Somerset Archaeological and Natural History Society*, vol. 133, 1989, pp. 195–6

Woodward, Donald, 'The Background to the Statute of Artificers: The Genesis of Labour Policy, 1558–63', *Economic History Review*, vol. 33, 1980, pp. 32–44

Woodward, Donald, 'Wage Rates and Living Standards in Pre-Industrial England', *Past and Present*, no. 91, 1981, pp. 28–46

Woodward, Donald, ' "Swords into Ploughshares": Recycling in Pre-Industrial England', *Economic History Review*, 2nd ser., vol. 38, no. 2, 1985, pp. 175–91

Woodward, Donald, *Men at Work: Labourers and Building Craftsmen in the Towns of Northern England, 1450–1750*, Cambridge, 1995

Worsfield, A. F. de P., 'Peacock's School, Rye, Sussex', *Sussex Archaeological Collections*, vol. 68, 1927, pp. 199–209

Worsley, Giles, ed., *The Role of the Amateur Architect*, London, 1994

Worsley, Giles, *Inigo Jones and the European Classicist Tradition*, New Haven and London, 2007

Worsley, Lucy, 'The Architectural Patronage of William Cavendish, first Duke of Newcastle, 1593–1676', unpubd PhD thesis, University of Sussex, 2001

Wotton, Henry, *The Elements of Architecture collected by Henry Wotton Knight from the Best Authors and Examples*, London, 1624

Wright, T., ed., *Three Chapters of Letters relating to the Suppression of the Monasteries*, London, 1843

Wroughton, John, 'Puritanism and Traditionalism: Cultural and Political Division in Bath, 1620–1662', *Bath History*, vol. 4, 1992, pp. 52–70

Wunderli, Richard M., 'Evasion of the Office of Alderman in London 1523–1672', *The London Journal: A Review of Metropolitan Society Past and Present*, vol. 15, no. 1, 1990, pp. 3–12

Youings, Joyce, 'The City of Exeter and the Property of the Dissolved Monasteries', *Transactions of the Devonshire Association*, vol. 84, 1952, pp. 123–41

Youings, Joyce, 'The Terms of the Disposal of the Devon Monastic Lands, 1536–58', *English Historical Review*, vol. 69, 1954, pp. 18–38

Youings, Joyce, *Tucker's Hall, Exeter: The History of a Provincial City Company through Five Centuries*, Exeter, 1968

Youings, Joyce, *The Dissolution of the Monasteries*, London, 1971

Youings, Joyce, 'Drake, Grenville and Buckland Abbey', *Transactions of the Devonshire Association*, vol. 112, 1980, pp. 95–9

Youings, Joyce, 'Tudor Barnstaple: New Life for an Ancient Borough', *Transactions of the Devonshire Association*, vol. 121, 1989, pp. 1–14

Index

Footnote references are confined to those places where the discussion enlarges on the text. All known dates of birth and death are included, including monarchs, or known working activity (e.g. artists) or holding office (e.g. abbots). References in *italics* are to pages where illustrations are found.